Advanced Praise for *Rain Making, 2nd Edition*

"*Rain Making* is an essential guide for anyone responsible for business development in the professional services industry. Ford Harding provides practical, concrete advice and tools that will be beneficial to professionals in our industry regardless of their level of experience."

Mark Mactas
chairman and CEO of Towers Perrin

"Ford Harding's ideas have had a big impact on how our firm thinks about marketing and selling our services. If you can only read one book on how best to develop and retain business, as well as service clients, read this one."

Jim McTaggart
founder of Marakon and CEO of Trinsum Group

"His guidance is practical and reveals an understanding of what it takes to sell professional services that could only be obtained by doing it and acute observation of others doing it for many years."

Prof. Dr. H.C. Roland Berger
founder and chairman of Roland Berger Strategy Consultants

"Ford Harding has a rare ability to deconstruct and then teach the intricacies of effective selling techniques that every professional must possess to compete in this global economy. He provides a road map enabling firms to develop processes to harness the entrepreneurial energy existing within their organizations."

Gerard M. Creagh
president of Duff & Phelps LLC

"I highly recommend *Rain Making* for younger lawyers starting to grow their practices, for more seasoned veterans trying to enhance theirs and for firm leaders interested in developing more systematic approaches to practice development."

Alan Kolod
chairman of Moses & Singer LLP

"The techniques and systematic processes developed by Ford Harding are essential tools to helping professionals within the business services industry become more effective at generating new business opportunities, and extending and developing strong networks. His frameworks help to instill and drive discipline, methodology, confidence, and ultimately, success into their business development pursuits."

Julie M. Howard
president of Navigant Consulting, Inc.

"Ford Harding's *Rain Making* is a tremendous resource for the professional who wants to win more clients. The book has had a great impact on our people. It has helped motivate engineers who don't think of themselves as salespeople to go out in the market and give it a try. It also provides the techniques that help them stay with it and succeed."

Michael J. Scipione P.E.
president and CEO of Weston & Sampson Engineers

"To be absolutely honest I did not fully appreciate the simplicity and elegance of this book when I first read it. However, the results were swift and the techniques Ford describes have easily become habits. It is now crystal clear to me that *Rain Making* is the most productive and definitive book on relationship marketing that I have read."

Rick A. Lincicome
CEO of Ellerbe Becket Architects & Engineers

"*Rain Making*, in its new edition demonstrates its position as the single most sensible, accessible guide to building a professional practice that exists."

David Maister
consultant and author of *Strategy and the Fat Smoker*

"By breaking down the complexities of what is necessary for success in business development into easy to understand concepts, Ford Harding has helped our employees develop new and better client relationships. The end result has been better business development practices at all levels of the firm, thus helping us to achieve significant top line growth."

David R. Gaboury, P.E.
president and CEO of Terracon Consultants, Inc.

Also by Ford Harding

Creating Rainmakers
Cross-Selling Success

RAIN MAKING

2nd Edition

Attract New Clients
No Matter What Your Field

Ford Harding

Avon, Massachusetts

Published by Adams Business
An imprint of Adams Media, an F+W Publications Company
57 Littlefield Street, Avon, MA 02322
www.adamsmedia.com

ISBN 10: 1-59869-588-6
ISBN 13: 978-1-59869-588-5

Printed in the United States of America.

J   I   H   G   F   E   D   C   B   A

Library of Congress Cataloging-in-Publication Data
is available from the publisher.

This publication is designed to provide accurate and authoritative information
with regard to the subject matter covered. It is sold with the understanding that
the publisher is not engaged in rendering legal, accounting, or other professional
advice. If legal advice or other expert assistance is required, the services of a
competent professional person should be sought.
—From a *Declaration of Principles* jointly adopted by a Committee of the
American Bar Association and a Committee of Publishers and Associations

Many of the designations used by manufacturers and sellers to distinguish their
product are claimed as trademarks. Where those designations appear in this book
and Adams Media was aware of a trademark claim, the designations have been
printed with initial capital letters.

This book is available at quantity discounts for bulk purchases.
For information, please call 1-800-289-0963.

CONTENTS

PART III

Sales Tactics: How Professionals Advance and Close a Sale • 163

PART IV

From Tactics to Strategy: What Works and What Doesn't • 265

Preface to Revised Edition

There is a saying among architects that the design of a building is completed when the project manager pulls drawings from under the designer's pen. So it is with books. They are never really done. Rather, they represent the author's thinking at the time the manuscript must be shipped off to an editor.

Since *Rain Making: The Professional's Guide to Attracting New Clients* first appeared in 1994, the world has changed. The old version doesn't even mention the Internet, an oversight acceptable then, but not today. The recognition that selling, if done correctly, is an honorable activity at a professional firm is far more accepted today than it was in 1994 and, broadly speaking, professionals are more sophisticated about the subject. Fourteen years ago, there were six big accounting firms. Today, there are but four. All but one of these have spun off their consulting arms, or they are currently rebuilding them. These are just some of the most obvious changes. My own knowledge has increased, too, the result of working with hundreds of additional professionals.

And so I offer this updated version of the book. For any readers of the old version, it may help you to know that chapters 6, 10, 11, 12, and 24 are entirely new. Also chapters 2, 4, 8, 13, 14, 15, 16, 20, and 21 have been either changed or added to substantially enough that they can be said to be quite different from the old versions. All other chapters have been updated, too, though less markedly.

Acknowledgments to the Revised Edition

With fourteen more years of experience than I had when the original version of this book was published, I have many more people to thank for helping me learn more about rainmakers and how to help professionals achieve that status. There are far too many to thank here, so I must limit myself to those who helped with specific parts of this edition.

Betsy Kovacs of the Association of Management Consulting Firms and Lisa Bowman of the Society for Marketing Professional Services helped with this book in many ways, large and small.

Roger Parker and Greg Mancusi gave me many valuable suggestions for making a Webinar work. I asked Matt Caspari of Caspari McCormick to provide Chapter 6 on the Web. My limited and his substantial knowledge of this subject made this a logical decision. Matt and his colleagues put together a knockout Web site. In writing Chapter 10, I received so much help from my partner, Mimi Spangler, and my colleague, Gary Pines, that I felt it only right to list them as coauthors. For the past ten years, Mimi has contributed in many ways to our understanding of rainmakers and to helping our clients learn how to achieve that status. Gary has done so for five years and brought our firm his almost thirty years of knowledge of selling actuarial and consulting services. Also contributing to Chapter 10 were David Nadler of Oliver Wyman Delta, Jim McTaggert of Marakon, and Tom Saporito of RHR International.

I received help from many people in describing network markets. Dallas Kersey contributed by exemplifying networking fitness. Dennis Simon and Ruth Ford of XRoads Solutions Group and Alan Kolod of Moses & Singer contributed to the description of the distressed-company network; Phil Ullom of Watson Wyatt Worldwide and my colleague, Gary Pines, to the description of the pension-and-benefits advisory network; and Guy Geier of FX Fowle Architects, Hether Smith of Julien J. Studley, and my partner, Mimi Spangler, to the description of the office move network. Jack Jolls of John D. Jolls &

Company advised me on the municipal water and wastewater network, and George Kolodka of Bernstein Investment on the high-net-worth advisory network. Many clients also contributed indirectly to this chapter. Amit Sabharwal's knowledge of graph theory enlightened the whole chapter. I hope I have not misinterpreted their insights too badly.

Barry Seymour provided much help on Chapter 13. Mel Bergstein, Alan Chimacoff, Mike Palmer, Charles Searight, and Craig Spangler offered insights that were most helpful to Chapter 22. Jerry Colletti of Colleti-Fiss contributed some of his wealth of knowledge of sales effectiveness to Chapter 25.

Barcy Fox and Liz Richardson helped tighten the book up when it needed it. My sister, Judy Harding, made it a better book in many ways through her editing. Jeff Herman again proved his knowledge and value as my literary agent. My editor, Peter Archer, improved my prose and managed me with tact and patience.

I am solely responsible for any mistakes that have slipped into this work.

The first edition was dedicated to my wife, Liz. I rededicate it to her now, loving her more than ever.

Acknowledgments

This book is the result of almost twenty years of learning and teaching the marketing and sale of professional services. During that time hundreds of prospects, clients, colleagues, and friends contributed to my education and, indirectly, to this book. I cannot name them all.

I wish to express my thanks to Maurice Fulton, who gave me my first opportunity in consulting and had the strength to let me stumble many times as I learned to succeed. Also to Jim Keane, who gave me my first opportunity to manage a consulting office and taught me so much about management. And to Bob Hillier, who introduced me to architecture.

Several organizations have been particularly helpful. These include IBM Executive Consulting Institute; the Institute of Management Consultants; and The Society for Marketing Professional Services. Participation in ACME, Inc., the Association of Management Consulting Firms, played an important part in my education, and its president, Ed Hendricks, has been a valued friend and advisor. It has been both an honor and a pleasure to be a part of the Network of Opportunity. Its members have been a source of motivation and practical help. Several, including David Gensler of Madison Pension Services, Norman Kallen of Ravin, Sarasohn, Cook, Baumgarten, Fisch & Baime, and Michael Seltzer of Insurance Planning Concepts, contributed their experiences to this book.

I have benefited from the example of many people. These include Linda Lukas, an exceptional business developer in the field of architecture; Joan Jorgenson of Executive Resource Group, an entrepreneurial executive recruiter; and Robert Leisk of Cagley; Harman & Leisk, the cheeriest engineer I know. Michael Paris of Michael Paris Associates, Ltd. has provided thoughtful advice over the years. Judy Koblentz of Jannotta Bray & Associates has been a source of so many ideas, introductions, and uplifting comments that I have lost count. Steve DePalma of The Schoor DePalma & Canger Group, Inc., saw his consulting engineering firm through a major turnaround under the toughest personal circumstances. His resolution and current success can provide a lesson to us all. It is hard to know how to thank Gail Atlas, who taught me so much in so little time. My life is better for her help. I wish Oscar Megerdichian were alive to thank for his mentoring and guidance. I miss him. Of special help in providing insights into specific professional practices were Ed Greene of Cleary, Gottlieb, Steen & Hamilton, whom I am fortunate enough to have as my brother-in-law; Mike Schell of Skadden, Arps, Slate, Meagher & Flom, with whom I built a tree house long ago; Charles O'Neill of O'Neill & Neylon; Terry Meginniss of Gladstein, Reif & Meginniss; Dennis Yaeger; Bruce Pritkin of Robbins, Spielman, Slayton & Halfon, who has probably given up camping for life after our last shared experience with our sons; Paul Taenzler; and Emad Youssef of Paulus Sokolowski & Sartor. The partners of the firm Herman Yula Schwartz and Lagomarsino have provided help either directly or indirectly. The questions and comments of students and clients at classes I have taught have sharpened and expanded my thinking. Thank you all.

Several times during the writing of this book I found I needed to discuss ideas with someone with a fresh perspective. Many people helped in this way. Particular patience was shown by Bill Shapiro of Price Waterhouse. Mary Wisnovsky, the most thorough of conference organizers, kindly commented on the chapter on seminars and conferences.

Edith Poor and Ed Myers, both authors, and Don Cleary taught me much about getting a book published. My agent, Jeffrey Herman of the Jeff Herman Agency, Inc., proved a faithful guide through the rigors of finding a publisher for a first book. Dick Staron, my editor, pushed me to make the book longer and better. Without him it would have had several gaps. I want to thank the *Journal of Management Consulting* both for originally publishing several of my articles and for permission to adapt and reprint them here. Chapter 3 originally appeared in the *Journal* under the title "Ten Rules for Better Networking," 1990, volume 6, number 1; Chapter 1 as "Make Yourself an Efficient Writer," 1991, volume 6, number 4; and Chapter 19 as "Rain Making," 1992, volume 7, number 1. Deborah Baxley's appendix on bios originally appeared in *The Professional Consultant* (July 1993). I also wish to thank that publication. Portions of Chapter 6 originally appeared in *National Business Employment Weekly.*

Finally, and most importantly, I want to thank my parents for teaching me to love books and Dinny and Judy and Jon for the close friendship that only family can give. My sister Dinny, a lawyer, also contributed directly to this book in several ways. Jon gave editing advice. My son, Charek, has inspired and motivated me and given up many hours with me while I wrote. I dedicate this book to my wife, Liz, for her tolerance and kindness and support, and because she is the love of my life.

Introduction

You must sell yourself to sell your firm. This is true of accountants, architects, consultants, engineers, and lawyers. It is also true of actuaries, executive recruiters, interior designers, public relations specialists, real estate brokers, and, increasingly, doctors. Though a buyer of manufactured goods seldom thinks about those who produced them, one who buys professional services almost always does. Unable to try out or even look at a service before buying it, the buyer does the next best thing by assessing what it would be like to work with the professional who delivers it. This means that, sooner or later, all professionals must market if they want to advance their careers and grow their firms.

This book is written for the professional in a firm who must make the transition from doing managing work to marketing and selling it, as well as for the professional who is already marketing and who wants to enhance his or her skills. It is also for the sole practitioner who must sell to stay in business. These are the people who must face the implications of what Warren J. Wittreich noted long ago is the buyer's desire to deal with a professional who sells rather than a professional salesman.[1]

Historically, training of professionals to win new clients has been haphazard. Law, accounting, engineering, medical, and architectural schools teach nothing about selling. This is also true of most business schools, surprisingly so, given that a sale is what defines the existence of a business. Many firms offer in-house education on technical issues, and almost all provide such training on the job, but marketing and sales training is spotty. Most of us must learn by trial and error.

So it was with me. My early career as a professional was swept along on the tide of a boom economy. Work flowed in, allowing me to learn my craft. I also learned how to respond to inquiries about our services, becoming a competent reactive seller. I got promoted, and life looked promising.

Then the tide turned. One month, we were struggling to keep up, wading deep in client work and not knowing how we would get it all done. The next, clients were calling to cancel projects, leaving many of my team unassigned. Prospective clients, who but a month earlier had pushed us for proposals, lost interest and stopped returning our calls. My colleagues and I were left stranded on the beach without work or much hope of getting any.

By this time I was running a small practice and was called into the corner office. Two senior members of the firm told me it was my responsibility to keep my team busy. They sent me out into the marketplace to find clients. Yes, they acknowledged, need for our services had ebbed with the economy, but there were still companies out there that could use our help. I was to go out and find them.

I didn't have a clue about what to do. Nothing in my previous education or career had prepared me for this. The initial advice I received was sound enough—write some tactful letters and call to see if you can get a meeting—but I was too green to understand what was meant.

Ours was a confidential service. If a company did need our help, only a handful of its people would know. However artfully written, a letter that asked if the reader would be interested in consulting services seemed tacky and unlikely to get a response. Both these logical conclusions proved true, but that didn't solve my problem.

Slowly, with a little mentoring and coaching and after my share of mistakes, I learned what to do. Knowing how to bring in business, and so build a practice, has helped ensure a good income and more control over my own destiny than many people have in this turbulent world. It has ensured a flow of interesting work with interesting people. It has allowed me to develop and maintain a team of professionals. It has earned me respect among my peers.

This book is a self-help manual for professionals wanting to enhance their sales and marketing skills. In creating it I have drawn on several sources, beginning with my own experiences from the time I developed as a marketer and salesperson at a consulting firm. This process convinced me that a more efficient approach must be possible and eventually led to my current practice. I have also drawn on my work with hundreds of professionals—architects, accountants, actuaries, engineers, consultants, publicists, recruiters, and lawyers, both in one-on-one coaching sessions and in classrooms. This experience is supplemented by surveys and studies conducted by me and others, and, of course, by literature on the subject.

Sales mean survival.

Have no doubt about it: You must learn to sell. The sole practitioner who cannot sell will lose his independence and have to go back to work for someone else. At most large firms, to make partner, you must be able to bring in business. The underlying economics of the firm make it so.

Even if it is not stated, the professional within a firm who does not market and sell has a far higher probability of seeing his career plateau than one who brings in new business. When times are tough, a firm will hang onto those who bring in business longer than those who provide technical support. These underlying economics are so relentless that they will require you to sell, even if for years top management has said otherwise with the best intentions. My firm, which helps professionals learn to sell, is currently working with two management consulting firms, where for many years a few top people sold engagements and those rising through the ranks were told not to try. But when the firms hit hard times, the policy changed. Now people have to bring in business to keep their jobs and to get promoted.

The head of professional development at a big accounting firm admitted to me that "we promote our people on the basis of their technical ability, and then it's sink or swim on whether or not they can bring in business. It causes a lot of turnover." My seat mate on a plane trip recently had just been made a partner at a large law firm. He told me he had not expected to be made a partner because he hadn't sold enough business, and now he was afraid for his job because he didn't know how to bring business in but was expected to do so. And not so many years ago, one of Wall Street's largest law firms terminated partners who weren't bringing in new business. Their high salaries could not be justified on the basis of billable work alone. Most had never expected to have to sell; nor had they received any sales training.

We recently worked with a large architectural firm that enjoyed a flood of work during the boom years. Partners and studio heads didn't have to sell. But when the boom ended, it was sell or leave the firm.

You may know that you face a similar risk in your firm, but if you aren't doing something about it now, you are endangering your career. The professional career path is strewn with the bodies of those who meant to get around to marketing someday.

Lack of time is no excuse.

The economics of the professional services compel firms to keep their employees' time billed to clients for as high a percentage as possible. This is especially obvious in project-oriented fields such as management consulting and architecture, fields in which most project revenues extend for only a few months. Such firms are also notoriously reluctant to hire new employees unless work is overwhelming the current staff. I know, and your management knows, that you simply don't have much time to develop business.

But that is no excuse. This is not a value judgment; it is a statement of fact.

Yes, during good times, management will cut you some slack because you have not had time to market. But when times get tough and the boss has to make layoff decisions, who will he hang on to? Those who bring in clients. And what about when promotions are handed out? There again, marketers will get the lion's share.

The consulting firm I used to work for went through an annual ritual that is common in many of the professions, with the same results. At the beginning of each year, everyone was asked for a marketing plan. Each practice had to have a plan, and each practice's plan was, in essence, the composite of the individual plans of its professionals. At the end of every year, the results were always the same. Most professionals had failed to complete the marketing tasks they had promised, always with the same excuse—they were too busy. By any fair measure, they *were* busy. But so were the few who marketed and met the objectives they had set. It was always the same few, and they were no less busy than those who had made excuses. Somehow they had found a way. The executive committee noticed this, and rewards went to those who marketed.

If you are a sole practitioner, the belief that you are too busy serving one client to market to others will not save you when work for that client runs out and you have no business to replace it.

You must take responsibility for your own development.

I have already noted that professional firms do a poor job of training their employees to market and sell. If you do not take responsibility for your own development, no one will. Be thankful for whatever help you can get, and then go out and take care of yourself.

There are reasons why firms have effective technical mentors but few selling mentors. Technical mentors tend to manage projects. They must work closely with junior personnel to get their own jobs done, and often their work is made easier if the junior personnel perform better. This gives them an incentive to mentor.

The best marketers, on the other hand, are focused *outside* the firm—on the market. The things they do to develop new business are often done alone. Moreover, time spent on mentoring can reduce their immediate contribution to the firm and create competition for scarce prospects. Skilled marketers are also aware of the risk that taking an unproven associate along creates, when one ill-chosen word can destroy an opportunity that has taken months to create. All in all, they have little incentive to mentor.

This book provides some of the knowledge a good marketing mentor might offer, but it cannot replace the personal attention of a true mentor. Most people have to learn on their own. You cannot let this stop you.

You have to get over the hump before it starts to be fun.

You probably did not become a professional in order to sell. Few do. More likely you wanted to serve, do interesting work, and earn a good living. You have prospered because you are client-focused, enjoying the recognition and power clients give to professionals who serve them well. You have come to enjoy the influence you exercise based on specialized knowledge and skillful management of the client relationship. It's not easy, and it's rewarding when you succeed.

Initially, selling can seem like a comedown from this heady status. Clients almost always return phone calls; prospects often don't. Clients listen respectfully to what you say, because they are paying for it; prospects aren't always sure they should listen to you at all. To a client you are an authority; to a prospect, a vendor. The hard work and adept application of technical, managerial, and client relation skills that can pull you out of a fix on almost any project may have no impact at all on a prospect. This sudden change makes many professionals feel they have lost control. The lack of prospect response can make you feel unprofessional and embarrassed. Surely you must be doing something wrong. Faced with this situation, many professionals quickly—too quickly—conclude they aren't any good at selling and they don't like it.

Don't let this happen to you. You have to develop new skills and go through the discomfort of gaining some marketing and sales experience, but once you do, it will enhance your sense of control over your own fate, add to your recognition with clients and peers, and become a source of pride and pleasure. An actuary friend of mine who made the transition said to me recently, "I suppose I was happy before when I was managing projects, but I would never go back. I'm having so much greater impact now."

My son learned to ride a bicycle a year after most of his friends. His inability embarrassed him. On the morning of the day he finally learned, he insisted, "I can't do it. I hate bike riding. I hated it last year, and I hate it this year." But on the way home from the parking lot where he finally got the hang of it, he chirped, "What a great day! I love bike riding. It's my favorite sport." It can be the same with selling. You have to get over the hump, and you have to fall a couple of times before it starts to be fun.

You must adopt new measures of productivity and success.

If you have worked in a firm as a doer and manager, you have been inculcated with certain beliefs about productivity and success that can obstruct your ability to market. Among them are the following:

- *I must maximize billable time.* Although you must do this early in your career, you cannot let this stop you from marketing. At times it is essential to expend time that could have been billed to a client on marketing efforts.

- When you catch yourself using this phrase as a reason for not marketing, replace it with, *I must optimize billable time and meet firm standards. I must also make time to market.*
- *Nonbillable time is wasted time.* In their efforts to maximize profits, good project managers often make statements like, "Don't waste your time on that; it isn't billable." Although true of many activities, this philosophy is not true in regards to marketing. Time spent on ten unreturned phone calls may seem wasted to someone with a production mindset; to a marketer, it is a necessary investment.
- *Salespeople are pests.* Professionals trying to maximize billable hours may perceive frequent calls from vendors as a nuisance. Abstracting from this, they often feel that they, too, become pests when they call a prospect.
    - There are several fallacies in this logic. First, it is doubtful that you see vendors who add value as pests. Second, the fact that you feel a call at this moment is inconvenient is far different from perceiving the caller himself as a nuisance. Persistence is okay so long as it is courteous. Third, people react to calls in different ways. Many will not be troubled by your calls at all, even if they don't return them.
    - If you view yourself as a pest, you will have difficulty developing new business. It will undermine your persistence, and you will become one of the many professionals who makes three calls and then gives up. Those are the ones who never become marketers. This book will help you find ways to ensure that your calls do have value and get through to the people you want to talk to.
- *I can get the outcome I want on a project if I just work harder.* When you face a production crunch, you work harder and longer, more work gets done, and your problem is solved. This isn't necessarily true in marketing, where the one-to-one correlation between effort and results is lost.
    - Marketing is a numbers game. You have to pursue ten or fifteen or twenty opportunities to win one. On average, if you work longer and smarter, you will win more new business, but this is not always so. Market conditions and other factors can offset all your hard work.
    - In baseball, some players have higher batting averages than others, but all strike out a lot of the time. It's the same in marketing. If you go to the plate, there is a good chance you will strike out, but you must go to the plate to get a hit, and the more often you go, the better your chances of getting on base.
- *Whenever my work doesn't produce results, I have failed.* When doing client work, this is generally true. Any professional working on a project who runs up a lot of hours without producing a tangible result either runs down profitability or is doing his client a disservice.

■ Just before writing this section, I finally reached a prospect I had wanted to talk to for several months. It took me thirty-seven calls spread among seven different people to get to this point, and I still haven't got any business to show for it. This isn't failure. It's how selling works. Selling is a numbers game. Each call was like drawing a card from a deck in a game where the high card wins. When I spoke to someone and the information I received got me closer to the person I wanted to talk to, I had drawn a face card. When I hit a dead end, I had drawn a two. Unreturned calls aren't failures; they are like jokers—they simply don't count in this game. There may be a lot of jokers in the deck, but it doesn't matter, because you can draw as often as you want.

■ In selling, you must learn not to see efforts that produce no results as failures, or you will become demoralized, and you will fail. Selling requires bouncing back from adversity.

• *Doing client work is practicing my profession. Selling isn't.* I have heard professionals say that they don't want to sell; rather, they want to practice their profession. That is, after all, what they went to school to do. They don't understand. Selling is practicing your profession at the highest level. It is in the sale that you translate the client's hopes and fears about a situation into the outline of a design, or plan, or case, or legal document, or whatever it is that your firm creates, to meet the client's need. Selling is being a true professional advisor. Name a leading professional in your field, someone universally respected as a major contributor to your profession, and chances are you have named someone who works hard at selling. There is no task more important to a professional firm than developing business.

If you sell work, it's good for the firm and it's good for you. If you sell work, the firm grows and there is more opportunity for all. The more opportunities you originate, the more selective you can be about what work you take. You can accept the most interesting and challenging work, the work that will increase your competence and your reputation, and the work that is most profitable. To be entrusted with responsibility to bring in work may be a challenge, but it is also a sign of respect and arrival.

Marketing is an emotional roller coaster.

In most firms, rainmakers are seen as more emotional than the staid individuals who manage projects. They are. They work in a win/lose environment where a misstep or bit of bad luck can wipe out months or even years of work, but where skill and good luck can have incredible impact on the firm and their own careers.

Someone who has not sold much in the past can find the emotional swings disturbing if he does not understand them fully and is not prepared for them. You must prepare yourself, or you will decide you don't like selling before you give it a chance. It's okay to feel frustrated when you can't make the progress you want with a particular prospect. But you must bounce back and try again. Eventually you will win.

You can gain a sense of control in business development.

Feelings of stress are highly correlated with a sense of lost control over important things that happen to us. Business development operates by such different rules from client work that many professionals feel a tremendous loss of control when they first begin to sell. When this happens, stress levels rise.

As a structural engineer who was pushed cold turkey into full-time business development once put it, "I had never had any marketing training. I thought my boss would mentor me, but he didn't. Later, I realized it was because he didn't really know how to do it himself. No one told me anything about how to do it. I couldn't quantify anything I was doing. The first six months were hell." After fourteen years performing and managing engagements, where he knew exactly what to do when, no wonder he felt a loss of control. No wonder he felt stressed! Though most transitions are less abrupt, most professionals feel the same way about their early business-development efforts.

As with learning to ride a bicycle, if your fear of falling stops you from pedaling, you will never learn. You won't go very far or very fast at first, and sometimes you will fall. But you will gain ability and confidence. My friend the structural engineer brought $2 million of new business into his firm this year.

It is always better to be doing some marketing than none.

When doing client work, a little planning can save a lot of trouble later. This is true of marketing, too, with the big difference that planning does not assure results. Effective planning can reduce risks on an engagement to minor proportions, but selling is a numbers game. All that can be said is that the better your marketing planning and execution, the higher your probability of success. Planning cannot eliminate risk.

A client of mine who provides litigation support in a technical area fell into a common trap. We had discussed repeatedly his need to develop stronger credentials through article writing and speech making. Wishing to pick the best subject, he analyzed litigation trends, and analyzed and analyzed. He wanted to be sure that he picked a hot emerging area so that he would reap the biggest results from his efforts. The problem was that beyond a certain point, he could not know what the emerging trend would be. No amount of analysis will let us divine the future. Rather, he needed to make an educated guess and then get into the marketplace. You too must realize that analysis in marketing will not reduce risk to the same degree it does in client work. Almost any reasonable *action*, therefore, is better than none.

The professionals who succeed at marketing are the ones who market. They always have some marketing activity underway. That activity may not be original or brilliant but unlike most of their peers, they are doing something, and eventually they get results. Marketers market.

That is not to say that marketers want to give up client work completely. Few do. Rather, they realize that making progress on marketing is as urgent as making progress on a client's project. They become as uncomfortable when they do not have some marketing effort underway as anyone else does who has a shortage of project work. At least once each day, you need to remind yourself that marketers market and that you should be working on something.

You need to get face-to-face with a prospect to make a sale.

Brochures, Web sites, newsletters, mailings, advertisements, press releases, and articles can strengthen your marketing, but they will not help you unless they or some other technique in your marketing mix gets you face-to-face with a prospect to talk about his needs.

If you have not sold before and lack basic selling skills, getting face-to-face with a prospect may feel uncomfortable and even scary. This book will help you develop the skills to get over this discomfort and succeed, but you must ensure that your marketing mix includes activities that will get you face-to-face. Marketing mixes are addressed in the chapters on strategy.

When you find yourself wanting a brochure or Web site, ask yourself whether you really need it or whether you are avoiding the hard work of engaging prospects in a dialogue.

Everyone can make a contribution.

There is no one right way to develop business. Whatever your particular skills and interests, you can make a contribution. If you don't want to write, you can speak. If you don't want to speak, you can network.

This is important not just for you but also for your firm. The organization that can mobilize the most resources has a significant advantage over its competitors. Lincoln realized this during the Civil War, when he directed his commander in chief, General Grant, to get all his generals to apply pressure on the Confederacy. "Those not skinning can hold a leg," he wrote.[2]

I was once asked to turn around a troubled consulting operation and noticed that the most troublesome competitor operated on the star system, with one individual doing virtually all the marketing. Borrowing from Lincoln, I reasoned that if we could mobilize numerous marketers, even if many made a smaller individual contribution to our firm than this competitor did to his, we would beat him. It worked. If you're not skinning, hold a leg.

When you win, celebrate.

Companies with large sales organizations spend fortunes motivating their sales forces. They recognize how crucial motivation is to sales success. If your firm doesn't celebrate a major success, do it yourself. Take your spouse to dinner or buy something that can serve as a trophy. You should certainly do this when you close a major sale. Landmark accomplishments such as your first publication or getting yourself invited to speak to an important audience also warrant a reward.

If motivation doesn't come from the firm, you must provide it yourself.

Now is the time to start.

If you have not begun to market yet, now is the time to start. Every day you delay will make it more difficult. Every week that passes is an opportunity missed to make a contribution to the firm.

Use this book in several ways.

Broadly speaking, there are three ways to increase your firm's revenues. You can increase the number of people you talk to about your services. All other things being equal, if you talk to 100 people about your service and I only talk to 50, you will sell more work. (I will call this *variable network size*.) You can increase the percentage of those who hire you and that, too, will grow your revenues. This requires keeping the clients you already have while adding new ones (called *percent buyers*). Finally, you can increase the amount of revenue that you get from each client (called *revenues per client*).

The skills to succeed at growing revenue one way are quite different from growing them another. For example, the skills required to find a new account differ from of those required to develop an old one. You don't have to be superior at all of them. If you are really good at one, you can succeed while being less skilled at others. You can partner with someone who excels where you don't. Everyone can contribute.

Other activities will help you grow your revenue by increasing both the size of your network and percent buyers. Giving a speech, for example, helps you meet more people and so helps you increase the size of your network. If it is a good speech, it may also predispose some of the listeners to hire your firm and so increases the percent buyers.

This book is organized into four parts. Part I shows how to get leads. It will teach you methods you can use to find prospects and to make it easy for prospects to find you (that is, to increase your *network size*). Many of the techniques described in this section, such as publishing and speaking, will predispose clients to hire you (and so increase the *percent buyers*). You can add the people you meet through these efforts to your network.

Part II is devoted to networks. It describes how to create, maintain, and increase lead flow from your network. Our research shows that rainmakers maintain large networks from which most of their work comes. Part III shows how to advance and close a sale once you have a prospect. Doing so is, of course, necessary to increasing the number of people in your network who hire you or, in other words, to increasing the *percent buyers* and your *revenue per client*. Part IV shows how to build a marketing strategy that is appropriate for you and your firm. It comes last because you must understand something of the tactics at your disposal before you select a strategy.

Use the book in two ways. First, read it all the way through to gain the understanding of the subject matter required to begin to market. Exhibit 0.1 arrays the chapters against the three variables for quick reference. Knowing that the book would be used for this second purpose has required me to repeat some concepts and information so that individual chapters can stand on their own. I have tried to minimize redundancy by referring readers to other chapters when appropriate, but some repetition has been unavoidable.

EXHIBIT 0.1

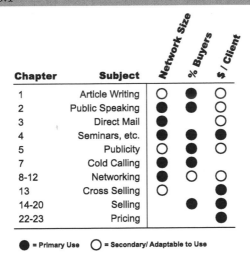

Chapter	Subject	Network Size	% Buyers	$ / Client
1	Article Writing	○	●	○
2	Public Speaking	●	●	○
3	Direct Mail	●		○
4	Seminars, etc.	●	●	●
5	Publicity	○	●	○
7	Cold Calling	●	●	
8-12	Networking	●	○	○
13	Cross Selling	○		●
14-20	Selling		●	●
22-23	Pricing			●

● = Primary Use   ○ = Secondary/Adaptable to Use

Because professionals must sell themselves in order to sell their firms, I have written about career as well as marketing strategies—about selling yourself as well as selling your firm. You must find the appropriate balance between the two, but you cannot do one without also doing the other.

Most of the content has been tested in training and one-on-one coaching sessions at a variety of organizations. I will know I have succeeded if those who read this book and follow its guidelines can say, "I tried it and it works."

PART 1

Marketing Tactics: How Professionals Build Reputations and Generate Leads

The founder of a civil and environmental engineering firm that today does $20 million worth of business each year told me how he became a marketer. "I never planned it. I started my own company because one client said he would give me all his business. A week later he died. I had a wife, kids, and a mortgage. That's how I became a marketer."

Most professionals who succeed as marketers begin by doing. They don't have a grand design. They aren't trying to build a firm. They're just trying to find a client. Such people are doers first and planners second. They are either trying to squeeze some marketing in amidst demands from paying clients or struggling to stay in business.

For the beginning marketer, doing before planning offers several advantages. It builds your self-confidence. It increases your knowledge, without which you will find it hard to plan. It puts you in contact with the market, the best teacher you will ever have. When you have developed basic skills, you can then create a more deliberate marketing strategy.

When you start, each marketing effort is a test. Even if the speech you give doesn't bring in a job, it will help you learn what works and what doesn't. Most professionals learn to market that way. I certainly did. I had worked as a management consultant for over ten years and sold many assignments before I received even an hour of formal training.

This portion of the book will help you learn to generate leads. It will reduce trial-and-error learning by providing practical advice on how to write an article, get an opportunity to speak, make a cold call, hold a seminar, send a mailing, and get quoted in the press. In one-on-one coaching sessions and in classrooms, as a manager of professionals and as a sales-and-marketing

1

consultant, I have analyzed what keeps professionals from succeeding at generating leads. I have used these analyses in developing the how-to advice found in the succeeding chapters. While working with this portion of the book, please note the following.

Learn by doing.

People learn more by doing than by reading. This portion of the book has many exercises that you should complete as you read the chapters. The text will guide you on what to do; the exercises provide a means to try out what you have read and help you internalize it.

You can't sell until you have a lead.

As a successful interior designer said to me, "It all starts with a lead. You have to have a lead to get a client." Some firms forget this. When a professional says, "I sold the XYZ job," he may mean that he generated the lead and then sold the engagement, or he may be thinking only of the accomplishment of having sold the job, forgetting the hard work that went into giving him the opportunity to do so. You should make a clear distinction: The first step is to get a lead, the second is to advance and close a sale. This, of course, implies that you know what "a lead" is. It's not so simple because the term is used loosely to refer to everything from a piece of information about a prospective client's needs to an invitation to talk about your services. In event-driven businesses, like disaster-recovery consulting, litigation support, or architecture, information that a specific prospect has a need has high value and may legitimately constitute a lead. In evergreen businesses, such as accounting, audit and tax work, and compensation consulting, every prospective client has an ongoing need. In such cases, a more useful definition of a lead is an opportunity to talk to a prospect face-to-face about a need that he has acknowledged.

You need prospects at different levels of development.

For your own business, you must gain a feel for two variables. The first is the typical gestation period from the time you first make contact with a prospect to the time you actually sign him as a client. Depending upon your business, this can range from less than a month to over a year. The second variable is the typical conversion rate from prospect to client. This may have several subsidiary rates, which you should also understand, such as the conversion rates from cool prospects with whom you are just talking to hot prospects who have requested proposals, and the conversion rates from hot prospects to clients.

A sense of these variables will suffice, at first, though you will probably want more precise measures later, since both variables change with market conditions. Understanding them will help you complete the following sentence, which underlies one of the key principles of marketing: *I need x prospects today to have reasonable assurance that I will have a new client in y months.*

Professionals often do not think enough about the implications of this sentence. They become focused on the pursuit of two or three hot prospects, and once these projects are either won or lost, they wake up to find that they have too few others in the early stages of development to generate the business they will need in the months to come. This is one of the major causes of *porpoising,* the radical and repeated swing from too much work to too little that so many organizations face.

To minimize porpoising, you will need to generate a continuing flow of new leads. This part of the book will show you how to get leads, however you define them.

Writing and Publishing
Your Article

Case example: *The author John liked to write. It helped internalize and organize things he learned, and he liked to see his name in print. Early in his consulting career he wrote an article that was published in a major business periodical,
and he found that by doing so, he had become the firm's expert in one of its small
practices. He wrote more and soon developed a personal plan to produce articles
for trade journals addressed to each of the major industries his firm did business
with and to each of the functional areas within corporations that his firm's consulting services supported. The exposure and increased stature the articles gave
him made it easy for senior partners to market him for major projects. When they
needed an expert on the insurance industry or on labor issues, John's articles gave
him the credentials. Frequently in front of clients, he soon began to get opportunities to sell as well. By modifying a piece for more than one publication and by
using articles as the basis for speeches, he leveraged his writing time. He rose to
become the leader of a regional office and a national practice for his firm.*

When I hire a professional, I want an expert. I know from the start that it's
going to cost me a lot of money; indeed, if my need weren't urgent, I wouldn't
be hiring at all. But my need is urgent, and I am going to pay—only I want
someone really good for my money. That's where my problem begins. I know
little about law or accounting or many other fields where I might have a need,
which makes it difficult for me to distinguish who is really good from who
isn't. My cynical nature makes me suspect that many more will claim to be
experts than really are. Publications provide one proof of who is real and who
isn't. Whether I see an article in a magazine or have a reprint handed to me
by the author, published work tells me that the author must have substantial
experience and that she has reflected more deeply on her business than some.
That the editors of the journal in which it appeared thought enough of it to

print it also counts for something. All other things being equal, the article will weigh more heavily than someone's self-acclamation.

This scenario explains why publishing an article is a logical first step in marketing. Professionals beginning to market need to build their stature, develop name recognition, and flesh out a resume. Articles do all of these things. Although they are not especially effective in generating leads, they do sometimes result in direct queries from prospective clients. Over a long consulting career, I have known articles of mine to lead to contacts that in turn resulted in jobs at companies like IBM and Ford Motor Company. My writings serve as proof of expertise. A future client from a major financial institution put it to me succinctly while holding up a reprint from a major business publication I had sent him: "Here's your credibility right here!" Reprints can also serve as mailers to remind past clients of your continued existence.

In spite of these benefits, professionals plan far more articles than ever get written. I have participated in so many discussions about articles that died aborning that I have come to believe professionals need more than an admonishment to go forth and publish. Additional guidance is called for.

Professionals will tell you that they don't write articles because they don't have time. It is axiomatic in professional service firms that production and sales pressures drive out marketing time. This is untenable. Firm management and individual professionals must preserve time for marketing and, at the same time, find ways to make as efficient use of their marketing time as they do their billable project time. It's not as difficult as it sounds. By learning some basic techniques, professionals can greatly reduce the time required to write articles while enhancing the probability of getting published.

In my experience, most professionals spend their article writing time unproductively. Lacking confidence, they waste too much time thinking in an unstructured way about what they will write. If an article gets beyond this point, too often it is constructed as a report or dissertation, and the resulting draft ends up long, ponderous, and dull. This means the author must rewrite it, a process the article seldom survives. Discouraged, he places it in a file, intending to return to it when the workload lightens, and never puts hand to it again. You can avoid this outcome.

It starts with an idea.

One way to increase your article writing effectiveness is to know what you want to write about when you find the time to do it. Whenever I have an idea for an article, I write it down on a slip of paper and put it in a file entitled "Article Ideas." I keep an electronic and a hardcopy version of this file. As other thoughts come to me on the same subject, I note them in the same place. I will clip articles, write down quotes that I hear, and make copies of data that pertain to the subject. The electronic material goes into the electronic file, and the hardcopy into the paper file. When I do get time to write, I have a packet of materials ready to work from. The files always have five to ten ideas in them, rising like dough in an oven, until I am ready to work with them.

If you do not have such a file, start one now. Take a few minutes and write down whatever ideas you have. Discipline yourself to write down additional thoughts on the subject as they come to you.

Most articles in hardcopy publications run between eight and twelve double-spaced, typewritten pages. A short opinion piece might run six, and a long, more academic one, over twenty. Electronic publications tend to want shorter pieces, perhaps three or four double-spaced typewritten pages. You may have to break your ideas down into smaller pieces to accommodate such demands. Consider offering the piece in two or three installments.

If you have an unexpected free morning or even a full day when you can write, you will find you can spend the time far more productively if some light research and many of the ideas are waiting for you in a file.

Know thy market.

Professionals often attempt to write articles without a specific journal in mind, viewing placement as secondary. This is akin to writing a report and then seeking a client to sell it to. By picking a target journal, you permit yourself to study several copies in advance, researching the journal the way you would any other prospect before attempting a sale. If you don't know what publications your target audience reads, ask; your clients can tell you. Leaf through the publications lying around your clients' reception area. Make note of periodicals a client has in her office. Search the Web for the publications of relevant trade and professional associations.

When reviewing a target publication, first determine who your audience will be. What is the editorial approach? Is it geared toward news items? Professional practices? In-depth case analyses? The article you submit must address the appropriate audience in a manner consistent with the journal's editorial policy.

Stop reading now and collect four or five periodicals—the more diverse, the better. Leaf or scroll through them, looking at each as a market rather than as reading material. Which periodicals are written by staff and which by contributors? This is an important difference. Staff-written magazines (such as *Business Week, Fortune,* or *Forbes*) will take no contributor-written articles, except (rarely) for a few specific purposes, such as a guest contributor column. If this is your target, your article must comply with the publication's strictures concerning length, format, and content. Occasionally a staff-written periodical will accept a piece in interview format or use a contributed article as a foundation for a staff-written one, in which case portions of your article will appear as quotes attributed to you.

Your best bet, however, is contributor-written journals (such as *HR Magazine* or *Urban Land*). Again, be sure to study past issues to identify the audience and determine editorial policies. Most publications provide "Contributors' Guidelines" or "Writer's Guidelines" on their Web sites, spelling out their requirements in detail. Media kits, used to market the journal to potential advertisers, are usually available for free and can provide useful information about circulation and editorial calendars. You can also query the editor by phone or mail about whether a subject would be of interest. Editors will state clearly if you are far off the mark, but they are otherwise cautious before seeing anything in writing. So save queries, unless your question clearly cannot be answered by studying copies of the magazine or reading the contributors' guidelines.

Refereed journals (such as *Harvard Business Review* or *Journal of Accountancy*) are those that submit articles for review to two or three experts. The decision to print will depend more on the votes of these reviewers than on the staff editor. Such journals tend to be academically oriented, and they usually require footnotes. The turnaround time between submission and publication tends to be long, often a year or more.

Some publishers, including professional associations, publish several periodicals to meet the different educational needs of their markets. ASAE, the Association of Association Executives, for example, publishes both *Association Now*, which is geared at current news of importance to its membership, and *Association Leadership*, a refereed journal devoted to weightier pieces adding to the body of knowledge about managing associations. Both take articles contributed by outsiders.

Reviewing journals is essential to selecting your market. The Web makes most publications readily accessible for your perusal. If you would like extra guidance, *Bacon's Business Media Directory: Directory of Print and Broadcast Business Media*[1] is an annual publication that provides brief information on many magazines, including an indication of whether they are staff or contributor-written.

Keep in mind the thing that every journalist knows.

Once you have a publication in mind, you next need to pick an angle, the point of view you adopt in writing about a subject. Choosing a clear point of view allows you to do the following:

- Address the article to a specific audience.
- Screen information in and out of the article.
- Provide focus, interest, and purpose.
- Develop an initial structure.

You should be able to state your angle in a single sentence. In this chapter, for example, I stated, "By learning some basic techniques, professionals can greatly reduce the time required to write articles while enhancing the probability of getting published." My audience is apparent: professionals who have difficulty getting articles written and those who are concerned about this problem, such as firm managers. The theme is circumscribed, greatly simplifying both my research and my writing tasks. Why? Because specific supporting information is called for.

Note how the sentence summarizing the angle for this chapter helps structure the piece. It cries out for an introductory paragraph or two on why article writing is important to professionals, followed by a description of why article writing usually takes so much time. It dictates a brief description of the required techniques. A good angle should provide this simple benefit to the author. Exhibit 1.1 lists some subjects and possible angles for articles.

EXHIBIT 1.1 Subjects and Angles

Review the exhibit and then, in the bottom portion, list a subject you want to write about, plus three alternative angles.

Subject	Angles
Library design	1. Ten common mistakes in library design can be avoided by skilled planning and programming.
	2. New technologies are radically altering the way that libraries should be designed.
	3. Libraries can serve different functions that require radically different designs.
Wills	1. You should review your will and possibly rewrite it when certain key events happen in your life.
	2. When a will is poorly written, it can stimulate the events the deceased specifically wanted to avoid.
	3. Preparing a good will should begin with a clear understanding of your values and goals.
Your subject	*Your angles*
	1.
	2.
	3.

Once you have picked a journal, you can test an angle against its audience by asking yourself whether it is really targeted to them. If your angle is too broad or too narrow, rewrite it to focus your piece and you will improve the probability of its being published. Many professionals have nipped writing careers in the bud by producing articles that were too broad or too narrow to appeal to the editor of any identifiable journal. Discouraged by working so hard for nothing, these professionals often give up article writing completely. Review the angles you prepared based on Exhibit 1.1 and ask yourself whether they are well targeted to the specific journal you would like to be published in. Adjust them as needed.

Once you formulate an angle, you must write within its constraints or reformulate it. Reformulating is usually required when the first angle does not truly encapsulate what you want to say. Be sure to check any revised angle against your target audience to make sure it still fits. Many teaching professionals often forget the limits and focus that a good angle requires. Those who make this mistake end up with wordy, rambling pieces. If you are having trouble with an article, check to see whether this is happening to you. Beware of *angle creep*. Every author, including this one, has ideas and stories he falls in love with, even though they don't quite fit the angle he is writing about. Part of the discipline of writing a publishable piece is to delete such items from your work. Save them for another article in which they would be more appropriate. Take the time to develop a good angle up front and then write the article to elaborate on it and it only.

Exhibit 1.2 provides a second exercise to help you understand angles.

EXHIBIT 1.2 Incomplete and Complete Angles

What is wrong with this angle?
Quality Assurance in the Property and Casualty Industry

Answer:
It is a subject, not an angle. It is not a complete sentence. A complete angle is "Quality assurance offers a means for property and casualty insurers to differentiate their services." This angle makes it clear that the author plans a marketing article rather than an operational/how-to or financial/cost-savings one. It clearly focuses on a specific audience and set of issues.

Artful use of angles also permits you to place an article where you might not otherwise be able to. A colleague and I once sought to place an article on research lab location in a trade journal read by many researchers. Therein lay the problem: The editor only wanted articles addressed to actual researchers, while the audience we had in mind was management. The angle we chose was this: "As part of your career planning, you should understand how corporations select research lab locations so that you can improve your chances of living where you most want to." It became an article suitable to both audiences and was accepted.

With a little practice, sitting down and listing two or three possible angles on a subject that will make it attractive to a specific periodical should not take long. Once you choose a clearly stated angle, your writing job will be easier, because the temptation to include too much information in a clumsy structure will be reduced. This focus also reduces research requirements.

The formula has power.

A formula is a set pattern for expressing ideas. It helps you determine the components of your article and the relationship of the components to each other. This chapter uses one of the most common formulas found in professional and trade journals, the how-to formula.

Though many professional writers use formulas unhesitatingly, I have had to convince my clients of their true value. Many feel that writing based on a formula is inherently of lower quality than other writing. This belief is simply wrong.

This outlook ignores the many examples of formula writing of the highest quality. The formula used by John Mortimer for his delightful stories about Rumpole, barrister of the Old Bailey, which have been dramatized on television, has been summarized neatly by Donald E. Westlake, an author of comic mystery novels.

> This is the Rumpole formula: A mystery is presented that contains the possibility of a subject to ponder—the workman's right to withhold his labor, say, or the citizen's right to remain silent when charged with an offense. Several of the other recurring characters in the series will then turn out to be engaged in activities containing variants on the same matter (for instance, shall Mrs. Rumpole withhold her labor from Mr. Rumpole's house?), allowing Rumpole's ruminations broader scope. Partway along, someone coincidentally will just happen to tell Rumpole the fact that solves the initial mystery. Once the theme and variations are complete, Rumpole will take that fact to court, confound the prosecution and judge and retire triumphant, with a wry parting summation directed at us, his audience.

No variation on the above is permitted, or even considered. If the subject is the citizen's right to remain silent, for instance, you may be sure no character in that particular story will be so inattentive as to be found withholding his labor instead. He will dutifully wait for the with-holding-his-labor story.[2]

The use of formulas is not restricted to light or popular fiction. The for-mulaic components of Shakespeare's plays have been carefully described by Mark Rose of UC Santa Barbara.[3] The gripping speeches of Dr. Martin Luther King, Jr., utilize formulas for sermons he learned in seminary.[4]

The power of the formula lies in productivity. I have illustrated this point in my consulting assignments by asking clients to say something funny, with the restrictions that they must not use something they have said or heard before and that they have only two minutes. Not surprisingly, most are struck dumb by this request. I then ask them to do the same thing with the following additional restrictions.

They must make their funny statements in five anapestic lines with the rhyme scheme aabba. The first, second and fifth lines must have three feet and the third and fourth two feet. The first line must be "There was once a consultant named Ford." Once the participants realize that they are being requested to create a limerick, they are usually able to struggle through the exercise. Votes after the exercise show that my clients unanimously prefer the second exercise to the first.

This demonstration shows that it can be much easier and faster to create within the confines of a formula than with total freedom. The formula liber-ates you from many of the requirements to structure your writing, allowing you to focus on content. Formulas for articles are less rigid than those for a limerick but benefit the writer in the same way structured verse does the poet. There is no shortage of formulas to choose from. Some of the most com-mon are these:

- **The list:** This is the most basic of formulas and one of the easiest to use. Commonly used in articles reporting trends, this formula provides brief write-ups on each of a list of items tied together by an overall theme. An article entitled "The Real Estate Industry in the Year 2020" might use such an approach, with descriptions of such factors as the changing roles of developers, the tendency for brokerage commission discounts, the increased focus on build-to-suit, and so on. The list of formula types you are now reading is another example, although shortened and simplified so that it can be subsumed within the how-to formula of the whole chapter.
- **The straw man:** A premise is set up and then knocked down, showing the benefits of a different point of view or approach. This formula is used

commonly when new practices sweep an industry. A piece showing why an accepted method of cost accounting can be misleading and proposing an alternative one might use this formula.

- **The other point of view:** A subset of the straw man, this formula takes a contrarian view to the one commonly held. So, when there was great concern about the ethicality of cross-selling, after the Anderson/Enron debacle, I wrote a piece for the *Wall Street Journal* pointing out the virtues of cross-selling when done appropriately.
- **The miniature case study:** A question is raised and answered through three or four brief case studies. An article answering the question, "Does quick response provide competitive advantage?" might use this formula. One case study could show how quick response can lower unit cost, another how it increases customer perceptions of quality, still another how it permits premium pricing, and so forth. Anecdotes, strong selling tools in any profession, are used to make the case.
- **The interview:** On three occasions I have interviewed others in the firm I was working for, and on one I sat at my word processor and interviewed myself. Another time I provided a list of questions to a compatriot who then wrote out responses. All four articles were printed in reputable journals. This approach is particularly useful with staff-written trade journals. An interview can have higher value than a bylined article in building your reputation, because the format implies you were sought out by the journal as an expert.
- **The fad:** Fads sweep professions like fashions. Whenever one emerges, articles explaining the fad to different audiences appear all over the place the way a trendy color suddenly shows up on everything from dresses to automobiles. Articles on e-commerce can and undoubtedly have been written to explain its value to metal stampers, discount retailers, bankers, and many other groups. Articles on the latest tax shelter and investment approach appear in magazines targeted at doctors, lawyers, yuppies, and almost any other identifiable group that might provide a market. These articles tell what the fad is and what its benefits are and provide a hint of how-to.
- **More and more or fewer and fewer:** These articles report findings of a survey or other study. A piece entitled "Corporations Are More Concerned About Flexibility in Office Design Than Ever Before" might show how corporations require designs that allow them to adopt new technologies, down-size and sublease, move business units frequently, and so forth.

I have found that my clients understand the concept of formulas better if I show them how a subject must be adapted to each formula. Take the admittedly trivial subject (but one that everyone can understand) of picking up dates in bars.

An article entitled, "How to Pick Up a Date in Bars" would use the how-to formula to provide step-by-step instructions on technique. One entitled "Are Bars the Best Places to Pick up a Date?" might be a straw-man article written by someone who is against this practice. It would first describe the reasons why people pick up dates in bars, then knock them down by pointing out risks or faulty reasoning. Finally, it would point out that a person has a better chance of meeting someone compatible by taking French classes, joining an athletic club, signing up with a computer dating service, or (ignoring the risk of a sexual harassment charge) attending office parties.

"Should You Pick People up in Bars?" might be a miniature case study article. After citing a few statistics about the number of people who do pick up dates in bars, the article would describe four specific cases. If it is an article opposed to the practice, each case might show a different and progressively more horrible outcome. "What's Happening in the Bar Scene?" might be a list article in a magazine devoted to the subject of dating. It would describe the latest trends at bars, in list format, which might include virtual reality games, a return to the ethnic bar, and who knows what else. The discussion of each item would include a comment on its implications for the individual seeking to pick up a date. "An Interview with Mr. (or Ms.) Pick-Up" would be just that, covering an expert's experiences and asking for advice and his or her vision of the future, given changes that are occurring in the bar world. "More and More People Are Picking up Dates in Bars" would be an article reporting survey findings on dating habits and the habits of people who hang out in bars.

Now pick a subject more pertinent to your business than the one in the preceding example and see how it would change by using different angles and formulas. You will probably find that one or two have potential for a real article.

Once you have mastered formulas at this level, you will begin to see others in the articles you read, or you can develop your own. Formulas provide you with instant structure, allowing you to write an article quickly. This matters in an environment where writing time must be squeezed in among hours devoted to billable projects.

When you have chosen a formula and angle, list all the points you want to make. Then rewrite the list, organizing it within the structure that the formula dictates. Delete and add points, as needed. Now you are ready to start writing.

If you wish to see how research, angles, and formulas can combine to make article writing easy, try this experiment. Review several journals in your field and select one that is contributor-written. Develop an angle for an article to be submitted to this journal that is a variation on the theme "Professionals in (your area of expertise) Provide Great Value in Certain Identifiable Situations."

Outline an article based on this angle using the miniature case-study formula. From your own experience or those of your associates, pick three or four cases, each illustrating a situation in which a professional provided a specific, identifiable benefit (confidentiality, objectivity, issue resolution, and diagnostic insight, for example). Then sit down and write your article and see how long it takes. The conclusion should reiterate your angle.

Know what editors like.

Articles have a better chance of being accepted if they are submitted in a way that makes working with them easy for the editor. Some publications will specify how they like to see submittals in writers' guidelines found on their Web sites. Otherwise, submitting in the right way means doing the following:

- *Leave wide margins (1¼ inches) and extra space at the beginning of the manuscript (⅓ of page).* These allow the editor to make notations easily, as many editors still edit on hard copy (though an increasing number request electronic submissions only). All articles should be double-spaced for the same reason.
- *Place your last name, the article's title, and the page number in a header at the top of each page.* Because many editors still work off of hard copy, if a pile of unstapled manuscripts is dropped, yours will be easy to reassemble. If, for some bizarre reason, you submit your piece in hardcopy, use a paperclip, not a staple, to hold it together.
- *Provide an approximate word count on the last page.* The editor will have to do this if you don't. Most word processing programs make this easy. In Microsoft Word, look in the Tools menu for the Word Count function.
- *Include charts, tables, diagrams, checklists, photos, or side bars to enliven the text.* Some journals require or prefer camera-ready copy.
- *Provide headings where appropriate.* Good headings do not just help the logical flow of a piece, they also engage the reader (and the editor) by catching his or her eye. Thus, "Avoid Overcharging" has less catching power than "Greed" or "Like Pigs at a Trough."
- *State in a cover e-mail that the article is being offered exclusively.* This way, the editor does not have to worry about accepting an article for publication then finding it in print in a competing journal.
- *In the same e-mail, provide a one-sentence statement of why the article is pertinent to the journal's readers.* Don't place the burden of figuring this out on the editor.
- *Describe the article in two or three sentences.* Be sure to show the main points you will make.

- *Include a suggested author's description, consistent in length, format, and content with those the journal typically provides.* This will increase the odds that the description says what you want it to.
- *Comply with any other submission instructions.* These are usually noted in the magazine or its writers' guidelines.

By following the approaches I have described, you will find that article writing becomes easier and faster and publication more frequent.

Increase the chance of getting leads from your articles.

Articles should not be relied on to generate leads. Although they can occasionally do so, they will never provide the predictable, steady supply of prospects that a primary lead-generating activity must.

There are, however, a few things you can do to increase the lead-generating power of the articles you publish. Be sure that your name, firm, and the name of the city your firm is located in appear with the article. This can usually be done in the author's description. A few journals will not reference the city from which you do business. In such cases it may be possible to mention it in the text of the article. Do so carefully, since most journals will not accept articles that are patently self-promotional, rather than educational.

Some journals, especially trade journals, will be happy to reference an offer you make to readers to send something of value to them. This is usually a report of some sort that you have prepared. By requesting the report, a reader identifies himself as a prospect. The editor will usually want to see a copy of the report to make sure that it is not simply a brochure or something that would embarrass him, like a reprint from another publication. Sometimes offers must be made in a letter to the editor following publication of your article. It is worth asking the editor whether an offer will be printed if you are interested in this approach.

Research, angles, and formulas can be as important to this aspect of your marketing effort as the technical tools of your trade are to providing professional services efficiently. They help ensure that articles are not just planned but also produced and published.

2   Finding a Podium

Case example: The Speaker

After teaching for two years at a law school and working for several more at a large law firm, Frank accepted a government appointment at a regulatory agency. Because of his new position, bar associations and universities frequently invited him to speak. Frank had noticed at a recent conference how ill prepared many of the speakers were and decided that audiences deserved better. Though he had not made many speeches previously, he brushed up the skill he had developed as a teacher, spent hours developing a speech that would have value to his audience, and rehearsed. The audience clearly liked his speech, and he was invited to make others.

As his speaking reputation developed, Frank continued to prepare carefully, seeking out new material to keep his content fresh. He sought to develop relationships with members of his audience and with those who had arranged for him to speak. After each speech, he reviewed the evaluation forms the audience had filled out to see what he could learn that might help him get better. He also followed up with as many people as he could by writing to them. He developed a reputation as a reliable speaker.

When Frank returned to private practice as a partner at a major firm, the invitations continued. Increasingly seen as an expert in his field, he began to receive leads from people who had heard him speak. As he learned about the power of the podium, he enhanced his efforts in several ways. He would convert speeches into articles, gaining added exposure for little extra work, and he began developing speeches on a specialized area of his field not often touched on by others, increasing the probability that he would be invited to round out panels and conferences. Because he was a successful speaker, others often sought his ideas for fresh content at conferences. Such discussions often resulted in additional invitations. Leads continued to come, and others in his firm also found it easy to sell him to their clients as an expert in his field. He became a recognized rainmaker in his firm.

Case example: The Raconteur

Wendy loved to tell stories and she told them well. Events that passed unnoticed by others became hilarious when she recounted them. People sought her out at gatherings and afterward remembered her. When they called, she remembered them and reminded them of an event that made them laugh. She was fun to be with.

Wendy translated this social ability into a personal marketing strategy. She sold consulting services to public sector and not-for-profit community groups, of which there were thousands spread across the country. Associations of these groups met annually in each state and region, and there were several national organizations, as well. They were always looking for good speakers. On the basis of her storytelling ability, Wendy was invited to speak at these events, and she soon proved as entertaining at the podium as she was in the conference room and over the dinner table. Better yet, her stories delivered a message.

In time, her speaking reputation brought her more invitations than she could handle. What had begun as an occasional, informal marketing task evolved into a central strategy. As this transformation occurred, she began to do the following:

- To charge fees for speaking, turning this activity into a financially self-supporting marketing campaign.
- To focus on selected key messages that supported the firm's central marketing positions.
- To leverage the time she invested in speaking by reusing the same speeches many times, converting them to articles and book chapters and collecting names from her audiences so that she could follow up with them by mail.

Eventually she developed a two-day seminar, which prospective customers paid to attend. Her career prospered, and on the basis of these and other activities she rose to become the president of her firm.

Speeches are articles with faces. Like article writing, public speaking helps build your reputation as an expert. The audiences are smaller, but the impression you leave is stronger. You are more likely to be remembered by someone who has heard you speak than by someone who has read an article you have written, because she or he has seen you. Face-to-face with your audience, you can develop an emotional linkage not possible with an article and so increase their comfort with calling you later. Your chances of conversing directly with the audience, and of obtaining names and phone numbers so that you can follow up, are greatly increased.

Like the speaker and the raconteur, some professionals speak frequently. They develop reputations as speakers, find platforms, and, if they are good at it, bring in a steady flow of leads for their firms. Other professionals speak seldom or never for one of three reasons: fear of public speaking, uncertainty about their own speaking abilities, or lack of a podium.

Understand the fear of public speaking.

Fear of public speaking is a common complaint. If you feel this way, it may help to understand that your fear is shared by thousands of others, including those who speak frequently. Even the most accomplished speaker will have a queasy stomach when standing before a group larger or more important than he is accustomed to. Frequent speakers learn to handle the fear and counter it with confidence in their own abilities. They do not let their fear stand in the way of their careers.

If you lack confidence in your speaking abilities, I recommend taking one of the professional training courses available from a variety of organizations. Even skilled speakers can benefit from such programs. Pam Yardis, former Chair of the Institute of Management Consultants and a successful professional, once told me that she tries to take a presentation skills course at least once a year. Successful public speaking results from your appearance, movements, and tone of voice as much as it does from content. You can control all of these, and the courses teach you to manage them effectively, taping your performances so that you can see the effects as you change behavior. I have seen many individuals dramatically increase both their skills and confidence through such programs.

If you are unable to attend such a program, there are several good books on the subject. You should also study effective speakers every chance you get and emulate them. And don't forget to read Chapter 17 of this book.

Whenever I attend a conference, I learn from watching other speakers. I not only learn from those who do well, I also find out how abysmal the average speaker is. Long ago I realized that one didn't have to have the oratorical power of Winston Churchill or Dr. Martin Luther King, Jr., to outperform most of the speakers on the trade-show circuit. Most speakers do not prepare adequately, and fewer still really rehearse; rather, they review their notes silently or read scripts. I will deal with this issue later.

Find a podium.

Some platforms are more competitive than others, but there is ample opportunity for everyone. Most organizations hunger for speakers and will be willing to give you a chance if you present your case properly. Developing a reputation usually requires building from small audiences to large and from humble to prestigious ones. Even Martin Luther King, the preeminent American orator of the latter half of the twentieth century, practiced before peers in seminary and at church congregations before earning the chance to speak to larger groups.[1] Early on, simply for practice, you should accept almost any opportunity offered. Some people I know have joined Toastmasters, an organization dedicated to improving members' speaking skills, in order to get this experience.[2]

You may already know many of the groups you want to address from your work. If not, you can try the following alternate approaches:

- *Ask others who would know.* I once wanted to speak to senior human resource officers and found that meetings of the largest trade association tended to draw lower-level managers. By asking around I learned that there was no single organization that fit my purpose. In each major metropolitan area some smaller group served as the gathering place of my target market. These groups had to be identified on a city-by-city basis.
- *Identify groups.* Consult the *National Trade and Professional Associations.*[3] This publication, available in most libraries and on the Internet (*www.associationexecs.com*), provides concise information on thousands of associations, their purpose, membership, meetings, and publications.

Once you have identified a group to speak to, try to attend a few meetings. Speaking formats differ from organization to organization. Some prefer individual speakers; others prefer panels. One organization I know almost always pairs a corporate employee with a previously hired consultant. By going to a meeting, you will find out what formats are available, as well as what subjects attract the most interest; you can also meet members and staff. If possible, review an organization's publications to get a sense of members' interests. Speeches made at conferences often appear later in article form in an organization's publications.

Staff and committee members can tell you about procedures for selecting speakers and what kinds of speakers they are looking for. However, most organizations are looking for two things: strong speaking ability and strong content. Most will sacrifice some content for a speaker able to excite or entertain an audience because they have seen the negative effects the expert bore on attendance. This means that you will want to demonstrate both your speaking ability and subject knowledge when offering yourself.

The two most common approaches to selection are often used in combination. The first is referrals. Members or other contacts are asked for suggestions. In such cases, you must know who to contact to request consideration. I would recommend a low-key phone call to the appropriate person, stating that you have heard the group is seeking speakers and that you are available to speak on a specific subject. Ask whether you could send a summary of what you would like to talk about, plus a little information about yourself, then get off the phone. Once the person has reviewed your materials, you can make a stronger pitch.

A second approach to selecting speakers is to solicit proposals with an application form. These forms usually request a concise summary of your speech and proof of your credentials.

Whether you are sending a letter or a completing a form, you should include the following:

- **A statement of relevance:** You should state why the subject you wish to present is important to the audience. You may also be able to tie the subject to the theme that many trade associations have for their annual meetings. The ability to adapt a standard speech to a specific situation often makes the difference between acceptance and rejection.
- **A concise summary:** A three- or four-sentence description focusing on benefits the audience will receive is usually adequate.
- **Expert's credentials:** The reader will want to know why you are qualified to present. A reduced version of your bio, focusing on your knowledge of the subject you wish to address, is the most obvious proof. Reprints of articles you have written and lists of other audiences you have spoken to on the subject are good supplements.
- **Speaking credentials:** By providing proof of your speaking credentials, you will distinguish yourself from the majority of applicants.

Finding someone who will stimulate an audience is a difficult task. A person scintillating and vibrant in one-on-one conversation can turn into a wooden mannequin on the platform. Program committees dread inflicting such a person on their fellow members. Anyone who can demonstrate an ability to speak well will have a strong advantage in getting selected. As in most selection processes, the one who presents himself best will usually win, whether or not his actual performance is superior. Anyone who aspires to be a speaker should develop a file of speaking credentials. These should include the following:

- **References:** You can supply two or three references for your speaking abilities from others who have heard you speak. Staff or elected officers of organizations you have spoken to are best, but the references can be from anyone who has heard you.
- **Lists of podiums:** Lists of organizations to which you have spoken also constitute a proof, as evaluators commonly make the assumption that if you have spoken often, you must speak well.
- **Testimonial letters:** Thank-you letters are often sent to speakers. Save any that say good things about your effect on the audience so that you can send copies with future requests for a podium. Better still, you can solicit testimonial letters and request that they make specific reference to your speaking abilities.

- **Speaker evaluations:** Many organizations ask attendees to fill out speaker evaluation forms. Always request a copy of the results. These are especially valuable if they show you in comparison with other speakers rather than in isolation. In cases where evaluation forms are not used, I often prepare my own. This has allowed me to demonstrate my abilities in forums not usually evaluated, such as in-house training courses. A typical form is provided in Exhibit 2.1. Results should, of course, be summarized. Reviewing evaluations will help you polish a speech. If necessary, edit your summary to focus on positive commentary.

EXHIBIT 2.1 Sample Speaker Evaluation Form

Event: _____

Date: _____

Location: _____

Speech title: _____

Speaker:_____

Please help us by completing the following evaluation:

Topic

Excellent	Very Good	Good	Fair	Poor
5	4	3	2	1

Speaker

Excellent	Very Good	Good	Fair	Poor
5	4	3	2	1

General comments: _____

_____

_____

_____

What did you find most helpful?_____

_____

_____

_____

What could be improved?_____

_____

_____

_____

Name:_____Company: _____

Use these proofs of your speaking abilities selectively. No one performs equally well on all occasions. Ratings will vary with the nature of the audience, the frequency with which you have given a particular speech in the past, and other speakers' abilities. If you follow a four-star orator, your ratings will not be as good as when you follow a dud.

All letters and applications should be treated with the same attention that you would give a proposal to a prospective client. They should be thorough, neat, clear, and attractively formatted to make life as easy as possible for the reviewer. This will communicate the seriousness of your interest.

The time has come to talk of many things.

Once you are invited to speak, you must prepare for the event. A few guidelines follow. However, this chapter is less about the preparation and delivery of a speech than on gaining the opportunity to speak in the first place and using that opportunity as a vehicle to build your reputation and develop leads for new business. A good book on speech preparation and delivery and a good blog on the subject are listed in the appendix, and most of the material in Chapter 1 on angles and formulas in article writing applies equally to the construction of speeches. Formulas, for example, are commonly used in speeches.

A few guidelines on the nature of speaking engagements not found elsewhere are offered here:

1. *Don't speak too long.* The most common formats for speeches before associations are the single speaker and the panel. Most run between an hour and an hour and a half total. Single speakers should seldom talk for more than thirty minutes, leaving half an hour for questions. If you use slides or transparencies, controlling the number you use is one good way to regulate the length of time you speak. I know that I cannot present more than fifteen transparencies in half an hour. When that is my time limit, I force myself to use no more than this number. This, in turn, forces me to make decisions about the content to be presented. Panel speakers usually have between ten and twenty minutes each for their presentations. If they fail to control themselves, they risk appearing insensitive to other speakers and to the audience.

2. *Be conversational.* Today's most successful speakers use a conversational style, as opposed to one of the more formal alternatives. Many people find it hard to retain an informal tone when standing before an audience. To do so requires that you avoid using long and formal words when simple ones will do. As you rehearse, listen to what you say, or have someone critique you, so that you can replace phrases like, "They were impressed with our

method" with "They liked what we did." Beginning your presentation with a direct question to the audience may help you to retain a conversational style. Ask for a show of hands or a few comments. This brief dialogue with your listeners will help get you started with the right tone.

3. *Rehearse without a script.* I usually write a speech prior to rehearsing it, but once the rehearsals start, I set it aside. At most I retain a four-or-five point outline and notes on any facts and figures I might not remember. The purpose of writing out a speech is to organize my thoughts, not to develop a script. Because starting off and finishing are difficult, I will sometimes memorize the first and last lines. For the rest, I count on rehearsals to make me facile with the material so that it will come to me as I need it. Be sure the opening line is conversational in tone. One architect and programmer I know was able to transform a stiff and stilted style to a quite charming one by beginning with a disarming claim for his own expertise: "By some strange quirk of fate I have programmed more conference centers than anyone else in the world."

If possible, rehearse with a coach who will critique you. Ask this person to interrupt whenever he finds his mind wandering. Many coaches are too polite to do this unless asked, feeling that it is their responsibility to pay attention rather than yours to hold it. When stopped for this reason, review your content and the words you are using to see what is causing the presentation to drag. Are you giving more detail than is needed? Will an anecdote illustrate a point better than a description? Is the value of what you are saying clear to the listener? Do you need to change your tone of voice, increase your volume, or inject more emotion into your delivery?

Don't expect to feel good during a rehearsal. Practice sessions seldom provide the adrenaline lift of the real thing, but two or three real rehearsals during which you stand up and speak aloud will help make the real thing better.

Knowing the size of the audience and layout of the room will also help you prepare. The host can usually give you an estimate of the former and can almost always describe the latter.

Use speaking engagements to generate leads.

Generating new business leads is the main reason for seeking a speaking engagement. You will be more successful if you are deliberate about it. Though you may be willing to speak to a wide array of organizations at first to gain experience, once you have established a reputation you will want to be more selective, focusing only on audiences likely to be productive. Evaluation factors include audience size, the percentage of potential clients as opposed to other attendees, and the cost in time and money of attending. I once accepted an invitation to speak to a group without conducting the proper research first, only to find that I had wasted two days, including travel time, to address a group that had not a single potential client. I never made that mistake again.

You should also plan to attend the whole event you are speaking at, whether it lasts for only an evening or for several days. This allows you to do the following:

- Stir up interest in your presentation, increasing attendance.
- Assess your audience in advance.
- Meet with members of your audience after the presentation. Build off your presentation. Informal discussions can build rapport that might turn into leads later.

Your ability to generate leads also depends on your subject and content. A tax accountant who built the largest practice in his firm and is a frequent speaker says, "I usually average one new account per presentation. You have to have a hook. It helps if you can show special expertise at solving a nagging problem or avoiding a painful one. A lot of speeches don't do that."

Most leads come when you follow up with your audience after the speech. This means you must obtain their names, addresses, and phone numbers. There are several ways to do this. One is to circulate a sign-in sheet. This is not always practical, and the resulting list may have to be shared with any competitors on your panel. It also creates a minor distraction as it is passed around. When it works, it is efficient.

A second approach is to offer copies of your presentation materials to all who leave you their business cards at the end of the presentation. This is a common and effective technique but deprives the audience of take-home copies that many would like to have. As an alternative, you can offer something else—a report on a study, for example. A final approach I have used with large audiences is to ask them to fill out a survey form, offering to send copies of the findings to all who also fill out the name and address section.

Follow-up should occur between one and three weeks after the presentation.

A brief letter thanking the recipient for his interest will personalize the mailing and refresh fading memories of who you are. You can then follow up by phone, taking the opportunity to inquire about the need for your services.

Speech making can be among the most effective ways to develop leads for a professional practice. It also builds your reputation and that of your firm.

3 Marketing by Mail

Case example: The Source

By chance, Dennis developed expertise in an emerging area of insurance law. He received one case as an outgrowth of claims work his firm was doing for a major insurer, and a couple of others followed. Dennis had seen a manual produced annually by a competitor on another area of insurance law and distributed free of charge to clients and potential clients. Seeing a void, he developed a manual on his new specialty, crafting it to meet the needs of middle managers at insurance companies. The first issue was only ten pages.

Over the next ten years, he revised it annually or semiannually, and it is now almost 300 pages long. Each time he updated it, he sent it out with a personalized letter. Over the years he has developed a proprietary mailing list of people interested in this particular area of insurance law by gathering cards at conferences, adding names of clients and prospects, and responding to requests from those who have learned about the manual from others. Today his name is synonymous with this particular practice, partly because of the work he does in the field but also because everyone with an interest in the field knows the manual. He has become the source for information in this specialized area. The manual confirms his expertise to new acquaintances, opens doors to people he doesn't know (if they work in this area, they will usually accept a visit from the manual's author), and provides a regular reminder in the form of a useful tool for those he has worked with in the past.

Maurice Fulton, who gave me my first job in consulting, once said that in the early days of his career, shortly after World War II, he could send out one big mailing and "make our nut for the year." The world has changed. Professionals compete intensely, and almost all employ direct mail in their marketing mix. Few see the results my former boss saw, yet they persist, for several reasons.

First, direct mail seems easy in comparison to many other kinds of marketing, especially now that it can be sent electronically. It lacks the potential for direct rejection inherent in a cold call. A mailing can be sent out quickly with a minimum of fuss, compared to writing an article or networking. Much of the work can be delegated to the administrative staff.

Second, it seems cheap, and even cheaper today with the advent of the Internet. We send out e-mails every day and, less frequently, letters, seldom thinking of the cost. Certainly it is a low-cost way to deliver a message to a large number of people. Lastly, it is an accepted way for professionals to sell their services.

Professionals who have little marketing experience almost always think about developing a Web page or a brochure, then suggest a mailing. That most mailings are grossly ineffective seems to deter no one.

Direct mail (and I include e-mails in the term) can be a productive way to market your services, but it has to be done right. When done right, it is neither easy nor cheap. To make it effective, you must work with a limited number of variables, which include these:

- Objective
- List
- Medium
- Frequency
- Message
- Offers

Many professionals miss one or more of these variables.

What are you trying to accomplish?

There are several legitimate objectives for a mailing, the most obvious being these:

- **To remind past clients, prospects, and market contacts of your existence:** The typical newsletter serves this function. Direct mail shows your continued interest in a past client the way a Christmas card shows interest in a relative you seldom see. Clients are more likely to think of you when they have a need, or when they talk to someone else who has a need, if you jog their memories this way from time to time. As a management consultant in Spain put it, direct mail says "Blink! I'm still here. Blink! I'm thinking about you. Blink! This is what I do."
- **To build name recognition:** Name recognition makes it easier for you to get in the door when you make a cold call. It increases the likelihood of a prospect's calling you if she is given your name by a friend. Even our best

clients may not know about the full range of our services, which, after all, change with time. Direct mail ties your name to a specific array of services.

- **To generate leads:** Few professionals can sell their services by mail, but they can generate qualified leads. This allows them to focus marketing efforts on prospects with the greatest potential of hiring.
- **To position a phone call:** Professionals often send e-mails advising a prospect that they will call to request a meeting. I discuss this use of e-mails in Chapter 7 on cold calling.

You can seldom meet all these objectives with the same mailing. You must decide on the primary objective of every mailing so that the remaining variables can be adapted accordingly.

Who are you mailing to?

Many of the direct-mail pieces you send will be tossed without being read. The quality of the list you use influences the percentage of waste. A mailing sent to a well-targeted list of prospective clients will have a far smaller waste factor than one for which the list has been chosen carelessly.

Most professionals use two kinds of lists: those they create and those they buy.

Created lists are made up of the names of past clients and prospects, vendors, employees and past employees, and other business contacts and friends. In my experience, most of these lists are in disarray. They are created casually to meet a specific need, grow haphazardly, and are maintained poorly. The first list, compiled for a specific mailing, say a change of address when a firm is small, may have 2,000 names. Ten years and twenty mailings later, it may contain 12,000 names, with no indication of when each record was added or last updated or who submitted the name, no way to tell who these people are (past clients, vendors, etc.), and little checking for accuracy or duplication.

Few firms have the attention span to fix the resulting mess. The formats for the entries often complicate correction. Title and department, for example, may have been allocated to one field in the original database. Practical use later may require sorting your list by one or the other of these, which will be impossible without splitting them into separate fields. Parsing a field, as any database specialist can tell you, requires a visual review and manual correction for each record.

The installation of a firm-wide client database tends to leave most professionals unsatisfied. They find that changing the data on their own contacts now requires multiple steps or may even be forbidden. They find that the whole firm now has access to information that a client gave to them, based on their personal relationship, information like the client's home phone number or the date of his birthday. The new systems also may require the resolution of issues that the professionals maneuvered around when each kept her own contact list. Most significantly, many client information databases now require that each contact be assigned to one person from the firm who has the primary responsibility for maintaining the relationship. The old system often left that unclear and, at times, opaqueness was an advantage. Before, when two partners both claimed ownership of an account, the issue could be left undecided and so, vague. Now, only one person can be listed as the account exec, meaning that one of the partners must lose.

If you already have a list that is in disrepair, you should fix it as soon as possible, since the problems can only get worse as it grows and ages. The appropriate repair sequence is as follows:

1. *Purge.* Conduct a detailed review of the list to eliminate as many records as possible and identify those you know to be inaccurate. This will reduce the number of records to be repaired.
2. *Repair.* Modify the database to fit the format of your client relationship management or contact management system. A list should be purged periodically, and your new database format will make this much easier. Alternative purging methods include: 1) a visual review of all records that have not been updated within the past two or three years; 2) a review by each professional of the names he or she has placed on the list; 3) an annual first class/return-requested mailing (this can simply be one issue of your newsletter or other regular mailing); or 4) an annual reader-response questionnaire of the kind used by controlled-circulation magazines.

Lists can be purchased from one of several sources:

1. *List merchants*
2. *Directories.* (You can either buy preprinted labels from the publisher or extract names from the directory by hand. Before doing the latter, you should carefully read restrictions placed on the use of names by the publisher. Most publishers deliberately include false names and addresses to catch those who use listings without authorization.)
3. *Magazines*
4. *Trade associations*

Many lists can be presorted for you, so that you purchase only those names most likely to be valid prospects. Names can be sorted according to geography, size of company, industry, and job title.

When preparing a list, you may wonder how many people to include from one company. Companies neither know about your services nor buy them; people do. The number of people in a company who should receive a mailing depends on the company's size (the bigger the company, the larger the number of people who should receive the mailing) and on the nature of the mailing (the topic may have broad or narrow appeal).

When planning a direct mailing, you must choose what list or lists you intend to use, since that decision will influence both quantities and content. For example, an environmental consultant mailing a white paper featuring a case study on underground tanks at a service station might want to purchase a list of service station operators to complement his own past-client list.

Should you distribute your message electronically or in hard copy?

The war between electronic and paper distribution is almost over, with a stunning victory for electronic media. Electronic distribution has these advantages:

- You can track who opened it and who passed it along to others. This allows you to identify people most likely to be interested in your services. This is a huge advantage over paper.
- It is much easier for the recipient to pass along your electronic document to others and to respond to you than it is with paper.
- Most people under fifty prefer electronic copy.
- It is usually less costly than hard copy, especially for large mailings.

Paper seems to have "lie around" advantages. Once an electronic document has been filed, it is seldom opened again. Paper documents tend to lie around a client's desk, allowing her to stumble across them and read them at odd moments. Older audiences may be more comfortable with paper.

If you are going to send paper, you had better have a compelling reason.

How often should you mail?

Like advertising, direct mail depends upon frequency of exposure for impact. You will have to make frequency decisions early. If you don't, you may find yourself short of time or money to complete an effective campaign. A one-time mailing may not be worth the effort, depending on your purpose and content.

Frequency decisions should be closely tied to purpose. A newsletter to remind past clients of continued interest should be sent two or three times a year, every year, especially if it is your primary vehicle for doing so. A direct-mail campaign to increase your reputation and name recognition within a specific industry will require at least three or four mailings closely sequenced. If you mail less frequently, a high proportion of your audience will forget about the first mailing by the time the second one arrives.

A campaign to find prospects might require only one mailing if it includes an attractive-enough offer. Offers are described on page 32.

What should you mail?

The success of a direct-mail effort depends heavily on the message you send and the form you send it in. Your objectives help you determine both. Here are some possible formats:

- **E-mails:** These are the low-cost choice for mailers. Add to that their flexibility (e-mails can be used alone or in combination with other materials), and it is no wonder they have become the preferred format for mailers. Yet many get trashed, unopened in split-second choices by executives and their assistants or automatically routed to junk mail folders. To reduce the probability of this happening, it's important to see the problem from the client's perspective. That isn't too hard because we all receive so much spam and bulk mail everyday. Why do you open some of this mail and not others? Experience suggests that we are more likely to open e-mails when the subject line is personalized and provocative.

  - Our knowledge of many of the people we send e-mails to gives us an advantage over the spammers. We can often address the recipient by her first name in the subject line, something spammers try but often lack the knowledge to do. If the recipient's name is Katherine, and we know that she goes by Kay, rather than Kathy or Kate, we can differentiate our mailing from the spam by using her name in the subject line. As one executive secretary told me, "Everyone likes the sound of his own name." Personalization also requires that Kay be the only person listed in the address column of your e-mail. In some cases we can further personalize the mailing by citing why the material in the mailing is important to her. ("Kay, Relevant to Your Richmond Facility?") If you can't do that, you can at least make it provocative. ("Kay, Are New Trends in Exec Comp Causing Turnover?")

- **Brochures:** Brochures make poor mailers because they tend to be bulky and expensive to mail, they lack the news value required to induce a recipient to read them, and they are usually not sufficiently targeted to a specific need or issue. This does not stop many professionals from wasting money by sending them.

- **Newsletters:** Commonly used and usually boring, most are expensive and ineffective. A high-quality newsletter requires a major, consistent effort. Don't bother unless you are willing to make the commitment. Since the advent of desktop publishing and electronic distribution, the marketing newsletter has been so overworked that some firms avoid the term and appearance. They depend on memos, reports, manuals, and other materials to serve the same purpose.

- **Reprints:** The time spent writing an article can be leveraged by mailing reprints with a cover letter. The fact that a journal published your article implies you are an expert.
- **White papers:** More proprietary than reprints, white papers let your targets feel they are receiving special information not generally available. Sometimes they take the form of a memo on an important topic.
- **Gifts:** The gift must be worth having; otherwise, it is trash. Gifts are best if tied to a message about your services. For example, an architecture firm I worked for once mailed bookmarks with pictures of libraries it had designed to librarians.

In developing a mailer, consider the following guidelines:

The message must be tailored to your audience and your objective.

A white paper on ways to reduce the operating costs of major facilities is likely to appeal to the director of facilities and might be suitable for chief financial officers, but don't send it to CEOs. Materials sent to senior executives should stress high-level benefits, such as increased sales or market share. Those sent to lower-level managers require a higher level of proof of your technical competence.

Mailings to current and past clients will also have greater impact if tailored to interest. This is clearly the trend among sophisticated relationship marketers. A Boston-area lawyer who has built a substantial estate planning practice classifies his clients by interest. He tries to send each interest group a mailing on a relevant topic or service a couple of times a year. Says the attorney, "They know I am thinking about them and their interests, and that helps build client loyalty."

Insist on excellent layout and graphics.

Most people make an almost instantaneous decision about each piece of mail they receive, categorizing it as wanted or unwanted. The recipient, who is often pressed for time, must decide whether to download an attachment. She is likely to lean toward bypassing the download and move on to the next e-mail. Because the decision is so quick, it is influenced by visual appeal more than by content. Here are some simple guidelines to increase visual appeal:

- *Retain a lot of white space on the page.* Pages that are crammed with information look time consuming and hard to read. Instead of putting a lot of information on a page, shorten your content and make sure that every word counts. Alternatively, if you really must, you can lengthen your document.

- *Make sure the print is easy to read.* The type size should be no smaller than 12 point. It is better to use serif fonts.
- *Keep paragraphs short.*
- *Use graphics.* Photos, graphs, tables, charts, and lists are all more accessible than large blocks of text.

Make high-visibility text especially compelling.

Titles, headings, first sentences, and first paragraphs require special attention. They must stimulate curiosity or create a sense of urgency to read further. After completing the text, revise these portions, as needed, to grab the reader's attention.

Personalize your mailing whenever possible.

Anyone is more likely to read a personalized letter than one that is obviously a mass mailing. There will be cases where the size of the mailing prohibits personalization, but today's database and word processing technologies are constantly increasing the size of mailings that can be effectively personalized.

The rewards of personalizing can be substantial. A group of accountants, all on the faculty of a university, decided to establish a firm to cater to the accounting needs of the affluent. They sent a series of personalized letters to high-income individuals in the market area they had picked, announcing the opening of the firm and playing on the cachet of their university affiliation. Initial responses to these mailings put them in business.

How can you generate leads from a mailing?

Many products are sold directly through the mail, including clothes, camping equipment, food, furniture, tools, and bric-a-brac. Companies selling these goods can rely on direct mail for three reasons: Goods are moderately priced, they are returnable, and they are convenient to purchase. Professional services don't meet these criteria and so cannot be sold directly through the mail.

Nevertheless, you can use direct mail to induce a prospect to call or otherwise tip his hand that he is in the market for your services. This is a great benefit because it allows you to focus your most expensive marketing on a prequalified list of prospects. One of the great advantages of mass e-mails is the ability of the sender to know who opened it and who didn't and who passed on the e-mail to others. Those who showed interest in a subject by opening an e-mail, downloading attachments, and sharing the mailing with others are prime targets for follow-up. To get this information, you must make what is known as an *offer*.

An offer is anything of value that the reader can obtain by responding to your mailing. To be effective in lead generation, it should require readers to reveal that they have a need that somehow relates to your services. Here are some examples of offers:

- **A checklist:** This can be a list of issues to consider when undertaking some kind of a project. Checklists have the advantage of being relatively easy for most experts to create. They are also perceived as reader friendly and useful. An architecture firm generated sixty qualified leads from colleges and universities considering building or renovating libraries from an offer for a checklist.
- **A booklet:** Put together a booklet of information on an appropriate subject. Large accounting firms make effective use of this kind of offer with booklets on doing business in specific countries or on specific tax issues.
- **An audit or review:** This can be a brief analysis of a particular aspect of a company's business. Real estate brokerage firms will often offer to review a company's leases free of charge. Among consulting firms, this kind of service is known as a fishing license because it provides such a good opportunity to identify sales opportunities. Though this service is often provided free, professionals sometimes charge a modest fee to further prequalify the buyer before making a significant time investment.
- **A white paper:** An appropriate white paper might be entitled "Do You Need a _____ (fill in the blank with such things as Marketing, Environmental, Cost Reduction) Consultant?" People debating whether to hire a consultant or anxious to convince their bosses to do so will often request such a document.

Offers must be clearly identified and easy to obtain. Prominently display your phone number and e-mail address on any document likely to be downloaded and printed. Also, you can require the reader to fill out a brief questionnaire in order to obtain whatever is being offered. Remember that offers must require only a low level of commitment; in your mailing you are selling your offer, not your full range of services.

Conclusion

Direct mail permits you to reach a large audience at a relatively low cost with a specific message. It provides a means of generating qualified leads worth approaching with more costly marketing efforts. Some firms market by mail. If you do, take the time to do it right.

Once you have identified a prospect through direct mail, you must convert him into a client using cold calling and selling techniques described in other chapters.

4

Organizing Seminars and Conferences

Case example: The Intrapreneur

Jim, an associate at a large consulting firm, recognized that American manu-facturers would have to modernize their manufacturing practices thoroughly in order to regain their competitiveness in world markets. An industrial engineer, he saw an opportunity to develop a practice of his own in advanced manufacturing methods.

With the firm's support, he put together a half-day seminar on the subject and took it on the road to six cities. He invited representatives from mid-sized manu-facturing companies unlikely to have in-house staff able to revitalize manufactur-ing processes alone, and limited attendance to roughly twenty people per session to ensure intense interaction. He followed up personally with each attendee who had shown interest in his approach.

Today Jim heads a substantial practice. "The seminars were the foundation of this business," he says. "The work they generated kept us so busy for the next two years that we almost didn't have time for any other marketing. They established us in this business."

The popularity of conferences and seminars results from the benefits they offer. Attendees prequalify themselves as prospects; if they weren't interested in the issue being discussed, they wouldn't come. You get to talk with them face-to-face, during presentations and during breaks, meals, and receptions. As a speaker, you are automatically classified as an expert.

Because seminars can run from a few hours to several days, they can be adapted to a wide array of subject matter and contexts. I have been involved in a variety of seminars and conferences, including these types:

- **A series of late-afternoon seminars:** These were geared to past and prospective clients spread over two years, each using a panel to address an issue of current interest from different perspectives. Each was followed by a cocktail party. Objectives included maintaining the hosting firm's reputation as a leading-edge professional in its field and strengthening relationships with past clients and prospects.

- **A half-day seminar:** This was arranged and paid for by a specific client about to undertake a major corporate change. Speakers briefed the management on personnel, facilities, and other aspects of the change. The objectives were to provide the client's management team with background it would need to oversee the change process and to demonstrate that the firm organizing the seminar could assist throughout the project.

- **A two-day conference:** This was run by a professional conference organizer on a highly technical business issue, attracting participants from across the country. The fundamental objective for the organizer of the conference was to make a profit.

- **A series of two-day training conferences:** This was offered at several locations across the country to teach the fundamentals of a business activity to those just beginning their careers. Though run at profit, the primary objective of these conferences was to develop long-term relationships with prospective clients.

- **A one-hour Webinar:** This was offered by a not-for-profit organization as a benefit to members.

Each of these programs resulted in new business for some of the speakers. Unlike most forms of marketing, you can sometimes charge for seminars, covering your marketing costs and even making a profit.

With these benefits come associated risks and costs, especially if you plan a large conference for which you will charge a fee. If it is a onetime event, a conference is a high-fixed-cost, low-variable-cost enterprise. The time speakers must invest to prepare remains constant regardless of audience size. Marketing costs are also usually fixed, consisting of a large mailing. This leaves the duplication of handouts as the major variable cost. A two-day conference can cost you a bundle if too few participants attend to defray the hotel charges. By forecasting your costs, you can easily run a break-even analysis to calculate how many participants you need at a given price to recoup your costs. The fee from every additional attendee is almost all profit.

A large conference requires many hours of preparation from many people. This differs from many of the other marketing techniques described previously, which can be done by a single individual. A small seminar, given over a breakfast or at the end of the day, can be set up and run by one person, if an extended period of planning time is available. But it is a method that lends itself more to an organization.

Exhibit 4.1 provides a checklist of the specific tasks you must complete to run a conference. Variables for setting one up include subject, length, timing, location/accommodations, mailing list, invitations/flyers, speakers, supporting materials, informal interaction time, and fee.

EXHIBIT 4.1   Conference and Seminar Organizer's Checklist

(*Note: List is not strictly sequential because some of the steps are iterative.*)

I. Select subject
    A. Brainstorm alternatives
    B. Review for conferenceability
        1. Is it educational?
        2. Is it urgent?
        3. Does it lend itself to solutions?
        4. Do we have the resources/knowledge to handle it?
II. Determine length (One hour, half day, one day, two days)
    A. Establish schedule
III. Set date(s)
    A. Set completion dates for key tasks
    B. Monitor and revise periodically
IV. Select speakers
    A. Brainstorm alternatives
        1. Internal
        2. External
            a. Past clients
            b. Other experts
    B. Review for suitability
        1. Knowledge
        2. Drawing power of name
        3. Speaking ability
    C. Invite speakers
        1. Invite and confirm availability
        2. Invite fallback speakers, as needed
V. Select site
    A. Review alternatives
        1. Internal
        2. Hotel
        3. Conference center
    B. Inspect site alternatives
        1. Meeting space
        2. Break-out space
        3. Socializing space

        4. Sleeping accommodations
        5. Food service
        6. Logistical support
           a. Photocopying
           b. Audiovisual equipment
           c. Business center
           d. Message service
           e. Rest rooms
        7. Financial terms
     C. Negotiate terms and reserve space
VI. E-mail invitations
     A. Create invitation list
        1. Brainstorm with planning team
           a. Internal
           b. Purchased
              i. Determine fit
              ii. Determine cost
           c. Provided by speakers
        2. Select and assemble list
        3. Produce invitations
           a. Draft copy
              i. Describe theme
              ii. Describe benefits
              iii. Note who should attend
              iv. Describe schedule and content
              v. Describe speakers
              vi. Describe logistics
                 (a) Time
                 (b) Place
                 (c) Fee and payment
                 (d) Registration/response form
                 (e) Accommodations
                 (f) Directions
              vii. Design and e-mail invitations
              viii. Create list of confirmed attendees
VII. Order refreshments/meals
     A. Select caterer/provided
     B. Select menu
     C. Place order
VIII. Rehearse speakers
     A. Schedule rehearsal
     B. Coach speakers

C. Determine need and arrange for audiovisual equipment
IX. Prepare materials
    A. Collect copies of speakers' exhibits
    B. Collect speakers' bios
    C. Collect white papers/article reprints
    D. Prepare title page and table of contents
    E. Duplicate and bind
    F. Prepare speaker evaluation form
X. Arrange and check seminar logistics
    A. Reception
    B. Registration
    C. Name tags
    D. Coat room
    E. Speaker introduction
    F. Writing materials for attendees
    G. Materials delivery
    H. Seating arrangement
    I. Water for speakers
    J. Podium and lighting for speakers
    K. Audiovisual equipment
    L. Heating and air conditioning
    M. Hosts and helpers from firm
XI. Hold briefing meeting for firm members who will attend
    A. Review guest list
    B. Assign responsibilities
        1. Welcoming guests and giving directions
        2. Attendance to specific guest
        3. General responsibilities as hosts
XII. Run event
XIII. Follow-up
    A. Thank you e-mails to attendees
    B. Thank you e-mails to speakers
    C. Phone calls, as appropriate

Is it conferenceable?

I once suggested a conference theme to a professional conference organizer. She thought about it for a moment then responded, "It's an interesting idea, but is it conferenceable?" Conferenceability was a new concept to me. It means that the subject for a business conference must meet the following criteria:

- *It must be educational.* People come to conferences to learn. Entertainment is a plus, but promotion of your business is acceptable only if it is heavily disguised. There has to be something worth learning.
- *It must be urgent.* There must be a need to know now. A conference on "The Population Explosion of 2090" is not likely to draw many people. AIDS conferences draw thousands several times a year. I use the term "urgent" here loosely to mean that there is value to learning something now rather than later.
- *It must lend itself to solutions.* The conference must offer attendees solutions or progress toward solutions, because people attend business conferences in order to solve problems better.

You should test any subject against these criteria. If it does not meet them, try something else. Hit a winner and you can draw a large crowd. One law firm offering a seminar on the North American Free Trade Agreement in Mexico City attracted over 200 representatives from Mexican companies.

Good subjects for conferences or seminars often begin with the following phrases:

- How to Plan, Design, and Build a Data Center; Protect Your Assets in the Event of (fill in the blank); Negotiate a New Lease; Build Effective Teams; Get Better Results from Your Advertising Dollar
- What You Need to Know About the New (fill in the blank) Law; Drugs in the Workplace; Terminating an Employee; Outsourcing; Doing Business in Europe

A brainstorming session of half an hour can usually provide you with a good assortment of subjects to pick from.

The conference may be a matter of hours or days.

Next you must decide on the conference's length. You can determine length by asking yourself the following questions:

- *How much time and support do I have to set it up?* A two-day conference requires much more work than an evening seminar. You must adjust the length to the level of effort you can put into setting it up.
- *How much content do I have to offer?* There is simply not enough material for a lengthy conference on some subjects. When the Americans with Disabilities Act first passed, many people needed to learn about it quickly, because there were potentially stiff legal penalties for noncompliance. However, the legislation was so new that many of its implications were still

uncertain. It constituted an ideal subject for a half-day or evening seminar, but few people had the knowledge to run a longer one.

- *Is my audience willing to pay?* A two-day conference gets expensive, and most firms expect to be paid for them. The audience, in turn, is faced with not just a fee but a substantial cost in time invested away from other duties. A longer conference must therefore deal with a particularly weighty, urgent, or complicated subject. Generally you must also have a longer mailing list to find people with budgets and schedules that will allow them to attend.

- *How many speakers can I attract?* Plenty of multi-day conferences use only one speaker, but if you try to hold the audience all by yourself, you had better be good. Using three or four speakers a day diversifies your risk. Some of the time the audience will be listening to exceptional speakers, even if not all are of equal quality.

- *How geographically scattered is my market?* Few people will drive more than an hour to attend a breakfast or evening seminar. Assuming a 10 percent response rate to your invitations (an optimistic target), you will need to invite 200 prospective buyers of your services to attract a twenty-person audience. Identifying so many prospects within a one-hour travel time is easy in some businesses but impossible in others, even when more than one person is invited from the same organization. The wider the geographic area you need to draw people from, the longer your conference will have to be to justify the longer travel times.

Timing will also affect attendance. Most are scheduled to avoid summer vacations and end-of-the-year holidays. Longer conferences tend to be scheduled for either the beginning or end of the week, allowing participants to travel on the weekend and perhaps enjoy a short vacation at the city where the conference is being held. In the suburbs, short seminars tend to run in the late afternoon, allowing attendees to leave work a little early and avoid rush-hour traffic. Center-city seminars often fare better over breakfast or lunch. By the end of the day, city commuters want to get home.

Select the ideal conference location.

Possible locations for your seminar or conference include your own offices, a hotel, a corporate or privately operated conference center, or space borrowed or leased from another organization. If your office has adequate meeting space and is close to the market you are trying to reach, holding the conference there provides you the opportunity to show the place off and introduce other members of the firm. The location serves as a subtle advertisement for your firm. At one seminar I ran, an attendee noticed material on work the firm had done in the Czech Republic. He was about to start a project there himself. This kind of serendipity is more likely if a seminar takes place in your office.

Hotels and conference centers offer logistical support unavailable at many offices for conferences of a day or more, including full audiovisual support, eating space separate from meeting space, and ample breakout space. Most hotels will provide meeting space free if you guarantee a minimum number of room rentals. Room rates are negotiable if you expect a large number of participants. More importantly, you will want to negotiate the cost of meals and break-time refreshments. This is because participants pay for rooms themselves, while you pay for meals and refreshments either out of conference fees or out of your own pocket. Talk to several hotels, see the space they plan to give you, look at rooms, taste the food, check out logistical support such as photocopying and audiovisual equipment, request rates, and ask for references from others who have held meetings there. You will then be in a position to negotiate with several hotels to get the mix of service and cost that suits your needs.

Pull them in.

Most seminars are marketed by direct e-mail. The longer the seminar and the more you plan to charge for it, the longer the list will have to be to identify an adequate number of candidates. A breakfast or evening seminar can get by with a much shorter list. When I ran a series of after-work seminars followed by a cocktail party, the first one had an invitation list of 300, which grew to about 500 a year later. The acceptance rate for each seminar was about 10 percent, and almost exactly half the people who accepted showed up each time. Review the section on lists in Chapter 3 when preparing a mailing.

Because the quality of your invitation or flyer greatly influences attendance, it deserves special attention. For a one- or two-day conference, the flyer should include seven things:

1. *The conference theme:* The reader should be able to determine almost instantaneously what the conference is about. The wording should be as compelling as possible. The title "What Is the Competition Doing?" will entice more people to read the flyer than will "Competitive Intelligence."
2. *A concise description stressing benefits:* Professional conference operators usually employ a hard sell and make a profit by doing so. If you tone down your flyer, be sure you don't obscure the benefits in the process. Don't leave it to the readers to figure out what they will get out of attending. Tell them up front. At your two-day conference on the latest developments in competitive intelligence, for instance, attendees will learn the following:
   New methods for determining competitors' pricing
   Little-known sources of information on competitor profitability
   Ways to check the reliability of industry "gossip"

3. *A description of who should attend:* This inclusive list indicates who the conference is designed for and allows the reader to say; "This is meant for me!" Your list might include the following job titles:

   Strategic planners
   Marketers
   Competitor analysts
   Business unit managers
   Strategy consultants

4. *A review of the schedule and content:* In this portion, list what will occur from the morning through the afternoon of each day, noting speakers and subjects followed by two or three bullets stressing the benefits of each:

   Day One: 9:00–10:15 a.m.
   Determining What You Really Need to Know, Dr. Roger Skulk
   * Setting Priorities in Information Gathering
   * Avoiding Information Gaps
   * How to Respond to "It Might Be Nice to Know. . ."

5. *A concise speaker description.*

6. *Logistics:* Describe particulars like time, place, fee, payment, registration, and accommodations. This should include directions to the site.

7. *A sign-up sheet:* This can be a tear sheet or a response card.

A famous speaker, of course, deserves top billing. If you have one, resequence your material accordingly. Invitations to short seminars will be less elaborate but should include most of the same information.

Choose the speakers.

People who organize seminars for the first time often see themselves or others in their firm as primary speakers. You can often do better by including outsiders, sometimes by using them exclusively. Doing this will make the seminar seem less self-serving, which frequently results in higher attendance. Many prestigious firms periodically host one-day seminars for key business leaders. These seminars almost always feature a big-name outside speaker, who draws in the crowd. The firms' professionals sit with the audience where they can discuss the seminar and develop relationships.

Among the outside speakers you can choose are past clients, representatives of companies in businesses that sell to the same clientele that you do, and experts. Experts include academics and a wide array of other specialists who don't compete with you. When selecting a speaker or speakers for a seminar, you will want to consider things like the following:

- **Drawing power:** Some names attract more attendees than others. A client with stature in his industry will often attract his competitors, who are probably good prospective clients for you.
- **Availability:** One of the most onerous tasks in organizing a conference or seminar is lining up speakers. This needs to be done early in the process because everything else hinges on it.
- **Knowledge:** The speaker must know the subject matter. Firms that use only their own employees as speakers often can do so because they are presenting highly technical material that is little understood by outsiders.
- **Speaking ability:** The quality of the speaking will determine the success of the seminar. Don't subject your audience to the expert bore. Rehearse the speakers.
- **Balance:** If you have several speakers, make sure they present different points of view.
- **Price:** Most firms want to avoid paying speakers.

If you decide to speak yourself or to use others in your firm as speakers, you can do two things to make sure that you will be perceived as an expert rather than a salesman. First, seek out someone else to sponsor the event. Firms that run conferences for a profit will often accept good ideas, especially if the firm suggesting a subject is willing to help pay for it. Alternatively, you may be able to interest a trade association or other group in sponsoring the program by stressing its benefits to members. Be careful. Outside sponsors will sometimes invite a competitor to speak with you and will seldom bar a competitor from sitting in the audience. If you have strong reasons for using an outside sponsor, I would not let this risk deter you. The benefits of getting face-to-face with a large number of prospects usually outweighs the risk of competition.

If you plan both to host an event and to speak at it, you *must* stress the content and benefits in your flyer. The more people understand about what they will learn, the less they are likely to fear an advertisement. Remember, people attend a seminar to learn, not to be sold!

Webinars, also called Webcasts, combine a traditional seminar with aspects of radio performances because the speaker can't be seen by the audience. This is such a different speaking environment that I have include a checklist of guidelines for speakers and organizers in Exhibit 4.2.

EXHIBIT 4.2 Guidelines for Webinar Speakers

In preparing these guidelines, I relied heavily on Greg Mancusi of Deltek, a true Webinar guru.

Content: Without the physical presence of the speaker, the audience's ability to absorb information goes down. Avoid overwhelming your audience by limiting yourself to two or three main points.

1. Structure: Use a logical structure that is easy to follow. This structure should be used in your visuals, too. One such structure is the following:
   - What: (Example: First 100 Days on the Job)
   - Why: (Example: Most People's Success or Failure Is Determined in That Time Frame)
   - How: (Example: Goals, Plan, Metrics, Assessments)
   - Example: Provide an example
   - Repeat: (Example: "Goals" becomes the next "What" followed by "Plan," "Metrics," and "Assessment," each with their own why, how, and example)
2. Word pictures: Make it easy to grasp your message by including examples of people doing something. That will allow the listeners to visualize what you are talking about. Abstractions like companies, consolidations, and ambitions are hard to visualize and so hard to concentrate on without an example.

Visuals: Because the attendees can't see the speaker, more attention is paid to slides or other visuals than in a regular seminar. Visuals bear a bigger part of the responsibility for keeping the audience engaged.

1. The 45–60 Rule: Keep the audience's attention by changing slides more often than you would at a regular speech. No slide should be on the screen longer than 45 to 60 seconds. Changes in slides can be small, like adding another bullet to the previous slide.
2. Three things slide: Make sure the audience gets the main message. Prepare a slide listing the three main takeaways of the talk for the audience. Make it visually different (such as by changing the background) and show it three times: in the beginning, near the middle, and at the end of the presentation.
3. Simplicity: Your slides will be moving past the audience fast, so keep them simple and readable. Limit them to twenty words or less. Use graphics, but keep them relevant (graphs and charts). Do not use elaborate builds or other software animation; the reception equipment of some of the audience may not be able to deal with them.
4. Timing: Practice your presentation so you know how to work through the slides rapidly while speaking.

Delivery: Keeping the delivery engaging is hard when speaking to the audience by phone and seeing nothing but the wall of your office.

1. Live audience: Always have at least one person with you during the Webinar, so that you can see someone while you talk. That person should behave like an engaged listener.
2. High energy level: Exude excitement. A highly excited delivery does not seem over the top when the speaker can't be seen. Rev it up!
3. Second speaker: Try to have a second speaker with a different voice speak up once or twice during the Webinar. That person might talk for five or six minutes on one of your topics, for example.

Prepared Q&A: Always request a question-and-answer period. Prepare two or three questions that can be used to get that portion of the meeting going. Prepare answers to those and other likely questions so that you can address them concisely.

Give attendees a chance to talk.

People attend seminars and conferences not only to hear the speakers but to talk to their peers at other companies. They want to compare notes, commiserate, look for jobs, and relax with others who understand their problems. These periods of informal interaction also offer you the best opportunities for building relationships and generating leads. Arrangements for this activity deserve careful attention. You need to block appropriate time for it—before a breakfast or dinner seminar, after an afternoon seminar, and at several convenient times during a conference.

You will need open space out of traffic flow where people can stand and talk to each other without interruption. Comfortable sitting space in small clusters helps, too.

During this time, you and others from your firm should play host, circulating to make sure you meet everyone, making introductions, and absorbing those at the fringes of the conversations into the center. Above all, get others to talk. They have had a chance to hear you during the presentation. Now it is your turn to listen and learn. Learn names, learn personal interests, learn business responsibilities and concerns. This information will allow you to follow up later with a personal note to each individual.

Have a few stock questions to get others talking, like, "What is your interest in coming to this conference?" or "What do you think of the seminar so far?" Also, have questions that will draw out the silent individuals in a group. If one individual dominates the discussion with his reason for attending, wait for a pause and say, "That's interesting." Turn to someone else and say, "Did you come for the same reasons or different ones?"

Using your networking skills, you should be listening for ways you can help those you talk with. An obligation to call a participant with information he is looking for creates a means of keeping the relationship alive later. Create a list of these obligations for use after the conference.

The opportunity to establish a relationship with your audience is one of the primary benefits of running a seminar or conference. The chance to do so is largely restricted to informal interaction periods. Work hard during these periods, and you greatly increase your chances of obtaining business later.

Keep a handle on the money.

Few firms charge for seminars running less than a full day. A one- or two-day conference, however, can cost thousands of dollars to put on. Because of the substantial educational benefits they provide, attendees are willing to pay for them, and most, though not all, firms charge a fee. You should consider doing so.

The more your conference looks like one run by a trade association or other third-party conference operator, the more you can charge attendees. This usually means several presenters from a variety of organizations, high-quality audiovisual materials, a binder full of training materials, and high-quality conferencing space. Individuals with unusually strong credentials as experts and trainers do present alone for two days and charge, but they are in the minority. For prevailing fee structures, review fliers for conferences that you receive by mail. As of this writing, they run between $1,500 and $2,000 dollars per attendee for most two-day programs. Charging a fee can enhance the credibility of your seminar. It shows that people will pay to hear what you say and is an indicator that you intend to educate, not advertise.

Provide something to take home.

For-profit conferences universally provide participants with material summarizing what they have learned. If your event is free, you must decide whether to do so. Materials you can use for this purpose include copies of exhibits used by speakers, white papers or reprints of articles on the subject, and speaker bios.

A high-quality package of materials adds to the professional appearance of a seminar and gives those who attend something they can save with your name on it.

Follow up.

Within a week of a conference's completion, follow up with letters to everyone you have met, thanking them for attending. If you have promised someone information, you can put it in the letter, or, if appropriate, call. As in all forms of marketing, follow-up has a major impact on lead generation and separates the serious marketer from the casual one.

Conclusion

Conferences and seminars demand more of those who sponsor them than many other forms of marketing. They are expensive, complex, and deadline oriented. Hundreds of tasks must be completed on time. You can postpone a cold call or a mailing, but once a date is established, you cannot postpone a conference.

These concerns must be weighed against the power of the conference. It is a marketing activity that can pay its own way in fees. You establish yourself as an expert. You do so, in most cases, without having to compete for attention, and you have a strong opportunity to develop personal relationships you can build upon later. Seminars and conferences will remain one of the most powerful tools for marketing professional services.

5

Getting Publicity

Case example: The Publicist

Glenda, a litigator in a Midwestern city, had a way with words. Part of her success resulted from using concise, colorful phrases that juries remembered. One morning when she came into the office, the senior partner complimented her on the good quote she had received in the city's largest newspaper. She looked at a copy and found that two phrases she had used with a reporter the day before had been quoted. The conversation had been casual and almost accidental. A friend had suggested the reporter call her because she had experience in product liability law that might be pertinent to a story he was writing. The afternoon the story appeared, she received a call from a small corporation with a product liability matter. It became the first client she sold entirely on her own.

She called the reporter to thank him for the quote, and he asked her about another story he was working on. She couldn't help him, herself, but referred him to two people who could, explaining exactly why it might be useful to talk with each of them. From then on she and the reporter spoke every month or so, and once in a while she would end up with a quote. Occasionally another reporter would get her name from one of these stories and call her, too. She would incorporate him into her network of press contacts. When she learned that a local radio talk show was going to do a story on dangerous Christmas toys, she sent a letter along with some press clippings to the host, who invited her to speak on the program. This time she received two calls from prospective clients. Glenda had become a minor media star, and by honing public relations skills, she was able to build much of her practice around the leads her publicity generated.

When the *Wall Street Journal* twice quoted a competitor on a subject I knew a lot about, I became so irritated that I began a campaign to obtain a similar quote for my firm. Three months later a reporter from the *Journal* referred to a study I had done in a small article that appeared well back in the paper. My study received but a sentence or two. I was not mentioned at all, and the name of my company only once, but the following week three prospects called as a direct result. Had I had any doubts, this would have convinced me of the power of media relations.

Media exposure will help build your reputation and generate leads. What is more, according to a study by D.F. Blumberg Associates, companies that call you because they have heard about you in the media are substantially more likely to hire you than those whom you call first.[1] All experienced professionals know this, at least intuitively. There are at least four reasons why it is true. First, such prospects have prequalified themselves on the basis both of need and of an interest in hiring you. As is explained in Chapter 28, this is especially helpful for those practices where client need is infrequent. In such cases, proactive selling approaches tend to be ineffective because looking for a client who has the need today is like looking for a needle in a haystack. This problem is compounded if the client's need is also confidential. Second, the publicity has reassured the prospect that you are a credible source of help, reducing the selling you have to do. Third, the majority of professionals are far better reactive than proactive salespeople, and responding to the prospect's call requires reactive selling only.

Prospects want to hire a firm that has relevant, successful experience, and publicity spreads news of your successes across the market. As one attorney said, "You have to let other people know you have done a transaction. That's what builds your reputation in this business. You do that by getting the right reporters to write about it."

If a prospect has read about you in the papers or heard you quoted on the radio or television, his willingness to give you a meeting or include you among the firms being considered for a project increases. Press clippings can also prove your expertise and reputation to prospects you have reached by other means.

Many professional firms do not understand the process for getting good coverage. The lack of knowledge keeps many from trying. Others try ineptly, fail, and give up. Some firms find it difficult to attract media attention because the businesses they are in don't offer much good material. An engineering firm that designs mechanical, electrical, and plumbing systems for grade-school renovations will have fewer opportunities for exposure than a consulting firm that specializes in disaster recovery, simply because disasters attract more publicity than school renovations. In spite of these deterrents, almost any professional who is willing to learn the process, can think creatively, and makes the effort can get media coverage.

Most neophytes to public relations hold a number of mistaken beliefs that diminish the effectiveness of their efforts. These are so common they warrant immediate comment.

Mistaken belief #1: My primary objective is to promote my firm.
Promoting your firm may be an underlying reason for making the effort, but when you sit down to talk with a reporter or write a press release, your primary objective should be to help the reporter prepare a good story. If you are not helping, he will quickly lose interest in you, not just for this story, but for others as well. You should ask yourself what you have that might help the reporter. Do you, yourself, have direct experiences that might be interesting? Can you refer the reporter to someone else he should talk to? Are there reports or studies the reporter should know about because they address the issue he is investigating? Use the reporter's time well, and you have a good chance of becoming a source now and in the future. Abuse it by treating him as nothing more than a vehicle to promote your firm, and he will soon catch on and talk to you only if absolutely necessary.

A surprising number of people must learn that the media do not exist to promote their companies and services. Rather, they exist to educate and entertain their audiences. If they fail, circulation or audiences decline, they lose advertising revenues, and eventually they cease to exist.

Mistaken belief #2: The process starts with a press release.
Press releases may be the logical starting place if you are reporting on promotions of firm personnel or other routine matters. They are not the best place to start on any major story. There are many things you need to do before deciding whether to write a release; these are described on page 52. In spite of this caution, releases remain a valuable tool.

Mistaken belief #3: Reporters are primarily interested in facts.
Of course reporters are interested in facts and information. That goes with the job. But in my experience, facts and information are relatively easy to come by. If you talk to enough people, you will usually get plenty for a story. Having information is a prerequisite to getting interviewed but by itself will not get you mentioned. Guidance on how to get mentioned is provided on pages 52 and 53.

Mistaken belief #4: If I help a reporter, I'm entitled to coverage.
When I first began to work with the media, I spent several days helping a reporter from *Inc.* magazine with a story. She needed a case study of a company move to fit a relocation theme issue. I identified a past client interested in the publicity, gathered background information, and spent a day driving her to the client for the interview. In total I invested several days, and time is money.

Shortly before publication, she called to inform me that her editor had decided not to run the story. I was speechless. Would my client be upset?

What would my boss think about the waste of time? I leaned on her and leaned hard, but of course she held her ground.

I look back on this incident with embarrassment. Up to the point I started leaning, I had done a professional PR job, earning the reporter's respect and gratitude. Had I accepted the decision to drop the story graciously, she probably would have wanted to help me in the future either by using me as a source or by passing my name on to other reporters. As it was, I lost not only the story but also a valuable contact.

Reporters have no obligation to use any source they talk to, even if that source has been extremely helpful. Especially at high-end publications such as the *Wall Street Journal, Business Week, Fortune,* and *Inc.,* evidence that a reporter included quotes in direct exchange for getting information could get him fired. The ethics of journalism dictate that accurate reporting and a good story must be the only criteria for deciding what gets included. This standard protects reporters from political and economic influence that might undermine the media and endanger both our freedoms and our wallets. (Some readers will recall an incident in which an influential reporter was caught using publicity in his column to manipulate stock values.) The more influential the media, the more carefully it will hold to this standard.

This means that sometimes you will work hard to help a reporter on a story, but you won't get mentioned. Or you will be named but not your company, so that no one reading the story can find you. It happens. When it does, accept the reporter's explanation graciously and supportively, thank him for his attention, and offer your help at any time he needs it in the future. Ethical standards aside, reporters are human and they do have a sense of obligation. When someone has helped them, they will try to give that person coverage if they can find an appropriate opportunity to do so. Keep at it, and you will get the press you want.

This high standard does not apply everywhere. Trade publications unashamedly boost a particular industry, profession, or trade, and no one expects them to do otherwise. In this context, the risk that your help will not result in publicity is greatly reduced.

Unabashed boosterism is far preferable to what you find at some less meticulous media. Smaller and more desperate for revenue, some regional and local organizations will inform you directly, or by inference, that advertising dollars can be swapped for publicity. Editorial staffs sometimes stand up to such policies, but during a recession when advertising dollars decline and everyone fears for his job, they are less likely to do so. You must decide whether the resulting publicity warrants the advertising expense and the sick feeling in your stomach that come with such a deal.

Having cleared up the most common misconceptions about media relations, we can now look at what the professional should do to get good publicity.

Know your market.

You must sell your story to the media by convincing them that it has value to their audiences. The first step in this process is to determine which media organizations serve audiences that might have an interest. You must know your market, and that means knowing what audiences are targeted by what publications and programs and also what approach they take with those audiences. You must know the kinds of stories they typically run and the kinds of content such stories require. How much data are they likely to want? How much reporting is done through interviews? Will they only interview one company in an industry, or will they always talk to several? This research is quite similar to the research you would do before writing an article. Sources of information include these:

- *Bacon's Business Media Directory:* Published annually, this source provides background information on the media. It is also available online.[2]
- **Personal inspection:** Familiarize yourself with any publication or program you seek to place a story with. If it is a newspaper or magazine, review back issues. If it is a radio or television program, listen to it several times. Does what you see and hear tell you something about what they are looking for? It should.
- **Advertisers' kits:** Many media companies produce kits of materials for advertisers that provide data on audiences, information on upcoming themes to be covered, and other information useful to you. The kits are usually on the Web and free for the asking.
- **Interviews with reporters or editors:** Take a reporter, or editor, to lunch and ask him about his primary audience and how his particular program, or publication, selects stories. Ask how you can be helpful. These people can tell you things that are not easy to find out in other ways. For example, some of the national business media are far more likely to publish stories on publicly held companies than privately held ones, because investors make up an important part of the audience. I only found this out by talking with their reporters.

Second, because people make decisions about what stories to pick up, you must know something about individual people within a specific media organization. Rather than blindly submitting your story, whether by press release or phone call, you will succeed more frequently if you direct it to the individual most likely to be interested. Reporters work beats, or subject territories. In an ideal world, if you misdirect a call or press release, the receiver will pass it along to the right individual. In reality, people make mistakes, get distracted, and get lazy about doing things that are not personal priorities. Getting the story to the right person first not only avoids these problems but also demonstrates your professionalism.

While reviewing back issues or listening to programs, try to identify reporters covering related stories. During your lunches with editors or reporters, ask who covers the beats you are interested in.

A little time invested in research before you begin to promote your firm will greatly improve your results.

Create a network of media contacts.

Networking is helping people. Networking is recognizing a lead for someone else when you hear it. All of these guidelines (delineated in Chapter 8) apply to media networks as much as they do to any other. Work your media contacts in the same way, and you will see amazing results. This means, of course, that you must understand what "help" means to a reporter. Help can be any of the following:

- A lead on a hot story, before others hear about it
- An approach to a story the reporter may not have thought about
- Names of people she can contact to help her with a story
- Good quotes (see page 56)
- Good use of her time, such as not wasting it with useless stories

In return, you increase your chances of learning about a reporter's story idea, since reporters will often discuss a concept with someone they trust and who they think can be helpful. This will give you the chance to help her frame it in a way that may get you mentioned. For many years Moran, Stahl and Boyer, a consulting firm, has helped one of the national business magazines rank American cities. The opportunity for such blockbuster publicity came from this type of conversation.

If you choose media relations as an adjunct effort, you can still see results from a more modest investment of your time than a full networking program requires.

Recognize a good story when you see one.

Every project you do, with the insights you gain from completing it, generates possible material for a story. The hard job is determining what approach to a story would have the most interest to a particular publication or program and its audience. In short, you need an angle.

Reporters always use an angle to work a story. An angle focuses material on the interests of a particular audience. By doing so, it helps the reporter decide what portions of the mass of information collected on a subject belong in the article. It provides a purpose to the piece that· pushes the writer beyond a simple recitation of facts.

The closer you can come to suggesting a good angle to a specific reporter, the greater the chances that he will see potential in the story. This means you must develop a nose for a good story.

When you evaluate something about your business as a potential story, ask yourself these questions:

- *What makes it news?* Most of the media are interested in subjects that can be classified as news. That means they must be current, informative, and, whenever possible, urgent. The tenth anniversary of your firm may be current, but it fails to meet the second two criteria for most media. A law or accounting firm might be able to report on how different kinds of clients are responding to a change in the tax laws; this meets all three criteria.
- *Can you tie it to a national or regional issue or trend?* One way to make something newsworthy is to tie it to broader trends. The prohibition against the use of Freon and halon in refrigeration, air conditioning, and fire suppressant equipment provides an opportunity for a number of architects, consulting engineers, consultants, and lawyers to get publicity for their projects or views. One large architectural firm received coverage in *Fortune* by tying its work to the corporate trend toward suburban campuses.
- *Can you tie it to someone who is newsworthy?* Your clients are often more newsworthy than you are. When a real estate broker fills a building with a nationally known firm, he may be able to build a story around the event, which becomes newsworthy in part because of the client's name. A transaction for a large client may provide its attorneys with an opportunity for publicity.

Completing the exercise in Exhibit 5.1 will increase your understanding of these three criteria.

EXHIBIT 5.1 Is It Newsworthy?

Make three copies of this form and fill it out for three projects or events you have worked on.

Project or Event: _____

1. Is it news? (*Is it current, informative, urgent? Who would it be news to? Why?*)	
2. Can you tie it to a bigger issue or trend? (*How does it relate to something newsworthy in your region or nation?*)	
3. Can you tie it to someone newsworthy? (*Is some person, company or organization affected who appears in the news for other reasons?*)	

Find ways to create news.

Do you have, or can you create, information that would be news to others? Many firms have done this and reaped publicity rewards.

There are four typical vehicles for creating news. The first is an event. Ground-breaking, topping-off, and opening ceremonies for new buildings have become events staged for the media. A seminar can also provide grist for a press release.

The second vehicle for making news is a report or white paper. New tax, environmental, labor, and other laws often provide an opportunity for a firm to prepare a paper on their implications. Reports on opinions also get coverage; some firms have conducted face-to-face interviews with past and prospective clients in order to collect them. Though expensive, the personal contact is seen as a worthwhile marketing cost. Still other firms have been able to extract portions of work done for a client, expand upon them, and issue the results as a report.

The third vehicle is a survey. Reports on surveys appear in the press almost every day. The contents need not be earthshaking to be newsworthy. At the peak of two recoveries, surveys I conducted showed that labor shortages resulted in increased turnover, rising compensation costs, and reduced hiring standards. Both times these less-than-surprising findings were reported on the front page of the *Wall Street Journal* and on radio because they filled a void. Reporters could use unemployment statistics to show that labor was scarce, and they had plenty of anecdotal information on the impact of the shortages, but my study provided the only statistical evidence that linked the shortage to problems.

Of course, the cost of conducting a survey can be high unless you have an artful way of capturing the data. Much of the data for my labor shortage survey was collected from personnel officers I made speeches to. By leaving a brief survey form on every seat, I was able to collect many responses at little cost. I have seen a major consulting firm collecting survey information at a trade show booth. Other organizations have been able to convince a publisher to incorporate a brief survey in a magazine with responses recorded on the reply card that allows readers to request information from advertisers. Data can also be a byproduct of normal business operations, such as the space availability studies prepared by many real estate brokerage firms.

A final category of "made news" is the manufactured statistic or ranking. These data may appear annually, quarterly, or on some other regular basis and provide indicators of business or other conditions and, so, are grist for a journalist's mill. An example is one leading strategy firm's most innovative companies list, which appears now annually in a major business magazine. Because innovativeness is an abstraction and abstractions can't really be measured, the ranking means little. Indeed, some firms seem to be measured for apples and others for oranges. So, Microsoft receives marks for a massive R&D budget, Wal-Mart for reducing packaging waste, and Disney for reducing bureaucracy and making an acquisition.

Usually such statistics are a byproduct of a firm's normal operations, but some companies have been able to take publicly available data and manipulate it in a way that provides something newsworthy. To develop a statistic that can be identified with your firm, you must identify how data that you have access to and to which you can provide a special interpretation can be related to nationally or regionally important trends.

Speak quotably.

I noted previously that having information may get you interviewed by a reporter, but will not, by itself, get you mentioned. To get mentioned, you must be worth quoting. As investigative reporter Carl Hiaasen put it in his comic thriller, *Tourist Season*, ". . . in my business, the coin of the realm is a good quote—it's the only thing that brings a newspaper story to life. One decent quote is the difference between dog food and caviar."[3] A good quote helps the writer and gets you mentioned. As a derivative benefit, it gets your name into the publication's files, increasing the odds that you will be called the next time someone writes on a related subject. This means that you must learn not just to help reporters but to speak quotably while doing so.

Look at the front page of any issue of the *Wall Street Journal*. You will see that an article has three kinds of sources. First there are those who are central to a story and must be quoted, if possible: the president of the company being discussed, a whistle-blower, or other key parties to an issue. Second there are people with inside information, like customers, vendors, and trade association heads. Finally there are outside experts, usually professionals like consultants, attorneys, and accountants. The best quotes are taken from each group. For most professionals, the biggest opportunity to get quoted is as an expert. Because there are usually so many experts to choose from, and because their comments are not essential to the story; experts must make a particular effort to speak quotably, if they want to get mentioned.

Some people have a knack for speaking quotably. For most of us, it requires practice. I must concentrate hard on speaking quotably when I talk to a reporter, and I still fall far short of several people I know. I have progressed to the point that I can predict with near-perfect accuracy which statements I make will get printed. Read some well-written newspapers and study the quotes carefully, especially those made by outside experts. See whether you can get a flavor of what makes them attractive to the writer. Some of these characteristics are the following:

- **Brevity and decisiveness:** Most quotes are short. They must capture an opinion or fact in few words. A reporter is more likely to quote two different experts with opposing opinions to create balance in a story than to quote one who is able to express both points of view. It makes better copy.
- **Color:** The more colorful the statement, the more quotable it becomes. Similes and metaphors often appear in the press, while some ("like Bambi caught in the headlights") are becoming clichés. Colorful words also help. For a while referring to someone as a "wannabe" almost assured a quote. Even a standard opinion can get quoted if it is worded originally.
- **Controversiality:** Controversy is generally more exciting than reason, and reporters strive to add spice to their pieces. Think of some people you know who get quoted frequently in the media and you will realize that they often say things that the rest of us would cringe to utter.
- **Cynicism or hope:** Reporters can often use cynical or hopeful statements to balance public relations hype or group despondency. By using such statements, the reporter proves that he is not accepting at face value what others say.

If you have a knack for the epigram or the *bon mot*, you should consider incorporating a media relations effort into your marketing program. Note that quotable statements should go into your press releases as well as into your conversations with reporters.

My clients sometimes feel self-conscious practicing speaking quotably, but it is essential to learn how. The importance of a good quote was brought home to me by another experience with the *Wall Street Journal*. A reporter called, and several people in the firm I worked for provided him with real help, including background information and, with the client's permission, a perfect case example. When the story appeared, our background information was used and our client was quoted extensively. Compelling quotes from two of our competitors, speaking as experts, also appeared. We were not mentioned at all.

The standards of the *Journal* required that the reporter interview our competitors, and I realized later that their statements had been much more quotable than the bland ones we had made. We had done all the work, and our competitors had gotten the benefit.

Exhibit 5.2 lists some statements that someone might say to a reporter. See whether you can come up with some colorful quotes to replace them.

EXHIBIT 5.2 Say It Quotably

Here are four statements to a reporter. Reword them to make them more quotable.
1. "The people laid off by (name an industry or company) will find it difficult to find another job."
2. "Most companies shouldn't spend time on that issue anymore."
3. "Depending on how you interpret the facts, he might have done it because he was dishonest or because he was naïve."
4. "We haven't given up yet."

There is no right answer, but examples of more quotable alternatives include these:
1. "Many will never work again" or "A few might find jobs in the industry, but most will have to find some other way to make a living."
2. "That issue is as dead as the flat earth theory."
3. "He may have been naïve rather than dishonest, but naïve people shouldn't be in this business" or "but that won't bring back the widows' and orphans' money."
4. "This is only round one."

A call from a reporter may be blind luck or may result from hard work to attract his interest. In either case you must make the most of the opportunity, for it may not come soon again. Stop. Think about what you are going to say. Speak quotably.

Involve your clients.

Your clients may be bigger and better known and thus more newsworthy than you are. Moreover, your expertise, knowledge, and accomplishments all derive from the work you do for your clients. To a large degree, your stories are their stories. Much of your ability to get good press depends upon your ability to use your clients' names.

Yet your clients have no obligation to help you publicize yourself. They have paid you for your services and have publicity needs of their own. They may not want any publicity. Under these circumstances your ability to get your clients to work with you can determine the success of your publicity campaign. To get as much help as possible from your clients, follow these rules:

- *When in doubt, ask.* If you have any doubt about whether a client would mind your using its name, ask. It is hard to imagine publicity so good that it is worth alienating a good client.
- *Learn the client's predisposition for publicity early.* If your clients are against it, this will save you the time you might devote to planning a publicity effort they will not accept. An architectural firm hoped to get a lot of publicity about a new headquarters it had designed for a not-for-profit organization, only to find that the organization's management was afraid such publicity would call attention to the cost of the new building. Publicity plans had to be adjusted accordingly.
- *Offer the client good publicity whenever you can.* If you know that a reporter is writing a positive story that your clients might be able to contribute to, find out whether the clients would like to be quoted. Helping them get good publicity may make them more willing to help you in the same way later. Clients that are not large enough to have a public relations staff are likely to appreciate your offer to serve as their publicist.
- *Work with your clients' public relations staff.* By knowing what kinds of publicity your clients plan around the project you are working on, you may be able to find ways both to help them and to get some publicity yourself.
- *Warn them about impending bad publicity.* By doing so, you show you are on your clients' side.
- *Get a commitment for help from as high up in the organization as possible.* Corporate public relations staffs will cooperate with you more fully if they have been asked to do so by the boss.
- *Show them what you plan to distribute, if you plan to use their name.*

By showing them the portion of any release that pertains to them, you avoid misunderstanding. Also, they may object to something that seems positive or innocuous to you. You can usually get a twenty four-hour turn around or less by using faxes. Public relations departments understand deadlines.

Recognize that reporters have different obligations and ethical standards from yours.

You must exercise caution when speaking to the media. You may know this, but understanding why will help you talk with reporters more effectively.

Everyone has obligations that supersede even close friendships. If, for example, you knew about a major financial problem at your company, you would probably feel obliged to withhold it from a reporter who was also a friend. Similarly, because of his obligations as a journalist, a reporter friend might feel obliged to publish a story or quote that you would rather not see appear.

Good stories aren't easy to write, yet truth, circulation, and the reporter's job depend on them. This creates pressures to do things that are not easy for an outsider to understand. Take the case of the Chicago reporter who called me about a large city agency long ago. The agency, at the time, was doing a lousy job, but I didn't want to go on record as saying that. I had to work with the people there. Still, his question seemed fair enough: "What were five good and five bad things that I could say about (the agency)?" I answered and went happily back to work.

The next day a friend commented that the agency must have really done something to make me mad. With a sick feeling I looked at the paper. There, accurately quoted, were the five bad things I had said about the agency . . . and nothing else. After smashing my coffee cup, I calmed down and analyzed what had happened. Obviously, no one had wanted to offend the staff of the agency. The story was filled with quotes that would have made a flack grin. Other sources had been smarter or more experienced than I was. They had stuck to the good stuff, leaving the reporter with a lopsided set of quotes. The reporter needed balance to keep his readers' and editor's interest in the subject. He needed someone naive enough to speak his mind. He found me.

I did not make this mistake again. When asked for an opinion, I answered much more carefully thereafter. Sometimes I have even told a reporter that I have had both good and bad experiences with the press, most of the bad ones involving being quoted out of context. I then offer to give him my opinion, if he will exercise caution not to do what the reporter in the preceding anecdote did. This has saved me similar embarrassment, but has also gotten me cut out of some stories altogether.

Always ask yourself how a reporter might use any quotes you give him before you answer, and then choose your words accordingly. Don't say anything, even off the record, that you would be unwilling to see in print with your name attached unless you know the reporter extremely well. Even off the record, the quote had better not be too tempting. Not all reporters are ethical; some will use anything you say, regardless of whether it is on the record or not.

If you understand the media and know how to work with them, you can enjoy publicity that will build your reputation and bring in leads.

6

A Few Words on the Web
by Matt Caspari

Web sites

At first, they were entertaining asides—self-indulgent hi-tech fluff that made us all feel cutting-edge but with no mechanisms for a real interactive dialog.

Then, seemingly in the next month, they became real fulfillment vehicles—a place where prospects, once pre-sold by advertising (what else?)—could instantaneously gather all the details, a kind of glorified brochure.

Today, seemingly ten seconds later, Web sites have become much, much more—not a follow-up, but an introduction; a place where complete strangers can look you up and, within seconds, evaluate you.

Your Web site is treated the same way you might be judged in a singles bar—a very rude and busy singles bar, where everyone is impatient and always looking. Appearances, of course, are important. The first words out of your mouth better be good. And if you behave in weird and unexpected ways—well, it's on to someone else.

Here's a primer to making it in that kind of environment.

Website creation: Take the critical first steps.

There are lots of ways to build Web sites.

Ideally, you want one where you can change most information yourself and one that is built in a way that doesn't restrict your options of what Web companies you can use to alter it going forward.

Most Web sites are built using a content management system (CMS), at least in part. Generally, the Web developer will create one or more templates in the CMS program, allowing companies to enter fields within a page and change copy with an administration tool that works as simply as Microsoft Word.

There are many, many kinds of CMSs. Some of them are free, open-source programs; some of them are proprietary, more complex systems that are licensed by the developers, and for which you may pay an ongoing fee. Many sites use a CMS for only some of the pages—it costs more to construct these pages initially, but if the pages contain information that changes more than once a year, it's worth it.

If a CMS is desired, one of the first things a Web company will do is choose which of the many CMS systems it'll use. Some companies are comfortable choosing among many. Some only know how to work with one. The Big Question for the client is this: "What kind of flexibility does this give me?" Web companies make their money as much in maintaining sites as they do in creating new ones—it's better for you if you only have to call on them occasionally.

First things first: Consider the branding element.

The first question prospects have when they encounter you electronically is "Who are you?" The second question is "What makes you so special?" These questions are usually answered by the first read—a prominent portion of the home page given over to an explanation of what differentiates you.

This explanation takes two forms: what you say, and how you say it—both verbally and visually. Your Web site creates an instant impression the moment it clicks into view; you want that to reflect your brand personality. Are you buttoned-up? Original? Friendly? An industry leader? The prospects know—or think they do—right away.

Many people are tempted to put their best foot forward technologically. Some open their Web sites with full-screen animated introductions that then invite you to the real home page. Entertaining as these can be, there are a couple of reasons why they haven't gained favor.

First, the Web—for better or worse—has taught users that they are in control. Anything that has to be waited through, even for a few seconds, frustrates them.

Second, extensive Flash elements—the animation in which these openings are rendered—befuddles search engines. These days, the name of the game is search engine optimization. This is the mysterious process through which your name, or your company's name, magically appears on the list when the appropriate keywords are logged onto Google or Yahoo or whichever search engine is being used. Coming close to the top of these lists is never easy, particularly in very competitive environments, and Flash—which appears as a black box to search engines—hinders rather than helps. A little Flash is nice, but an appealing, intuitive design and crisp presentation may be better.

Information architecture: It's about them, not about you.

While it's your Web site, the prospects are the ones using it. The question is not what you want to tell them. It's what they want to know. What services do you provide? What work have you done in the past? Who can a prospect expect to work with? Big buckets of information like these make up the main navigation.

Each of these major buckets has information that fits within it. This is known as the subnavigation. Again, divide topics by their interest to outsiders, not insiders. You may divide the business by your offices in New York, Stamford, and Lexington. But your prospects may care more that you have experience in aeronautics, agriculture, and architecture.

There are some things you have to say that don't speak directly to the main sell but instead interest a secondary audience. These include the history of the company and information for job seekers. These belong in the utility navigation.

Last, there are things that are more technical requirements than elements of interest to any but a handful of really bored people. These include things like terms of use and privacy policies. These are usually contained in footer navigation, at the very bottom of the page.

How pages are arranged differs from site to site, but this is becoming more and more standardized. Buttons are usually lined up horizontally close to the top of the page or down the left hand column, both considered prime Web real estate.

Remember, architecture goes beyond the home page. If a prospect decides to pursue an avenue of the site, he still wants all his original options. The main navigation should remain constant throughout the site. The word most often used to describe good information architecture is *intuitive*—the prospect should be able to feel his way around, without ever having to pause to wonder where he goes next.

Content: In a word, brevity.

Let's keep this short.

No long blocks of copy.

Unlike magazine pages, Web pages can go to any length you wish. Chances are, however, that the prospects' computer windows won't display even the equivalent of a typical letter-sized page without scrolling. Unless you've hooked them above the fold—the area of the screen initially displayed—prospects aren't looking to scroll for more information.

Don't be afraid to break up information, and empower your prospects to explore it at the depth they want. If you've written a fascinating 10,000-word article, tease them with two lines on the home page. Give them a 100-word overview when they click through. Then invite them to download and print the whole article.

People's attention spans are short. And they're never shorter than when on the Web.

Be warned.

Functionality: It ain't over when it's over.

A lot of energy is expended in the creation of a Web site. After it goes live, everyone tends to exhale and celebrate a job well done. But depending on how it's organized, a Web site may be more like a periodical than a book. And all you've completed is the first issue.

When designing a Web site, people tend to think big. Wouldn't it be nice if we included a section on current news about the company—or better yet, wrote a weekly blog on subjects of industry-wide interest? Wouldn't it be nice if we did Webcasts?

That depends.

If an ongoing feature is a repurposing of something your organization is doing anyway, by all means, include it. If you've got a Webmaster whose sole job it is to create content for the site, good for you.

Just remember: nothing looks worse on a site than blank pages or out-of-date information. The Webcast that made you look cutting edge when it was produced five years back will make you look foolish if it's still sitting—alone—in a grandiose section of your Web site five years hence. A section for press releases is great, unless your company never has time to write them.

Speaking of looking professional, make sure all your links *work*.

Search engine optimization (SEO) and search engine marketing (SEM) are critical.

Let's consider search engine optimization (SEO) first. Everyone wants to get their name on top of the search engine rankings. You may have heard tales about secret techniques—like invisibly imbedding your site with hundreds of hidden words—that will ensure you disproportionate prominence.

This may have been true in the Wild West days of the Web. But today, search engine companies know their survival depends on the quick delivery of useful information. They're increasingly hard to trick, and when tricked, increasingly retaliatory.

While a number of carefully guarded factors determine ranking, there seems little debate about the following:

1. *How your pages are indexed is important.* This is a bit technical, but when Web pages are created they are labeled—sometimes with words, sometimes

with strings of code. These labels are read by search engines, and words tell them far more than code.

2. *Depth of interest is important.* Do visitors come to stay, or do they leave right away? The longer visitors stay on your site, and the more pages they click through, the better.

3. *Linkages are important.* If information on your site is useful to others in the field, as demonstrated by the number of other sites that point to your pages, it is thought that you rank higher.

4. *Natural rankings take a while to establish.* There is no silver bullet that allows your site to come out of nowhere instantaneously. If someone claims there is, be wary.

Search engine marketing (SEM) is not the same as natural optimization. You can buy your way to the top of the rankings for any keyword you wish. It's a pretty simple process, too—you bid on a keyword, and, if you win the bid, you pay for every time a prospect clicks on your link. You can determine a budget figure, meaning you won't get charged millions, and the search engines will take down your link after a specified number of hits.

As with anything else, a little information can be a dangerous thing. The more desirable the keyword, the more bidders, and the higher the per-click cost. If your keyword is too broad, or (in some cases) not geographically qualified, you may get hits from large numbers of non-prospects. And buying keywords is only the tip of the iceberg in the SEM field. As with buying traditional media (newspapers, magazines, radio, and television ads), there are people who can help you get more value for your money than if you place ad words alone. SEM experts—if they're really experts—are worth the money.

Here's a final thought on the Web.

The Internet intimidates us all.

I'm sure there are super Web geniuses out there who can single-handedly design sites that look good, are intuitively organized, ideally optimized, and perform every function known to mankind, all very affordably.

I have yet to meet one.

A good Web site, at a minimum, takes a good brand thinker, good designer, good information architect, and a good tech person, all respecting each other's abilities and importance to the outcome. As someone who knows your business really, really well, you are no less part of this collaborative effort than any one of those other individual experts.

A good Web company will welcome your involvement, maybe not in leading the charge, but as a respected member of the partnership. Don't settle for one that doesn't.

Eliminating the Dread of Cold Calling

Case example: The Cold Callers

Alex saw an unfilled niche in the market and went for it. A principal at the largest architectural firm in an Eastern state, he noticed that most of the hospital work in the state was being done by nonresident firms. Wouldn't the administrators prefer to work with a local firm with offices close to their hospitals? Wouldn't they rather work with a firm whose employees and their families lived in the hospitals' service areas? A quick poll of a few administrators brought back the answer, a resounding yes, with the caveat that the local firm had to have hospital experience. Alex's firm had little.

He set to work with Laura, the firm's premier business developer. Unlike many people, Laura had no fear of calling people she didn't know and asking for interviews. She began to line up meetings for Alex with administrators at all of the major hospitals in the state. Through frequent calling, she got to know the secretaries by name. She would send them cards when they had been ill and would call and thank them for every bit of help they provided. They worked quietly in her behalf to help set up meetings with their bosses.

At the meetings, Alex learned about each hospital's needs, its decision-making process for hiring architects, and the administrators' experiences, both good and bad, with other firms. The administrators learned about his acute interest in their problems and the high service and design quality his firm offered.

Through cold calls, Alex and Laura learned about impending projects early and established relationships with prospective clients. The administrators advised them on which projects were worth pursuing and how to pursue them. Starting with small projects, they established their reputation in the state as health-care architects. Over time, they built a strong health-care practice based on this work.

A cold call is a visit initiated by you to a prospective client to introduce your firm and its services. While many professionals feel uncomfortable with other kinds of marketing, almost all loathe the cold call. Giving speeches at least conjures up the idea of recognition, respect, and listening audiences. Networking implies camaraderie and mutual exchange. Cold calling conjures up a vacuum-cleaner salesman, an image that few professionals embrace.

Your reaction to cold calling depends, in part, on your profession. In the built-environment industry (architecture, interior design, and consulting engineering), most professionals would acknowledge its usefulness, whether or not they make any cold calls themselves. Accountants, actuaries, lawyers, and management consultants are far more likely to dismiss this approach. Many protest too much, however, when they claim that cold calls don't work in the professions. There is ample evidence to show that they do for many practices.

Between 1987 and 1990, a consulting firm specializing in strategy implementation grew its revenues fivefold, to well over $100 million a year. An active cold-calling program was the source of most of its new clients. Through cold calling, a friend of mine at a large compensation consulting firm developed a profitable practice from a base of zero, in spite of protestations from others in the firm that it could not be done. A large law firm succeeded in a major geographic expansion, largely through the cold-calling efforts of a small team. Such examples prove that cold calling can work for both individual professionals and for firms.

When in doubt, give it a chance. No other technique will get you face-to-face with so many prospective clients to learn about their specific concerns and to talk directly about what you can do for them.

There are three basic parts to a cold call:

1. Getting a meeting
2. The meeting
3. The follow-up

Take the steps to get a meeting.

The cold-calling process tends to follow an iterative pattern shown in Exhibit 7.1. You initiate contact through a referral from a mutual acquaintance or through an e-mail. You then phone the target to request a meeting. Once you have met, the process begins again. You follow up with a thank-you letter and request a second meeting, either with the same target or with someone he refers you to. The pattern continues until you make a sale or reach a dead end. At each stage in the process, your objective is to build relationships and obtain increasing commitments that will ultimately lead to a sale.

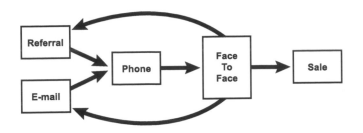

EXHIBIT 7.1 Cold Calling Follows an Iterative Pattern

Establish contact.

In your initial e-mail, you may request a meeting, but your true objective is to induce the target to take your phone call. This is a more limited commitment than agreeing to a meeting and so is easier to get. To get it, word the letter in a way that makes a negative response difficult without the benefit of a phone conversation. This means the e-mail should be short; the more information you give, the easier it will be for the target to decide not to meet.

The e-mail should begin with a clear request to talk or meet briefly. It should mention a subject or choice of subjects likely to be seen as important to the target and about which you have specialized knowledge. Subjects might include trends affecting his industry, impending legal or regulatory issues, or opportunities he is likely to be pursuing. This part of the e-mail should include a one-sentence description of why you would be worth talking with on this subject, if the target is likely to be unfamiliar with your firm. It should close with a vague offer to induce the target to take your call for clarification before deciding whether to meet with you. Exhibit 7.2 provides examples of such e-mails.

EXHIBIT 7.2 Sample E-mails

Dear Mr. Hansen:
I will be in Boise several times over the next two months and would like to meet with you. My firm specializes in cost reduction and has recently completed a study of overhead cost structures in the frozen food industry. It covers thirty-two firms and looks at twenty-eight different variables, correlating each with profitability and market share. I thought a discussion of trends in the industry might be of mutual interest.

I will call in the near future to see if we can arrange a meeting.

Sincerely yours,

Dear Ms. Perez:

I would like an opportunity to meet with you. My firm specializes in retail design and our recent work for Rachel's, Mr. Harper's, and Clothing Bazaar has increased floor space by an average of 7 percent at their downtown stores. All report increased sales since renovations were completed. I thought a discussion of trends in floor layout and design might be of mutual interest.

I will call you in the near future to see if we can arrange a meeting.

Sincerely yours,

When writing the e-mail, avoid being presumptuous. Don't say, for example, "Executives in your position need to know (fill in the blank)." Instead, base your claims on your experience: "Many of the natural-gas suppliers I work with have wanted to know x, y, and z." Don't be arrogant or egotistical. Don't say, "My knowledge of this issue would be valuable." Once again, build off your experience. It is better to sound tentative than to sound as if you know the target's mind: "I thought the experiences of others in your industry might be of interest to you."

Avoid making the target feel he will become obligated by meeting with you. Don't say, "I would be happy to fly to Boise to meet with you." He won't want to bear the burden of asking you to incur such an expense. Say, "I will be in Boise on other business over the next month and would like to take advantage of the opportunity to meet with you." As stated, keep the offer vague: "I hope an exchange of ideas on this issue might be mutually beneficial." He will have to talk with you to figure out what that means. After writing the e-mail, reread it and see whether there are places where you can replace "I" with "you" by rewording it. This will make it sound more prospect-focused.

Follow up by phone.

Once you send such an e-mail, be sure to follow up. Most people don't.

Your next goal is to get the target on the phone. Has this ever happened to you? You call to ask for an appointment with a prospective client. "Is Mr. Arbuthnot in?"

"No," the secretary responds. "He's out until tomorrow. May I take a message?" You hesitate, decline to leave a message, and say you will call back later. Hanging up, you feel disappointed, but you are also relieved that you did not meet with clear rejection.

What about this? You call a prospective client and are answered by a voice mail system. You leave a concise message that receives no response. A week later you do the same thing with the same result. After that you make no further contact.

Getting a meeting requires working with secretaries and voice mail systems.

I prefer to deal with secretaries rather than with voice mail and e-mail systems. I can have a conversation with a secretary. If I treat her properly, she can provide me with information and help. One of her principal jobs is to serve as gatekeeper, a role that many professionals perceive negatively. What they forget is that gatekeepers are responsible for letting people in as well as keeping them out.

Rose Begnal, a former executive secretary who later worked for an out-placement firm, once put it this way: "To get past the secretary you have to empower her to become your friend. Her impression of you may also be the first impression her boss gets when she talks with him, so remember: Your first interview is usually with the secretary."

So how do you get a secretary on your side? As one former secretary put it too me, "Give her the respect and the information she'll need to talk with her boss about you, and don't ever let her get the impression that you're trying to deceive her." Secretaries are often faced with what she calls the "fool-you factor," epitomized by the person who calls up using the boss's first name and pretending to be a friend. Such ploys aren't appreciated, since it is the secretary's job to help the boss manage time wisely.

Instead, demonstrate an understanding of the boss's problems ("I know he must be very busy"). Then ask the secretary to help you, letting her know concisely what you want—presumably, a brief meeting—and why the boss might benefit from taking the time to meet with you. The reason for your call must be carefully selected to provide value to the prospective client.

When establishing a reason for making a visit, you must work with two criteria: information and urgency. If you offer information of value to the prospective client and there is some urgency about the visit, you can often get a meeting. If you simply want to describe your services, your chances of getting face-to-face are lower. With some reflection, most professionals can come up with an array of information of value to prospective clients, including the following:

- **Industry information:** As a professional, your knowledge of what is going on in an industry or particular field of activity (such as product liability or salesperson compensation) gives you information that many targets would like to have.
- **Techniques or practices:** Is there some aspect of your service that differs from that of your competitors? Does it solve problems your target faces? Are they the kind of thing that a well-informed person in your target's position would want to know about?
- **Project information:** Is there a project you have recently completed that the prospective client would like to hear about? Some professionals are

precluded from discussing past projects by confidentiality agreements. Others can use recent projects as a subject for discussion even with direct competitors of the past client, so long as they show reasonable discretion.

- **Study results:** The results of a study can provide a sound basis for a meeting. Some firms conduct surveys as a part of the projects they do for clients and then offer to discuss survey results with participants as a benefit for participating. These follow-up visits are thinly disguised cold calls.

A prospective client is most likely to agree to a meeting if he perceives some urgency associated with it. I am not recommending panicky insistence that he must meet now before it's too late, but rather a statement that there is strong reason to meet sooner rather than later. Urgency can result from factors such as the following:

- **An opportunity that will be lost:** You can state that you will be visiting the prospect's city in two weeks and are not sure when you will be back again. There can also be opportunities specific to some professional practices that will be lost if too much time passes.
- **A problem that will be avoided:** Changing tax laws and other time-sensitive legislation are examples of factors that can create a need for a client to get information quickly. Several environmental consulting firms in New Jersey were able to use regulations dealing with underground storage tanks to create reasons for meetings.
- **A need to stay current:** Your prospect may benefit from being the first to know about the information you are providing or from knowing about it when his boss asks.

Obviously there can be other reasons for urgency, and you should reflect upon the specific nature of your practice in order to identify them.

I frequently receive calls from salespeople who want to introduce their companies and services but offer no special information or claim to urgency. I seldom meet with them, being too busy for casual meetings. When I do, it is because they have called me at a time when I feel at least a modestly urgent need for information they might have. In other words, I am supplying the rationale for the meeting, and they have simply gotten lucky and reached me on the right day. When making cold calls, you yourself should identify the value of a meeting for the prospect and reduce to a minimum your dependence on luck.

Get the most from the gatekeeper.

When you call to ask for a meeting, your manner must communicate that it will be worthwhile. You must sound confident and well organized. Even so, the chance that you will be able to speak to the boss immediately is small. The late Bruce McNaughton, who could get a meeting with anyone and from whom I learned a lot about cold calls, taught me that when this happens, you should make the most out of the opportunity to talk with the gatekeeper. From her you can learn the following:

Are you, in fact, speaking to the prospective client's secretary?

Good networkers and salespeople always establish who they are talking to at the beginning of the conversation. The secretary can provide a lot more help than others who answer the phone. If you aren't speaking to the secretary, you may have accidentally determined when she breaks for lunch or coffee. This can be useful information, as you will see.

What is the secretary's name?

A helpful secretary can make your job a lot easier if she wants to. Showing a personal interest by asking and remembering her name is always worthwhile.

"For most people," Rose Begnal says, "there's no music sweeter than the sound of their own name." As you get to know the secretary during the follow-up calls and visits, she is likely to prove increasingly helpful if you make the effort to establish a relationship. The same, of course, applies to receptionists and people who back up the secretary when she's away from her desk.

Is the secretary disposed to be helpful?

Some secretaries are more willing to help than others, depending on their personalities and the boss's instructions. Those few who feel it's their obligation to bar anyone trying to sell anything, often with instructions from the boss, pose a serious obstacle. By testing a secretary's attitude with a few easy questions about the boss's availability, you can determine whether your future calls should be planned to coincide with her lunch break.

Breakthrough sometimes comes when you circumvent an unhelpful secretary.

After repeated efforts to reach one prospective client, I decided to call on Christmas Eve, a time when his secretary might be out, while he, being Japanese, would almost certainly be in. It worked.

When is the boss expected back?

Professionals who sell successfully make efficient use of scarce marketing time. Knowing when the boss will return saves precious minutes that can be used productively elsewhere. By calling when you know the boss is in, you increase your chances of reaching him.

Asking when you might call back has another benefit. It's often answered with information on the boss's activities. "He's in Europe this week"; "She's in budget meetings all day"; "We're in the midst of an acquisition, and I'm afraid she's not around much"; or "He's in the hospital" are tidbits that give you a sense of the boss's activities and provide subjects of conversation to help you develop rapport when you do speak.

When is the best time to call?

A good secretary is likely to know at what time of day her boss is most receptive to answering calls. Knowing this gets you through at a time when the boss can focus on your concerns. If you have been playing telephone tag, setting an exact time to call is particularly important.

Has the e-mail you sent been received, and if so what has been done with it?

If you have written in advance of calling, the secretary probably knows how the boss wants you treated. If he wants to see you, the secretary will take aggressive steps to arrange it. If you have been passed on to someone else, she can connect you immediately. If the boss has decided not to meet with you, she can let you know before the boss has to say so directly. With this information, you can back off and plan another way of gaining access.

Can the secretary schedule a meeting for you in the boss's absence?

Many secretaries have the authority to schedule meetings for their bosses. If you have a sense that the boss may have a strong reason for meeting with you, but you are having difficulty reaching each other by phone, ask the secretary whether she can set up a meeting for you. Failing that, she can probably schedule a time for a telephone conversation as a first step.

Is there information about the company or her boss that she can provide you?

Most secretaries can send annual reports or brochures on their company, and sometimes even a bio of the boss. In one case a secretary told me that her boss had formerly worked at a chemical company. I was able to incorporate several chemical company examples in the description of my services to good effect.

At times, the secretary can also help ascertain which aspects of your services might be of most interest. "I want to make the best use of his time," you might say. "My firm assists in both acquisition and divestiture of real estate. Is your boss more focused on one of these areas than the other?" The answer to a question like this can improve the value of the meeting you have with the boss for both of you.

Secretaries are also natural sources of information on the correct spelling of a boss's name, title, and address, as well as the person's direct phone line, directions to the building, and similar details.

Can she ask the boss a question for you?

If this isn't your first call and you are simply seeking a bit of additional information from the boss, the secretary can probably get it for you if he is unavailable. The boss will appreciate this efficient use of his time, and the secretary will appreciate the opportunity to help you both, since that is her job.

Can you help me?

When efforts to approach the boss fail and the secretary seems disposed to be helpful, a direct appeal for guidance can produce surprising results. The work you have devoted to developing a relationship pays off at such times. Once I was frustrated in my efforts to recontact a prospective client after an initial show of interest. I finally told the secretary that I feared the project I was pursuing would slip between my fingers if I didn't reach the boss soon. Could she help me? She suggested I call another individual who was also working on the project. I did. I was given a meeting, and we were eventually awarded the job.

Use the voice mail system.

Voice mail systems have proved the bane of cold callers who have developed a knack for working with secretaries. How can you develop a relationship with a machine? You can't, but you can begin an admittedly one-sided relationship with the person who listens to your messages. You develop this relationship with your tone of voice and the words you choose. This means you should be upbeat, businesslike. Start by stating your name, your firm's name, and your phone number. When you leave your phone number, say it slowly, so the listener can write it down easily. If, however, he must replay the message to get the number right, he only has to listen to the opening seconds of the tape to hear it, again. Then briefly and clearly state the reason for your call. Ask for a return call, promising that you will keep the conversation short. You must keep this promise later.

People who use voice mail instead of a secretary often answer their own phones when they are in the office. By calling at different times of day, especially early or late, you can sometimes catch them in. Finally, many voice mail systems provide the option of reaching a secretary. If you have found an urgent reason for calling, you have good reason to try this approach. When the system offers no way of reaching a secretary, try hitting the pound (#) key, the pound key followed by zero, or just zero. You will often be connected with a human being. If this doesn't work, try calling the main number of the organization and asking for your target's secretary.

Use your time wisely once you're connected.

Whether working through secretaries or voice mail systems, you will eventually be connected with most of the prospects you target. Keep the conversation short and to the point. State who you are, what you want, why a meeting might benefit your prospect, and, if you have one, your reason for urgency. Then wait for a response. If the prospect cannot meet with you in the near future and puts you off, ask whether you can schedule a visit for three months from now. If he declines, acknowledge that he must be busy and ask whether you can call back in three months. He will have a hard time saying no to this request, and by granting permission creates an obligation to take your call.

Your objective should be to keep the phone conversation to less than five minutes. Longer than that and you risk holding the meeting over the phone, which you must avoid. A friend of mine once did this on a project he felt well positioned to win. The prospect began to question him, and he responded as helpfully as he could. After the phone call, the prospect could see no reason for a face-to-face meeting. My friend had answered all his questions. When the prospect finally awarded the job, it went to a competitor who had met face-to-face and built a rapport.

Once a prospect agrees to a meeting, you have achieved an important goal. You will usually get in to see him, even if the visit is postponed several times.

Be persistent.

An electrical-engineer-turned-business developer at his Rochester, New York, firm once commented to me how difficult his associates said it was to work on cold calls. The large number of telephone calls required to arrange a meeting discouraged them. That many prospects don't return calls hurts many professionals' pride, and they do not want to appear a nuisance by calling repeatedly. I know this because I ask many professionals how many calls they would make to a target before giving up. Most say either three or five. In doing so, they grossly underestimate what it takes to get a meeting.

Such reticence results from transferring standards developed when dealing with clients to cold calling prospects. When working with clients, you enjoy a certain importance in their eyes; when working with a cold-call prospect, you don't. When a prospect doesn't return a call, it should not be seen as a reflection on you, personally, but on the absence of a relationship. That is what you are working to change. Repeated calls are not usually a nuisance. The prospect can always continue to ignore you, just as you may ignore calls from someone you don't know who is trying to sell you something. Do these calls make you angry or contemptuous, when done respectfully? I doubt it.

Persistence differentiates the casual caller from the serious. Many times I have finally reached a prospect after weeks of leaving messages, only to be greeted with an apology for the lack of response. An agreement to meet almost always follows. It has taken me up to a year to get meetings with some prospects. The wait has often been worth it.

To give you a sense of what persistence means, I have included two diagrams of efforts I have made to get meetings with potentially large accounts. (See Exhibit 7.3.) In both cases, I tried to reduce the coldness of the initial calls by finding contacts either inside or outside the company who would provide me with a referral. The diagrams show the multiple paths I explored to find a route in, some of which were abandoned because I succeeded in getting a meeting with a key player. Had that effort failed, I would have pursued the alternatives further. Note that in both cases it required thirty calls to get a meeting, while the target contacts required ten calls each over a period of about two months before I reached them and lined up meetings.

EXHIBIT 7.3 The Importance of Call Persistence

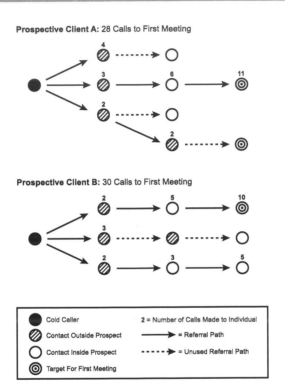

Prospective Client A: 28 Calls to First Meeting

Prospective Client B: 30 Calls to First Meeting

The professional unaccustomed to cold calling also has to learn that the total time required for such an effort is not great; in the examples used for Exhibit 7.3, I spent perhaps an hour and a half at most on the phone for all the calls made to each prospect. This investment was well worth it, given the potential for business both offered. Besides, neither target was upset with the frequency of my calls. Rather, both were apologetic about being so difficult to reach, and both readily gave me a meeting, in part to make up for not responding. Rather than hurt me, my persistence distinguished me. You need the call discipline to be persistent, to maintain an untiringly courteous phone voice, and to use a little ingenuity. I finally reached Prospect 2 by calling her at 8:00 A.M., when she answered her own phone.

I will discuss call discipline more in Chapter 8. To succeed at any marketing activity requiring relationship building, whether it be networking, cold calling, relationship marketing, or publicity, you must have call discipline. You have to find a way to make dialing the phone an important part of your schedule. Whether you set aside an hour each day or a morning each week or commit yourself to making a specific number of calls each day does not matter, so long as you make the calls. When most experienced cold callers sit down at the phone, they make a couple of easy calls first, calls they know will be taken. This warms them up for the hard ones.

Many firms employ professional business developers to relieve professionals from the burden of setting up meetings. These individuals are generally college-educated and trained in the firm's services, markets, past projects, and staff. They develop relationships with gatekeepers and prospects and get the professionals they work with in the door. It can be a highly successful approach, if you can afford it.

Prepare for the meeting.

A partner at a big accounting firm described his problem this way:

> Our people are good at getting leads, but they don't know what to do with them. They attend an event and collect business cards, but they don't know how to follow up. They sometimes set up a meeting, but they don't know what to say when they get there.

A partner at a large consulting firm expressed the same concern after we discussed the need for call discipline. "I've thought of setting up meetings, but I don't know what we should do when we get one." Confusion over what should happen at a cold-call meeting inhibits many professionals from arranging them. Whether through experience or intuition, they sense, correctly, that simply making a presentation will not produce results. So what else can they do?

Cold-call meetings are in many ways indistinguishable from sales meetings. Detailed information on how to handle such meetings is provided in Part III of this book.

There are a couple of primary objectives of a cold call:

- To learn enough about the prospect to determine whether she might have a need for your services, what value these services would return to her, and what should be done next to establish whether there is a match between you and the prospect.

- To provide the prospect with enough information about your firm to give a preliminary sense of the value you can provide her, if any, and commit to another meeting, if appropriate.

This sequence—learn first and provide information second—is important, because until you learn, you don't know what information to give. It is also problematic, because having requested the meeting, you have created the expectation that you have something to say. Successful cold calling requires that you flip this expectation so that the prospect sees the meeting as hers.

In order to obtain the meeting, you have promised to provide information of value—the results of a study, a review of a project you have completed, or information on your services. You must deliver it. Begin with a *short* introduction of yourself, your firm, and your subject. Rehearse it so that it takes no more than five minutes. Then turn the meeting over to the prospect by saying something like this:

> There are many things we could go into about (the issue of concern to your industry, our new service, the project we completed for the XYZ Company, our study of firms in your industry), and I want to make this time as useful for you as possible. Would you tell me a little about your company and its situation and why you were interested in taking time for a meeting on (our services, the project, the study)? That way I can focus on the aspects most important to you.

In other words, you can provide more value if you understand the prospect's situation first, a truth that gets her to talk. It also shows you are focused on her needs instead of selling your services.

Once she begins talking, your objective is to keep her going using the questions described in Chapter 15. Specifically, you want to find out what value the solution to a particular problem would have to her company and to her personally. Questions like, "Why hasn't action been taken on this situation before?" and "What difference would it make to you (your company) if it were fixed?" help establish the value that your service would provide.

As she describes her situation, you must ask yourself, "What parts of my knowledge of (the issue, my services, past project, study) relate to these needs?" If no parts do, but you feel your firm could help the prospect with her concerns, make her an offer: "We had planned to talk about (our new service, past project, study), but it doesn't really pertain to the issues you have raised. There are other ways we could help you. Would you like to talk about that or stick to the original agenda?" Most will accede to the suggestion and change the agenda.

If you see no match between your services and her needs, say, "I'm not sure how (our new services, past project, study) relates to the situation you have just described. Let me give you an overview; you may understand better than I do. Feel free to interrupt me at any time." In such cases keep the presentation short, unless the prospect demonstrates strong interest. You don't want to waste her time by going over material of little interest.

By the end of the meeting, you should know whether there is an opportunity to pursue. If so, either suggest a specific follow-up or ask the prospect how you think the two of you should proceed. Make it clear that you would be delighted to visit again at no obligation. Kind prospects often hesitate to take advantage of you when you wish they would.

If there is potential for a sale, always try to advance in a way that requires some commitment from the prospect, be it more time, arranging a meeting with others, or sending you material to review. Her willingness to take action is a sign that she is working to make something happen and not just taking your time. If she is unwilling to commit to one action, suggest another that requires less commitment. If possible, leave the meeting with an obligation to get back to her with some piece of information she wants.

If you see no fit between your services and the prospect's current needs, acknowledge that you don't, thank her for her time, and ask whether it would be acceptable for you to call back in six months to see whether her circumstances have changed.

Plan your meeting so that you don't exceed the time allotted to you. When you leave, you should have talked no more than 30 percent of the time.

Just as you need call persistence, you will need meeting persistence. Scheduled meetings with prospects will get canceled or postponed. Occasionally you will be stood up. A large percentage of your meetings will lead nowhere immediately. If cold calling is to work for you, you must have the resilience to keep at it. Marketing is a numbers game.

Don't neglect the follow-up.

Always follow up a cold-call meeting with a letter. By the second or third meeting, you should have moved from cold calling into either relationship marketing (Chapter 13) or selling (Part III).

Conclusion

Cold calling requires a long-term commitment, time, technique, and a tolerance for rejection. But no other marketing technique will put you one-on-one with so many prospects talking about issues of concern to them. That is why cold calling is among the most powerful marketing techniques available to you.

PART II

Building a Network: How Professionals Develop a Sustainable Source of Leads

The founder of a 400-person accounting firm has told me that finding new opportunities gets easier every year. And if you're doing it right, it does. This is because the power of a referral network grows geometrically as the number of people in it increases. Why this is so is explained in my book, *Creating Rainmakers*. All of the rainmakers we studied maintained large networks, which they built up over the years, and reaped big rewards from doing so.

This part of the book is devoted to referral networks. Professionals add people to their networks in many ways. They meet them when they are working with their clients, when they give speeches, when they make cold calls, when they give a seminar, and when they attend association meetings. This part of the book describes how those networks are built and maintained.

8 Networking: The Alternative to Cold Calling

Case example: The Man Who Knew Everyone

Oscar Megerdichian grew up in the rough-and-tumble moving industry in New York City and never went to college. Combining social skill with business acumen, he built a consulting firm specializing in move management. An intelligent, self-educated man, he liked people. He liked talking and was always on the phone. He honestly cared about his business friends and tried to help them whenever he could. He knew thousands of people. I once introduced him to a client. As we toured the building, we met five different people. During five-minute conversations, Oscar identified mutual friends with each. "What a small world," he would say each time with a quizzical smile. When this happened a month later at another company, I knew I was dealing with someone special.

Once you met Oscar, he didn't forget you. He would call periodically to see how you were doing. Better still, he often offered useful pieces of information. His real help came from introductions. He was always introducing people who could help each other. He introduced me to several people who later gave me large consulting assignments. His calls, needless to say, were always welcome, though they did sometimes make me a little uncomfortable that I had not done enough for this nice man who was working so hard for my benefit. I sought ways to return his help in kind.

By the time Oscar died, he had built a substantial firm. More importantly, his life had been warmed by many friendships, and those of us who knew him reflect on him often with affection.

Case example: The Man Who Saw Value in Everyone

John is a recruiter running the Cleveland office of an executive search firm. Prior to becoming a recruiter, he worked at an automobile manufacturer. He had spent his time there working on internal issues and so had few external contacts when he left. To be effective in his new job, he had to meet a lot of people fast. He set out to meet everyone he could. "Everyone," he says, "is either a potential buyer of our services, a potential candidate, or a potential source of information that will help me find good candidates." He has acted according to this belief for many years. One place he learned to meet people was on airplanes. Over the past twelve years, he has picked up ten searches that way. "One came from talking to a flight attendant about her husband's business. Two months later he called me; I went to see him and he gave us the search."

One key to successful marketing is gaining access to a decision maker while he has a high concern about confidentiality and is still formulating his needs around a specific problem. This means knowing him so well that he confides in you early. More likely, you must know someone who enjoys such a relationship with the decision maker and who will introduce you. In short, it means networking.

Networking is one of the most referenced and seldom realized activities in business. This is because so many who try to do it don't understand it. When training people to network, I ask what *networking* means. Typical responses include:

- Using your friends to get business
- Doing lunch
- Calling people a lot on the phone
- Asking people you know to help you get business

These views are either wrong or reflect form rather than substance.

Done correctly, networking can greatly expand your sales force and bring in business. Done poorly, it is a waste of time. I suspect that more time is wasted on so-called networking than on any other area of the professional services. This is disturbing because the value of time spent on marketing far exceeds the value of out-of-pocket expenses in most firms. That so much is spent for so little shocks my puritan soul.

In an effort to remedy this situation, I conducted a study to identify key aspects of successful networking. I interviewed and observed the most effective networkers I could find in a range of businesses, including consulting, law, engineering, accounting, architecture, construction, railroading, insurance, and office supplies, to name but a few.

One example is the late Oscar Megerdichian, the man I described in the example at the beginning of this chapter. At the peak of his career, he could gain access to almost anyone he chose in the New York area through his extensive network. I sat with him when he phoned high-level executives who dropped what they were doing to take his calls. It was transparently clear that he knew things about networking others did not.

Here are seventeen basic networking rules I have learned over the years:

Rule #1: Networking is helping people.

This is the most basic rule and the reason selfish people fail at networking. At its simplest level, it means that if you have a choice between presenting your services to a compliant but less-than-enthusiastic contact or giving him a ride to the airport, you are probably better off doing the latter. Your contact will remember you better and be more inclined to help you later. You can have a nice chat while you drive.

Giving often precedes receiving in networking. In the architectural and construction industries, which rely heavily on networking for new business, the admonishment "You have to give to get" is often heard. I first heard it from Linda Lukas, perhaps the best networker in the architectural industry. If you cannot or will not help others who can live very well without you, why should they go out of their way to help you? We are not talking about charity or social responsibility here; we are talking business and even friendship. Business associates and friends help each other, though perhaps in different ways and for somewhat different reasons. This is why it can be difficult to network with those you dislike.

Exhibit 8.1 provides a checklist of kinds of help you can provide. In different businesses, help is defined differently, so you must adjust your definition of "help" to your contact's point of view. A successful insurance salesman I know, a superb networker, wants to be introduced to prospective customers or people who have influence with his prospective customers. He does not consider information to be real help.

In contrast, many people tied to the real estate market, be they brokers, developers, architects, consulting engineers, or construction managers, covet information. As one successful real estate broker put it to me, "I don't need an introduction. What I need is information that someone is considering a move. I trust our people to get in the door." In varying circumstances, leads, information on prospects, introductions, sales assistance, references, and ideas are but some of the kinds of help provided by networkers. If you need to verify what a contact considers helpful, simply ask. The key is to keep asking yourself, "How can I help this person?" rather than "How can this person help me?"

EXHIBIT 8.1 Help Checklist

Examples of help you can provide a network contact
I. Information
    A. About a prospective client
        1. Need for service (a "lead")
            a. Description of need
                i. Size
                ii. Timing
                iii. Reasons for need
                iv. Issues
                v. Contact
                    (a) Name
                    (b) Title
                    (c) Address
                    (d) Phone
                vi. Decision-making process
                vii. Buyers/influencers
                    (a) Names
                    (b) Titles
                    (c) Roles in process
                    (d) Concern
                viii. Competitors
                    (a) Names
                    (b) Strengths and weaknesses
                ix. Changes
                    (a) In need
                    (b) In buyers
                    (c) In decision-making process
                x. Reasons for winning or losing sale
    B. About an existing client (or contact)
        1. Changes
            a. Personnel
            b. Reorganizations
            c. Major business events
        2. Problems (client is having with contact)
            a. Existence of problem
            b. Reasons for problem
            c. Impending actions
        3. Actions of competitors to win away contact's client
    C. About competitors
        1. Problems/changes

     2. New clients

     3. Successful practices

     4. Facts (number of employees or offices, etc.)

     5. Key personnel

   D. About attractive new markets

II. Introductions, referrals, and references

   A. To prospective clients

   B. To network contacts who can help get business

   C. To vendor who can help improve service

   D. To prospective employees

III. Ideas and advice

   A. On how to approach a prospect

   B. On how to solve a business problem

IV. Personal support

   A. Congratulations

   B. Condolences

V. Free or discounted services

VI. E-mail invitations

   A. Create invitation list

     1. Brainstorm with planning team

       a. Internal

       b. Purchased

         i. Determine fit

         ii. Determine cost

I have watched while a lot of highly paid executives talked about synergy between their firms and possible strategic alliances (*synergy* and *strategic alliance* are two more overworked and under-realized terms), but they could not figure out where to begin. Often all it takes to get such a conversation off the dime is for someone to give the other side real help without setting any conditions. It is amazing what a freeing experience this can be.

Does this mean you will sometimes help someone without seeing any return?

Of course. So what? When you want a favor, it will be much easier to get if you have been of real help to the person you are asking. The more significant the help, the greater the desire a reasonable person will feel to help you in return.

Rule #2: You must learn to recognize a lead for someone else when you hear it.

Though there are many ways to help people, what you can probably provide most frequently are leads and introductions. To do this, you must know enough about your contacts' businesses to recognize a lead when you hear one. Ask them to give a presentation to you. Ask what services they provide to what kinds of organizations. Ask what situations and conditions are likely indicators of a need for their services. Exhibit 8.2 provides a list of questions you can ask. When you find yourself listening to clients, prospects, and other business contacts for needs statements that apply to others' practices as well as your own, you will know that you are becoming an effective networker.

EXHIBIT 8.2   Questions to Ask a Prospective Network Contact

- Would you please describe your company and its services (or products)?
- Who are your clients (or customers) by industry, company size, geography, etc.?
- Who at the client companies buys your services?
- What are some typical indicators that show there might be a need for your services?
- What are a few questions I could ask to confirm whether there is really a need, if I uncover one of these indicators?
- Who are your major competitors?
- How are you different from them?
- How do you go about finding new clients?
- How can I help you?

Leads for others can appear at any time but are particularly likely in certain situations. Every firm receives inquiries from individuals who need a service that does not quite fit with those the firm offers. Every time you turn away business, you have a lead for someone else. I always try to make referrals in such situations.

We have all had the experience of hearing a client complain about a problem unrelated to the one we are working on: "The coffee here is lousy" or "Send it to me by courier. If it comes in the regular mail, it will get delayed in our own internal mail system." Statements like these represent opportunities for someone else. Do you know anyone who could help solve these problems?

Rule #3: Networking is sincere effort rather than keeping score.

Having been thoroughly indoctrinated into effective networking techniques by the pros, I am stunned by the amateurs who, upon learning rule one, help someone and then say in effect, "I've helped you, now it's your turn." Life is neither that simple nor, I hope, that mercenary. Would you expect such a tit-for-tat relationship from a friend? Then why would you expect it of incipient business friendships? What does it matter if you provide five leads to an individual and he provides you his one good lead of the year? He has done his best for you. You have done your best for each other. Excellence in networking, as in anything else, requires your best effort.

Rule #4: Networking is a sense of urgency and obligation.

You do want sincere effort, and the coin of sincerity in networking is the sense of urgency and obligation to return help received. If someone helps you, you should feel an increased need to do something for her. The sense of obligation should sharpen your attention to possible leads for the contact. Scan through your Rolodex, thinking about your contact's services as you look at each name. Is there someone she should know? Someone who could help her even if you cannot? If you are not sure, call your contact and ask. She will then know you are thinking of her interests, and the conversation may help clarify how you can help, or perhaps spark a new idea.

Can you do a favor for a friend of the contact who has just helped you? Even if it does not help her business directly, it may do so indirectly later. Passing on chits for favors goes on all the time among networkers.

Rule #5: Show how your services can add value to a contact's business.

Of course, you want others to help you as you are seeking to help them. This is easiest for them if you can describe how your services enhance the value of their own. The more clearly they perceive that by helping you they help themselves, the more they will be willing to do for you.

Will incorporating your services help a contact differentiate his services from that of a competitor? Let him know how. A friend greatly expanded his consulting business by showing real estate brokers how they could use his services in this way. Is there a possibility that the help your services provide in solving a problem will speed progress on a project that may require your contact's services at a later date? Explain this. Whenever possible, you must position your services in a way that shows their value, not just to the ultimate prospect, but also to your network contact.

Rule #6: Networking is showing gratitude.

When someone helps you, you must show you appreciate it. This is particularly true if the help pays off for you. If you receive a lot of information on a prospect from a contact and then win the job, let him know you appreciate the help. Call! Write! If he provided a reference or an introduction, take him to lunch! Networking is based on friendship, and friendships require appreciation and recognition.

Rule #7: Networking is maintaining trust.

The biggest inhibitor to networking is the fear that someone will take advantage of you or embarrass you. You can help overcome this fear in others by extending a hand when they need it, but that is not enough. Maintaining a high level of trust is essential to developing a network.

Maintaining trust requires several things. First, it means that you will provide a high-quality service. It doesn't pay to network with hacks because your reputation will be sullied by theirs. It also means that you will go the extra mile to clear up any problems that you might have with a client or in some other relationship.

This is good practice in any event, but by itself it is not enough to maintain trust in networking; you must also be forthright with your contacts. If client confidentiality or some other obligation prohibits you from providing a contact with the help that he desires in a specific instance, you must tell him so. If he understands networking, he will accept your explanation. If he does not, you will want to cut him out of your network anyway.

This rule further means that you, yourself, will hold off pursuing an opportunity if pursuing it might embarrass your contact. This can be very hard to do when you are under pressure to make a sale. One respondent to my survey told this story:

> I was once given a lead that I didn't pursue because I sensed that the person who had given it to me didn't want me to yet. She called me later and asked if I had gotten the business. I told her I had not and explained my reason. She was as surprised as I was embarrassed, but it was worth it in the long run. Knowing she could trust me, she became a lot more open, and I've gotten a lot of business out of her over the years.

Maintaining trust also means that you do not help one business contact by placing a burden on another unless you are in a position to request an outright favor. Rather, your objective is to help all parties involved. This means, among other things, that you shouldn't feel an obligation to introduce a member of your network to a client unless you think it will be beneficial to both and you can convince both of a meeting's potential value.

Exhibit 8.3 provides a list of do's and don'ts for maintaining trust with your contacts.

EXHIBIT 8.3 Do's and Don'ts of Developing Trust

Do's

- *Ask a contact how confidential his information is.* If you have any doubt, it is better to ask than to violate a confidence.
- *Always ask permission before mentioning a contact's name as a source of information.*
- *Call the contact who provided a lead to let him know the results of your pursuit.*
- *Show gratitude.* This applies especially when you win a job that a contact helped you win. Call. Write. Take him to lunch.
- *Help a contact who has helped you win a job by getting him a chance with the new client.* For architects and some other professionals, this means putting the contact on your team. In other fields, it means an introduction later.
- *Tell a contact when you cannot help him because of a prior commitment to a competitor.* If you take a contact's information, but you plan to work with a competitor, you are using your contact. Users get a bad reputation in a network.

Don'ts

- *Don't share confidential information.* This is the most commonly violated networking rule. You will be strongly tempted to use any information at your disposal in the bartering of networking, but you will get the reputation of being untrustworthy if you violate confidences.
- *Don't ask where information comes from if a contact is providing it hesitatingly.*
- *Don't share information provided by a contact with his competitor.*
- *Don't go around a contact to his boss when you wish to share information with his firm.* People help you, not companies. Return help to those who give it so that your contact gets credit for generating a lead.

Rule #8: Networking sometimes means selling other people's services.

From what I have said so far, you will understand why this is true. Helping someone else sell his services is the ultimate form of assistance in business networking. If you believe in what you are selling, you are helping the buyer, too. Those who work for themselves will find this rule easy to implement. Those who work for someone else can find it harder to justify. "Jane, sales are 15 percent behind budget. What are you doing about it?" the boss asks you. If you answer, "I helped Surprise and Delight Consulting sell a $75,000 job," he may not understand. You must educate him in anticipation of such an event. The best education is showing him how such help has been returned in the past, so keep track of your successes.

At first, helping sell someone else's services may seem awkward. After all, what business is it of yours? A few successes will overcome this concern. People are often most appreciative of a friend who introduces them to someone who can solve a problem. I once introduced a furniture dealer to a contact whose need for interior-design services were so small in scale that the firm I worked for could not help him. I told him that the dealer provided a high-quality service and would give away design in order to win furniture and carpeting business. Both the buyer and seller were delighted. The buyer called me two weeks after the job began to thank me for making the referral. He had not bought design services before and had been nervous about making a mistake. He was getting first-rate work and had saved his company some money. His boss was pleased. The seller received an order worth over $200,000. When you help one person in networking, you often find you are helping two.

You will also find that it is often easier to sell someone else's services than it is to sell your own. Because your perceived self-interest is low, you gain credibility. In the example just cited, I was able to tell the buyer that the furniture dealer was honest and would quote a fair price. This kind of thing is hard to say credibly about yourself, even though it is true.

The value to you of selling other peoples' services is epitomized in reverse networking. Everyone has someone he knows but from whom he feels uncomfortable asking for business. This may be because the relationship is too personal. At some golf clubs, for example, it is considered bad form to solicit business from other members. One person I know wanted business from the father of his son's friend but was reluctant to ask. Or sometimes it happens that the person in question has a strong tie to a competitor, and initial overtures have been rebuffed. In such a case, you may be concerned that too much pressure will damage your relationship.

Reverse networking is one way of overcoming such obstacles. Here's how it works. John, an accountant, wanted to do business with Ed but was uncomfortable raising the issue. He introduced Ed to a consultant, Mary, who he knew could help Ed with a problem he had mentioned. Mary made the sale and later reversed the networking by helping position John. "Who is your accountant?" she asked Ed later. On hearing that it wasn't John, she responded in surprise, "You mean it isn't John? He's the best in the business. Since you know him, I thought for sure you would use him."

Rule #9: Networking is keeping good data on the people you meet.

A contact list is the fundamental tool of networking. Unless you keep one and keep it complete and up to date, you aren't serious about networking.

You need to get all of your contacts on your list and add new contacts as you make them. A good place to start your effort is by reviewing whatever form of list you keep to make sure that it includes all the people you know already. Chances are that you already know people who can give you business or refer you to those who can. Others may not be able to give you business today, but they will in the future as their careers progress.

Because the business you win and money you make will come from them, it follows that the people you know are an asset. Like any other valuable asset, this one must be managed. As a first step to helping you with your finances, a financial advisor will ask you to list all your assets in one document. That allows you to manage them. It allows you to answer key questions: What is my current financial position in terms of my total wealth, its rate of growth, and my exposure to risk? Am I likely to have enough wealth to take care of critical future needs like college tuition and retirement? This information allows you to begin to plan for your future. By updating and reviewing this information from time to time, you get a clear picture of your financial progress.

A contact list is the sales equivalent to this summary of your financial assets. It is the basic tool of business development. If you don't have one, you aren't serious about selling. A list of your contacts also allows you to answer key questions: Whom do I know, and what does that tell me about my ability to meet my sales objectives, now and in the future? Do I know enough of the right kinds of people? How well do I know these people? How frequently do I talk with them? Answers to such questions arm you to manage and grow your contact base intelligently.

So, a first step to becoming a rainmaker is to figure out who you already know who might be a valuable contact. A contact is valuable from a business development perspective if the person meets the following criteria:

- He or she can hire you.
- He or she can influence someone to hire you.
- He or she can provide you valuable information about, or information valuable to, someone who might hire you.
- He or she is likely to be able to do one of these things in the future.

This last group is especially important if you are young. If you are, say, thirty and it takes a contact ten years to arrive at a position of influence, you will still have fifteen or more years in your career to benefit from the relationship.

Exhibit 8.4 provides a checklist that will help you identify all the people you know who might make good networking contacts. Take some time to gather as many names as you can from the different sources. If you are still in doubt about whether a specific name belongs on your list, err on the side of being inclusive. You don't have to call someone just because her name is on the list. But if the name isn't there, you won't. Preserve the option.

EXHIBIT 8.4 Ten Ways to Grow Your Client List

It is easiest to start networking with people you already know. Here is a checklist of places to look for names to add to your list.

1. **Old client files:** Look through all your old client files to get the names of people you have worked with, even briefly, on a case or project.
2. **Old prospect files:** Do the same with old prospect files. That a person considered hiring you is strong evidence that he or she is a good contact.
3. **Stacks of old business cards:** You have been saving them all these years for a purpose. The time has come!
4. **Phone directories from employers:** Your current and former colleagues can be good referral sources.
5. **School alumni directories:** People you went to school with are often interested in meeting people and developing business contacts.
6. **Colleagues:** Other people who work for your firm can be great sources of referrals.
7. **Affinity group directories:** People you know from memberships in special-interest organizations can be good contacts, especially those in professional organizations.
8. **Alliance partners:** Put your contacts from these important organizations on your list.
9. **Others serving your clients:** Your clients' accountants, lawyers, investment bankers, and other professionals who serve them should be added to your list.
10. **Friends and family:** Some people aren't comfortable doing business with this group. If you are, add them to your list.

Contact lists are so critical to business development that there is an array of software programs to help you manage yours. These include ACT, Outlook (both excellent programs), and many others. Use the one that is standard at your firm, but if for some reason that proves hard, go out and buy a program that works for you. It won't cost much, and developing a good contact list is too important to let a small expenditure get in the way.

Another option is to sign up for one of the online networking programs, like LinkedIn or Plaxo. The full value of these systems remains to be seen. Most of the people I know have obtained real value from the signing-up process. They would have received some of that benefit from any contact-organizing effort. The systems provide a powerful tool for tracking down contacts you have lost touch with by working through the network to identify a third party who has kept in touch with both of you.

The majority of the people I have spoken with received little additional benefit after signing on. But people who get much more from the systems turn up with increasing frequency. They appear to have the following characteristics:

- *They use the system more than the average user, even if they have to pay a fee to do so.*
- *They work hard to get all possible names into the system and so tend to have more contacts in the system.*
- *They get the most benefit inside a limited geographic area, within which they can refresh old contacts and get introduced to new ones in face-to-face meetings.*
- *They develop techniques designed for this kind of system.* One LinkedIn member with over 500 contacts in the system would e-mail contacts with information about himself, hoping to get information on the same subjects from his contacts. He found that often people would do just that. If he described his biggest business challenge, they were likely to tell him theirs. When a response suggested that the contact might have need for his services, he would arrange a lunch.

Resist the temptation to rely on a simple spreadsheet. These work well with small networks, but spreadsheets quickly become unmanageable as your network grows and you want to record more data for each contact. Delaying conversion to contact-management software only makes the change over more difficult later because every week you will be adding names of the people you meet to the list.

Enter key information on each person in your contact-management file. At a minimum, you want to include the following for each contact: name, title, company, address, phone number, cell phone number, and e-mail address. Also good to have are alternative phone numbers and e-mail addresses, facsimile numbers, home phone numbers and addresses, and the names, phone numbers, and e-mail addresses of assistants.

There will be gaps in your information. Big gaps are especially likely with people you haven't spoken to in years. Put their names down anyway. Gaps can be filled.

Rule #10: Networking is meeting more people.

Over the course of a year, most professionals meet more people who would be reasonable or even extraordinary network contacts, if only they realized it. You must adopt a mindset like the recruiter whose story began this chapter, who treated most people as potentially valuable contacts.

To do that, I recommend setting a goal of new people you will meet and add to your network over the next year. If you think you see a lot of new people based on the work you do, set this goal at 100 to 120. If you meet but a few, because you tend to work with the same few people at the same clients, set it at fifty to sixty. The number you commit to should be one you believe you can achieve, but you will have to stretch to do it.

Got a number? No, not yet? Take a minute set a goal. It should push you to ask these new people more questions so you can learn about them. Got it, now? Good. Put it in a place where you will see it often. That will help you focus on each person you meet as a potential network contact. If you find yourself surprised at how many new contacts you meet per month, move the goal higher, until it forces you to stretch.

There are many ways to meet people, and you can use all of them to some degree. But successful rainmakers usually focus on one or two, especially early in their careers when getting started. If you don't know enough of the right people, you will need a vehicle for meeting them. Exhibit 8.5 lists some of the ways to do it.

EXHIBIT 8.5 Ten Ways to Meet More People

Rain making is a numbers game. The more people you know and talk to, the better the chance of winning more business. Here are ways to meet people:

1. **Get to know everyone who attends client meetings.** Often we walk away from a client meeting attended by five or ten people only knowing one or two. Get to know as many people at these meetings as you can. Ask for their cards, and follow up with an e-mail. Use time before and after the meeting and breaks to establish relationships with people you don't know.

2. **Attend an association meeting.** It is perfectly acceptable to introduce yourself to a stranger at such meetings. There are no gatekeepers in your way. (See Chapter 9 for advice on how to work an association meeting.)

3. **Give speeches.** If you arrive early and hang around afterwards, a speech is a great place to meet people. Those who attend prequalify themselves as potentially valuable contacts because they have shown interest in the subject you are talking about. (See Chapter 2 for advice on how to get speaking opportunities.)

4. **Ask satisfied clients for referral.** A client who is happy with your work should be considered for such a request. Make the request as specific as possible.

5. **Ask a connector for introductions.** This same approach can be applied to anyone who is happy with you, both within your firm and at other firms. Of the people these contacts work with, whom would you like to meet?

6. **Join an affinity group.** Participation in sporting, political, charity, or other organizations can help you meet people.

7. **Conduct a survey.** Conducting a survey as a basis for a study for a client, for an article, or for a speech, provides a reason to call people you don't know to interview them. It's a good reason for asking third parties for introductions.

8. **Make cold calls.** This is a direct way to get to know people. Are you going to a town for a short meeting? Extend your visit and make cold calls.

9. **Talk to people on airplanes.** If you travel a lot, conversations with people you sit next to on airplanes can turn up contacts.

10. **Run an event.** Provide an educational and networking event and invite those you want to meet, as well as some you know. This can be a small dinner for ten to twelve, plus a speaker, or a holiday open house, for example.

Rule #11: Networking is following people from account to account.

Networkers stay in touch with their contacts for years. This has many benefits for both the professional and his contacts. The professional finds it easier to help someone he knows well. The better you know someone, the more efficient you can be about helping that person. By following a contact who changes employers, a professional can often get a new client. One rainmaker I know followed one contact into five different companies over twenty years.

Following contacts from one account to another can be seen as building what are known as *client trees*. Sit with a rainmaker and map out his client trees, and you will find that a significant portion of his business comes from keeping track of migrating executives. As will be seen in Chapter 11, this is especially true in professions where there is strong loyalty between professional and client.

Networkers follow their contacts from account to account.

Rule #12: Networking is time consuming.

You cannot build a network without spending time doing so. Effective networking requires long-term, consistent efforts; trust and a track record of mutual assistance cannot be developed in a week. A major project came to me after three years of helping one trade-association contact with odd bits of advice and information and a lot of listening. It was the first time he had hired a consultant in those three years, and the project took little direct selling when it came.

Your contacts must be nurtured by regular contact in the same way you must water a garden regularly to make it grow. A financial consultant who has built a successful practice in two years as a sole practitioner has said to me several times, "It's amazing how quickly the leads stop coming in if you stop calling people." Jim McTaggert, one of the founders of Marakon and a true networker, reports the same thing: "When you stop making calls, the calls stop coming back to you. I monitor my inbound calls, and when the inbound calls start dropping off, I know I haven't been making enough calls out. You can always tell seasoned networkers because they all complain about activities that cut into their phone time."

This means you must schedule time for networking. Oscar Megerdich-ian, who built a good business networking, spent the majority of his time at it. Another person I know blocks out a portion of each day to be on the phone. A third blocked out every Tuesday morning to make twenty-five calls. He would do no other business until they had been made. He didn't reach everyone he called, but the return calls would keep him in the market for the rest of the week.

When I began to network, my schedule defeated all efforts to organize in this way. The solution was to develop a list of contacts and turn to it at every brief period of inactivity. I picked up the phone when waiting for planes in airports, when a colleague was late for a meeting or when I was early, and at other loose moments. However you do it, you must find a way to structure networking calls into your schedule. The best networkers guard their tele-phone contacting time tenaciously and will struggle to protect it when other demands begin to distract them.

Trade associations provide a structured environment for maintaining net-work contacts. Most experienced networkers participate heavily in one or two such organizations. Similar benefits derive from formal networking groups, which are discussed on page 115.

Several software programs can also help you organize yourself to network. (My favorite is ACT. Microsoft Outlook also works well as a contact man-ager.) They combine the functions of your Rolodex, calendar, to-do list, tickler file, and vertical file on prospects and contacts. They will remind you to make calls, prompt you on possible follow-up to each call, keep all your records on a contact in one easy-to-access file, and otherwise help you get the job done. I recommend that anyone actively involved in networking investigate such programs.

Keeping in contact shows you are serious. It demonstrates your commit-ment. More practically, you will find that direct contact with people forces you to think about how you can help them and how they can help you. Over and over again, networkers give and receive valuable information that would not be passed on if they had not contacted each other for another reason.

I once called a friend in a construction company simply because I had not spoken to him for a while. We discussed a variety of projects that we were pursuing, and I learned that the decision maker for a 350,000-square-foot interior design project we were pursuing used to work at my contact's firm. My friend was able to help me with both advice and a reference, assistance that became a major factor in my firm's winning the job. Had I not made the call to touch base after a month of little contact, I wouldn't have learned of his relationship, and he would have been unable to help me.

Exhibit 8.6 lists ways that you can build the development and maintenance of your client network into your weekly routine. Try one out. If it doesn't work, try another.

EXHIBIT 8.6   Making Time for Client Development

Making time for client development is often the biggest hurdle that professionals face. Here are some ideas that may help you.

1. **Rethink your priorities.** You are trying to squeeze client development into an already over-packed schedule, when you should be rethinking how you allocate your time. Perhaps you need to reorder your priorities and redesign your schedule accordingly.

2. **Organize yourself for the effort.** The effort will require much less time if you are organized. Be sure your contact list is up to date and easily accessible so that you can make contacts efficiently. Then establish a routine. Common patterns for routines include the following:

   - *Blocking time:* Some professionals block a specific time every week or every day to make their calls and write follow-up letters.
   - *Establishing quotas:* Others set requirements for making a specific number of contacts a day or a week.
   - *Scheduling time:* Still others schedule a time for making calls in their calendars. This commitment then can be moved if there is a conflict, but it cannot be cancelled.
   - *Using downtime:* Many professionals set themselves up to make good use of downtime, such as time spent waiting in airports or waiting for others to arrive for meetings, to make calls.
   - *Setting up a nag system:* Contact-management software programs allow you to schedule calls in advance. Your computer then reminds you when you need to make a call.
   - *Getting it on your to-do list:* If you work from to-do lists, make sure that client development activity makes it onto the list every day.
   - *Using a group to create structure:* Some professionals commit themselves to participating in professional associations or other group activities. Time spent preparing for meetings and participating in committee work, then, helps make sure that they allocate time to client development.

3. **Leverage your time.** Whenever possible, leverage billable time for client development efforts. Examples of such leveraging include these:

   - *Getting to know every participant at client meetings:* When attending a meeting with a client, get to know everyone else who attends.
   - *Stopping by clients' offices when you are in their building for other reasons:* When you go to a meeting at a client's site, arrive early or stay late so that you can drop in on some people you aren't scheduled to see, just to say hello.
   - *Asking advice:* Asking a client for advice on a project you are working on for his or her company is an excellent way both to do better work and to stay in touch. Preparing a speech, writing an article, or launching a new service provide additional opportunities to ask clients for advice.

4. **Socialize with clients.** Many professionals also leverage their personal time by socializing with clients and prospective clients. You must decide if this approach is acceptable to you and practical given the location of your clients' residences.

5. **Say no.** You got to where you are in your firm by saying yes to most requests for help. But you are in a different place in your career now. It is all right to say no sometimes to preserve time for client development.

6. **Off-load.** You can't always add more to your days unless you eliminate something by delegating it to someone else. Twice a year, ask yourself what you are doing now that you don't want to be doing six months from now. The things you off-load will give you more time for client development.

Rule #13: You must be selective about who you network with.

You must spend a lot of time with your network contacts. You will be actively trying to help them. You will sometimes be putting your reputation on the line for them. You had better be careful whom you network with.

First, you will want to focus on those who are good at what they do. They are the ones who have something to offer your other business contacts. Second, you will naturally want to work with those who understand networking and are willing to develop an effective networking relationship with you. Third, you will want to focus on those who have business contacts who can help you. This means working with others who sell to the same people that you want to sell to.

You will try to network with many people but sometimes find you can't make it work. You give but get rejection. Before you take further action, reflect on the reason it isn't working. Those you wish to avoid or weed out include people who only want to receive help and are not inclined to give it. You will meet such individuals. They simply don't understand how networking works. They do not listen for leads for other people and so never hear them. Even if such a person has many valuable business contacts, the contacts are useless to you because you will never gain access to them through this kind of person.

Learning to recognize those who do not have a networking mindset will help you weed them out early. I once thought I was establishing a good networking relationship with another consultant. I helped him get a large job, and he helped me get a small one. Over the next two years I helped him get four other jobs but received little help in return. When I finally raised my concern, he responded, "But I don't ever hear of leads for you." I should have seen the signs earlier. Though I had been calling him every couple of months to stay in contact, he had never called me unless he wanted something. He couldn't help me because he didn't understand networking. I dropped him.

More troublesome are those whom you enjoy meeting with but who cannot really help you, although it seemed at first that they could. Cutting such people from the network can seem cold and personally dishonest. This can become an excuse for continuing to waste time and money on them. The solution is simple: Keep them as friends, but stop fooling yourself and wasting company resources—money and your time—by treating them as valued business network contacts. If you do not really want them as friends, either, it is time to ask what you are getting out of the relationship. Is your ego involved, by any chance? In such cases it often pays to be direct and say, "I like you and wish I could help you, and I suspect that you feel that way about me, but though we've both tried, we can't seem to make it work. I feel that we just can't make good introductions for each other. I deal with marketing issues, and people don't see me as a source for financial service advice. I suggest that we go on trying to help each other, but reduce the number of meetings we have, and instead talk by phone from time to time. How does that sound to you?"

Also problematic is the full-up contact. This person knows the right people and knows how to network but doesn't help you in any significant way. This remains true even after you help him out. The reason? He has a long-term networking relationship with one of your competitors. He is so close to the competitor and owes her so much that he gives all the introductions he can to her, leaving no room for you. It is easiest to simply write this person off. Other options include a direct conversation in which you ask if he is so locked in to the competitor that you should devote your energies elsewhere. A good networker will give you an honest answer. Another option is to give less frequently, but to keep giving in case there is a falling out between the contact and your competitor or if the competitor for some reason leaves the market. In that case you will be well positioned to replace her.

Keep this in mind: There are far more people worth networking with than you can possibly have time for. Since your own time is the most valuable resource you control, you will want to focus it on those networking relationships where there is the greatest potential for mutual benefit. One that may look like a non-giver but is worth your attention is the proto-networker.

Rule #14: Networking is helping other people learn to network.
Many people want to network but don't know how. They can be called proto-networkers. The more skilled you become, the more it will benefit you to help these new networkers learn the ropes. If someone is predisposed to be helpful, especially someone you have done a favor for, make specific suggestions about how the person can help you. You will be surprised at how many generous and interested people need such suggestions before they can act. They don't yet think like networkers.

I tried to network with a consultant for many years but got nowhere and eventually gave up. One day I met someone else who could benefit greatly from knowing him, so I introduced them. They got along famously and were able to help each other. Having made this useful introduction, I decided to try networking with the consultant again. He had always seemed to want to help, even if he had never done anything. This time, instead of asking if he knew anyone who might want my services, I asked if he could introduce me to some specific people. Though he had not responded to a general request for help, he was more than willing to introduce me to the people I named. An inexperienced networker, he needed coaching on how to help me.

When providing this kind of coaching, you must avoid the appearance of too much pressure. Be sure to include caveats to your request, such as, "We must each decide what we are comfortable doing with our contacts, and I don't want you to do anything that you would find uncomfortable or think would be ineffective, but would you be willing to . . . " This lets your hearer know that you understand that you are not expecting the unreasonable.

Rule #15: Networking is figuring out who knows whom.

There are some introductions you want badly. When cold phone calls are either ignored or passed to a lower and inappropriate level, or when you don't know anyone inside, a friend of a friend can get you in the door. You must ask yourself who might know someone at an appropriate level in this company. This requires research and a good fix on who it is you want to talk with. Who has the likely business and personal contacts? What schools did the person you want to talk to attend? Does he serve on any boards? Does he belong to any trade associations or clubs? Where does he live? Networkers know the truth in the saying that there are never more than six people between you and the person you want to talk to. My brother and I once made a game out of it and traced paths well within the six-person limit to such diverse individuals as Saddam Hussein, Queen Elizabeth, and Boris Yeltsin. Within the business world, the chances of being able to trace a short path are even greater.

All experienced networkers trace such paths and use them. Watching Oscar Megerdichian trace a path of contacts back to someone he wanted to meet was awe-inspiring. An actuary who runs the Phoenix office of a large firm told me, "This office has been here a long time, and we have some kind of contact with anyone we would want to work with. When we start a pursuit, we first look for that contact. There is always one. Someone at the company we are pursuing is a good friend of one of our people's neighbors or used to work for someone we know; there is always some kind of connection. We don't always choose to use it, but it's always there." When you can do this yourself, you will know you have become a pro.

Rule #16: Networks age.

The unavoidable consequence of this truth is best illustrated by the following story.

When I first began networking, I received immeasurable help from Oscar Megerdichian, who provided me with new business leads and several introductions that led to the signing of important projects. More valuable still, he taught me the fundamentals of networking. He was the single most valuable network contact I had, and he died.

With Oscar's death, I lost a friend I have thought of with surprising frequency, given that our relationship was basically a business one. With his death, he also taught me one final and important lesson. You must keep expanding your network, or it will contract. I have since noted several marketers who lost their value and sometimes their jobs because they had relied on an established network that had stopped expanding. Gradually, through retirements, deaths, job changes, and relocations, their networks had disappeared.

This never happened to Oscar. To the end he developed new contacts, many, like me, much younger than himself. His network never shrank, and, I believe, he had a richer and more personally rewarding life because of it.

Rule #17: Motivation is the most crucial ingredient in effective networking.

Networking comes most naturally to extroverted individuals who make friends easily. More introverted individuals often find the concepts intimidating and so risk discarding this approach to marketing without making a serious attempt to try it. This is a mistake. I have qualified as an introvert on every psychological test I ever took. In my experience, an individual who understands the guidelines outlined in this chapter and applies them deliberately and rigorously can outperform many more natural networkers who lack focus. More importantly, he can successfully bring in business. He can also develop relationships of lasting personal value.

What is most important is a strong motivation to succeed and a sincere desire to help people. If you have ambition and get real pleasure from helping others, you should consider giving networking a serious try for at least a year.

Networking involves ethics.

I must conclude this chapter with a few comments on networking ethics. Networking is ethically neutral. There are those who use the techniques described here for legitimate business purposes. There are others who use them to fight cancer and promote world peace. Still others use them to peddle drugs, launder money, and fence stolen goods.

The most serious ethical issues for most people surround the exchange of money for introductions, references, or information. When in doubt about the propriety of any money exchange in a networking context, ask yourself these questions:

- *Is it legal?* If it's illegal, don't do it, regardless of how willing others are. Stay away from anyone who has engaged in illegal money exchanges. Just knowing about them may place you in legal jeopardy. Be particularly careful to establish what is legal if you sell to local, state, or federal governments, where you are most likely to run into laws governing exchanges of money for help.
- *Does the client know about and accept the exchange?* If it's legal and the client who is being introduced has no complaints, it is hard to see why anyone else should care.
- *Is it accepted practice?* In some industries this kind of exchange, under the name of a "finder's fee," is standard practice. You can assume that most clients know about it without getting into a discussion. Be careful. This criterion becomes murky, with ample room for self-justifying activity that can cause you trouble later.
- *Is it against the rules of any organization you belong to?* Many companies and some trade associations and formal networking groups prohibit this kind of exchange.

Confidential information is another area of common concern. Such information is often more valuable than easy-to-get information. Before giving out confidential information, ask yourself these questions:

- *Do I have a clear obligation to keep it confidential?* If you have signed a confidentiality agreement or verbally promised to keep a confidence, you should do so.
- *How strong is any implied obligation to keep it confidential?* This is a tough judgment, which you will have to make.
- *Has the information become public through some other source?* If so, your obligation often ceases.

A final area of concern lies in networking with competitors. This can take two forms. First, you may want to exchange information or other help with a direct competitor of your own firm. Before doing so, ask yourself a couple of basic questions:

- *Is it legal?* Some exchanges of information among competitors are against the law. This is especially likely to be true of pricing information. Avoid any such communications or any that might be interpreted as such.
- *How much do you actually compete with the other firm?* The services of many firms overlap a little. Many furniture dealers offer some design services. Real estate brokers may offer some consulting or space programming

services. If there is only a small amount of overlap, you can probably go ahead and network to mutual advantage. The overlap implies a commonalty of interest. Exchanging information with direct competitors may help them win jobs and can get you fired.

When networking with two or more firms that compete with each other, you must also be careful. Sharing information received from one with another is considered unethical among experienced networkers. If you get caught doing it, you will be shunned. Once you have learned the information from another source, the restrictions are often eliminated.

Conclusion

Networking offers one of the strongest business development techniques for professionals. If you are not networking, you should consider doing so. To get started, you may want to structure your efforts through a trade association or formal networking group. The next chapter will describe some of the special aspects of marketing through such organizations.

Special Rules for Special Networks: Trade Associations, Formal Networking Groups, and Internal Networks

Case example: The Man Who Learned to Market

When the firm opened, no one at Madison Pension Services really had to market. The business poured in, and management focused its attention on handling the workload. Actuarial firms were like that in the late 1970s and early 1980s. But it didn't last. Tax acts, especially the 1986 Tax Reform Act, eliminated many of the financial incentives that businesses had for creating pension plans, and companies began to drop their programs. Boom turned to bust.

"I never planned to be a marketer," says David Gensler, the firm's president. "I had become an actuary because I had a gift for mathematics. I didn't think of myself as a people person. I was happy just being an actuary. Still, when business began to evaporate, I had to do something. I began to call on our clients, a thing we hadn't done enough of. I also began to call on accountants and lawyers who could refer us business."

Two years after he began to market, David joined the Metropolitan Business Network, one of the oldest formal networking groups in the country. "About 10 percent of our new business each year comes from referrals from the members. That's important by itself, but the group has helped me in many other ways. There was no one in my firm who I could learn to market from. The other members of the network were generous with their help. Participation helped me build my skills, confidence, and morale."

As the number of pension plans continues to decline, David's firm remains strong and has even grown. "I wouldn't go back to the old world in which I didn't have to market, even if I could," he says. "I feel that I'm making much more of a difference now. I'm leaving footprints at the firm."

Every networker builds his personal network over a career. It can be slow work. You can speed up the process by working through an organization, and most good networkers do. The organization may be an association, a formal networking group, or your own firm. This chapter describes the special characteristics of working through organizations.

Trade and professional associations are worth joining.

Trade and professional associations provide one of the few opportunities to meet large numbers of potential clients at one place. They offer a legitimate avenue for developing a relationship with prospective clients outside of a strict buyer/seller context. This helps lower the defenses a prospective client may erect when he feels he is being sold. Because others who seek to sell to the same people you do also attend the meetings, associations offer an excellent way to broaden your network of outside contacts.

So much marketing is done through associations that they merit a separate section of their own. My comments pertain to associations where your prospective clients constitute the primary membership—with you, your competitors, and others who sell to these people constituting an auxiliary membership. Generally, professionals attend meetings of such organizations for different reasons than functions of organizations in which they and their peers make up the primary membership. At the former they market; at the latter they learn.

Learn to work a meeting.

The most common vehicle for developing contacts through a trade association is the meeting, be it an annual, national, or international gathering lasting several days or a monthly, regional gathering lasting only a few hours. It was my first attempt to work a meeting that drove me to learn more about networking. Feeling lost and intimidated, I walked into a room filled with several hundred people I didn't know. I had a drink, nibbled appetizers, and talked uncomfortably with several people. Later I listened to a dull speaker over a rubber chicken dinner. I left feeling like an outsider. I had wasted my time, and I was just telling myself "Never again," when I ran into two acquaintances on the elevator. Both praised the meeting as one of the most useful and enjoyable they had attended. Obviously I had missed something. It was then that I began my networking survey, described in the preceding chapter.

In my experience, the principal complaints that professionals make about marketing through trade associations are these:

- **Crowd intimidation:** For many people, attending a large event at which they know few people is torturous. After all, there are more shy people than gregarious extroverts. Learning specific techniques for working a crowd can help overcome this fear; so can recognizing that it takes two or three meetings to know enough people in an organization to begin to feel comfortable.

- **Inability to access the in-group:** At every trade association meeting you will find people who are upset because they don't feel a part of the in-group. They complain about the standoffishness of the regular members who make up the clientele everyone else is trying to meet and about rules that maintain distinctions between this group and those who wish to sell to them. Don't be distracted by such nonsense. Every community of human beings has an in-group and an out-group. Your need is to become a part of the in-group or, if you cannot, to benefit from the organization while remaining part of the out-group. Complaints often come from those who know least about how to work the organization. I have attended the committee meeting of the associate members of one organization every year for five years and heard the same litany of concerns about this subject each time. While others complained, I obtained leads and contacts by working the meetings that have, on average, resulted in one new client per meeting.
- **Cost versus return:** Trade associations absorb both time and money. Naturally you expect a return on this investment. In my experience, those who complain about inadequate return usually tie it to the concerns already mentioned. Because they are intimidated by the crowds and find it hard to break into the in-group, they reason that the cost of participation does not justify the return. If you overcome the first two concerns, this one should also be resolved. On the other hand, it's possible you may be participating in the wrong organization.

Here are some guidelines for working a trade association.

Work on introductions and relationships rather than selling.

The primary purpose of attending association meetings should be to meet people and develop relationships rather than to sell your services. Once you have a relationship, you can arrange a meeting to discuss your services outside the context of the association. As at most country clubs, it is considered bad form at most association meetings to solicit business unless invited to by a prospective client. This protocol forbidding selling protects members from being inundated with sales pitches every time they go to a meeting, which they attend for another purpose. Prepare a one-minute description of your services to deliver when someone politely asks what your firm does, and reserve any direct selling for appropriate times, such as the following:

- When someone asks you how you would deal with a specific situation
- Running a booth, if you are willing to spend the money for one
- Meetings set up for this purpose after the conference is over

Some organizations explicitly prohibit direct selling, while at others social pressure provides the primary means of communicating appropriate behavior. Acceptable behavior includes the following:

- Introducing yourself
- Exchanging business cards
- Talking about almost any subject other than your interest in doing business with the person you are talking with
- Asking for information about a company. The opportunity to gain information is one of the great benefits of trade association meetings.
- Asking whether you can call in a week or two to discuss your company, if a person seems receptive

Meet as many people as you can.

Since the primary objective of attending is to meet people, you should avail yourself of every opportunity to do so, beginning as soon as possible and lasting until the bitter end. You can meet people in airports and flights bound for a city where the meeting is to be held, especially if it is taking place in a mid-sized city. If 3,000 people are to descend on San Antonio or Barcelona on a particular Sunday afternoon and you are taking a flight in from a large one like Chicago or Paris, the chances are pretty good that there will be other meeting attendees on the plane with you. Look around the waiting room for signals that fellow passengers are going to the meeting. Is there someone reading the brochure to plan which events she will go to? Introduce yourself to the person sitting next to you on the plane. I have made several valuable contacts by sharing cabs to and from airports.

Lines for food provide good opportunities for casual conversation with those waiting in front of you and behind you. So are lines for hotel registration and meeting check-in. Tours, exhibit halls, and meals provide other opportunities. When you attend a session, introduce yourself to those sitting on either side and behind you. Although it is considered odd to walk up to someone on the street and introduce yourself, this behavior is expected at an association meeting. Take advantage of this rare benefit.

Keep the conversation light. Say something nice about the other person's company or ask a few questions about it. Talk for a while and then move on to someone else.

Breaking into a group that is conversing at a reception or other quasi-social event at a meeting is perfectly acceptable, so long as you show appropriate sensitivity. Most conversation is small talk and is open to anyone. You can enter a group holding such a conversation in several ways. The easiest is to find someone you know in the group and stand next to him or her. Otherwise, observe the group for a moment or two to see who is dominating the conversation. Enter the group and listen politely, and then ask this individual a question. This shows that you are sensitive to the dynamics of the group. After you get your answer, ask another question of someone else. This shows you are sensitive to other people's desire to talk. Occasionally a group will be engaged in a serious conversation about a business or personal issue. Unless you have something significant to add, you should politely move on.

Avoid getting trapped by the lost soul who doesn't know anyone and is unwilling to make the effort to meet people. He will bend your ear all night. Polite breaking-away techniques include going to get another drink or appetizer, seeing someone you have to talk to, or introducing the lost soul to a third individual (you don't have to know the third individual to do so) and shortly thereafter leaving them to talk with each other. It is also acceptable at this kind of event to say, "Well, it's been nice talking with you. I think I need to circulate a little" and then move on.

You should also avoid hanging around with those you know and are most comfortable with, especially other employees from your own firm. Staying with those you know is particularly tempting during the first meeting you attend, when you know few people. If you work hard at making new contacts, you will find the temptation much lower at your second or third meeting, as you find yourself with a much broader range of acquaintances.

Arrive early at local meetings held over a meal or in the evening. Most socializing occurs before the formal meeting begins, and participants usually depart promptly to get back to work or home once the event is over. If I sit down to dinner at such an event and find the people I am sitting with aren't potential network contacts or clients, I will eat my salad, make the excuse that I have another commitment, and go home. There is no need to stay longer because after the dinner everyone will leave quickly.

Keep track of whom you have met.

Exchange business cards as often as possible. As soon as possible after meeting someone, without being obvious, make a note of his or her name and company so that you can follow up later with a letter. It will help you recall them later if you make a note about them on their cards. A few words, like "Loves rottweilers," or "Used to live in Hamburg," or "Tie with penguins" will help you recall a whole conversation and personalize follow-up e-mails, if you write them soon enough. Effective networkers keep careful track of whom they meet. After a meeting at which you have met between a dozen and a hundred people, memory will fade quickly unless you keep a record.

Large annual meetings usually provide lists of registrants. Review these when you arrive, and note whom you want to find. Each evening, review the list to monitor your progress. At local meetings, name tags are often laid out on a table at the door. Arriving early allows you to peruse the tags to see who will attend.

Make it easy for people to know you.

Of course, your sole objective isn't just to get to know other people; you also want them to get to know you. Make this as easy as possible. Wear your name tag on the right so that it is turned toward a contact when you first shake hands. If you fill the tag in yourself, take pains to make your writing large and legible. When you introduce yourself, speak slowly and clearly. If possible, create some immediate link to the person you are talking with. Are you likely to know someone in common? Explore the issue. I have already noted how good Oscar Megerdichian was at this. Since meeting him I have met several others who do the same thing. They are all superb networkers. Have you or your firm worked for the new contact's company? Make note of the fact.

When you meet someone, keep up strong eye contact and devote your full attention, whether or not you perceive the person to be an important contact. This is not just polite, it is also good business. You never know who knows whom and who can help you. Some of the people who have provided me the most help over the years did not look at first as if they could. If you are at a loss for conversation, ask a question or two. Most people would rather talk than listen and will be flattered to have the opportunity. Those who do 80 percent of the talking are most likely to remember the interesting conversation they had with you, especially if the 20 percent of the talking you do is thoughtful and makes them feel good or laugh.

Be cooperative with others who are there to market.

You are unlikely to be the only individual attending a meeting to market. Cooperating with others who are there for the same reason will often bring benefits.

You will also be more memorable if you play host, introducing new people into the group, drawing out those who talk the least and otherwise oiling the machinery of the conversation. This is particularly important at meals, where you may be tempted to monopolize the conversation of a prospective client on your right while ignoring the others at the table, especially the people on your prospect's right and on your left. Make a strong effort to bring them into your conversation. Others trying to make contacts are particularly appreciative of such help and will be more likely to help you later when you want an introduction. The prospect will also be impressed by your courtesy and mark you down as a reasonable person.

Find reasons to recontact prospective clients after the meeting.

An important objective of attending a meeting should be to obtain a reason to follow up later with as many prospective clients as possible. The best way to do this is to find some small favor that you can do for them that obliges you to recontact them later. The obligation may be to provide a book reference, a referral to a business contact, a clarification of some technical issue, or the name of a good restaurant in Nice. It doesn't much matter, as long as it's something the prospective client wants.

The obligation ensures that he will take your call later when strictures about selling are less severe. It also distinguishes you as an individual who is helpful rather than someone solely interested making a sale. It gets the relationship off on a friendly footing. That is why an effective networker will come away from a room full of people with five or six small things to do while the ineffective one will come away empty-handed.

Follow up after the meeting.

Once the meeting is over, you must follow up as soon as possible, preferably within one week but at least within two. During this period your contacts' memories of you and their lingering sense of obligation to be friendly remain. These things decline over time. Break the list of contacts you have made into two groups: those requiring a phone call and those requiring an e-mail. Only once have I received business from someone I met at an association meeting whom I did not follow up with later, and I have been more effective than most. I have a friend who worked a particular association for many years and was inherently more extroverted and effective at small talk than I am. However, he never followed up after a meeting, and he produced many fewer leads and sales than I did.

To be effective, an e-mail must sound personalized, even if several sentences are repeated in many letters. This is where my notes on attendees' business cards come in handy. I can write that I have a new appreciation for rottweilers or comment that the conversation about Hamburg brought back many memories. One of the most effective networkers I know owes a lot to his brilliance at personalizing follow-ups. His letters and phone calls always make you feel selected and specially recognized. This should be the objective of all of your follow-ups. Exhibit 9.1 provides right and wrong examples of leads to e-mails.

EXHIBIT 9.1 Personalized Follow-up Has Much Greater Impact

Right

Dear Arnie:

Ever since the ADVAC meeting I have laughed every time I recalled your comments on small-town Iowa. They took me back to my own childhood in Minnesota . . .

Dear Jenny:

I enjoyed our stimulating conversation about national health insurance at the ADVAC meeting. Until you told me, I didn't realize the cost to our country of having so many people uninsured. You have explained the issue better than anyone else I know. It is . . .

Wrong

Dear Peter:

It was good to meet you at the ADVAC meeting. If you ever need a . . .

Get to know the staff.

Make a point of meeting and getting to know the staff of the trade associations you participate in. The staff often influence who participates in committees, who gets selected as speakers, and who gets offered the chance to serve as officers. They can provide information and guidance in a number of areas. Often they need help, too. They may need someone to do committee drudge work or write an article for the association's journal. Knowing and helping such people will help you participate more effectively in the organization.

Participate regularly.

A trade association's strength is measured according to the support of its members. The most fundamental measure of support is member participation. Year-to-year attendance levels at national meetings are tracked with as much attention as year-to-year sales are tracked by a corporation. You will not be considered a serious player if you do not participate regularly. You will never make it into the in-group. Regular attendance is often a prerequisite to committee participation and other signs of advancement within the organization.

You will also wish to volunteer selectively to help in committee work. This will give you an opportunity to work with prospective clients in a non-selling environment, which in turn will help greatly in establishing relationships. When a committee you are serving on looks for a secretary, consider volunteering. This job provides you particularly good opportunities to work with other members. Public speaking and writing articles for an association's publication are other ways to increase your visibility. Committees that are especially good for making good contacts are the membership committee and the speakers committee.

Pick the associations you work with carefully.

It is not always easy to tell at a distance whether a particular organization is worth participating in. Often you will have to attend a meeting to find out, and sometimes you will have to attend several. Regional and national meetings of an organization can attract very different cross-sections of the membership, and participation often varies heavily from region to region. It may take several meetings to sort out who the other participants are and whether participation is likely to produce long-term value.

When I first participate in an organization, I look to see whether I can find any past clients or prospects among the attendees. If I can, this is a strong signal that other prospective clients will be there, too.

The *Encyclopedia of Associations* provides information on most trade associations in the country. You can find this reference book on the Internet and in most libraries. You can also acquire it on-line from the publisher at *http://gale.cengage.com*

Trade associations play an important role in the marketing of professional services. Where else can you find so many prospective clients gathered in one place, free from the corporate gatekeepers who screen their phone calls? Where else is it so acceptable to introduce yourself to total strangers? The regular pattern of meetings also provides a structure to marketing efforts that many professionals have difficulty imposing upon themselves. These last two advantages are shared by formal networking groups, which warrant a few comments of their own. (See page 115.)

Exhibit 9.2 is a checklist that you can review prior to going to an association meeting.

EXHIBIT 9.2 Working an Association Meeting

I. Key Objectives
   A. Meet people: At association meetings you can meet people that you might have difficulty meeting at other times, because you would normally have to get past a gatekeeper, because they are based far from where you live and work, or because you don't have time. It is a great place to build your network of contacts.
      1. Prospective clients
      2. Third-party contacts (software vendors, etc.)
      3. Association staff
      4. Presenters

B. Recontact people: It is great place to catch up with a lot of people you want to maintain contact with at once. Make the most of it.
   1. Former clients
   2. Third-party contacts
   3. Firm alumni
   4. Association staff
C. Advance relationships and commit to getting back to people: You can advance relationships by doing small things for people you meet, such as introducing them to someone else at the meeting who they would like to know. Also, you make commitments to call people back after the meeting, if you can identify a piece of information you are going to supply them later. This provides you with a reason for the next call.
D. Identify speaking opportunities: You can look for opportunities to speak at the association in the future.

II. Tasks
   A. Meet as many people at you can.
      1. Where
         a. At airports
         b. On airplanes going to and coming from conference
         c. In taxis and limos
         d. At registration line and in any other line
         e. At receptions, meals, and coffee breaks
         f. Visiting booths
         g. At your own booth
         h. At educational sessions, before and after presentation begins
         i. At hospitality suites
         j. On tours
      2. How
         a. Obtain attendance list and scan for people you want to meet.
         b. Start conversation with stranger with a question. Often you can identify a standard subject. (Bad weather: How was your trip in? Logistical mess-ups: How long did registration take you? etc.)
         c. Introduce yourself and get the person's name and, if appropriate, his or her card. Have a two-sentence description of yourself and your firm prepared.
         d. Find out about the person by asking questions.
         e. Record three or four words to remind you of conversation on card or attendance list as soon after conversation as possible. That will help you recall what name goes with what person.
         f. Ask someone who wants to help you, like a satisfied client, to take you around and introduce you to people.

      g. Follow up later with letters and, when appropriate, phone calls.

      h. Personalize letters to all key contacts with information recalled from conversation.

         ii. Make letters sent to secondary contacts sound personalized, even if they aren't.

  B. Recontact people.

      1. Schedule meetings for free times, such as breakfasts and dinners, in advance by phone.

      2. Agree to go on tour together.

  C. Find ways to help people.

      1. Ask questions.

      2. Listen for needs and dissatisfactions.

      3. Talk to wallflowers and introduce them to others.

      4. Introduce people to people they would like to know.

III. Don'ts

  A. Sell your services unless someone asks you to.

  B. Spend too much time with one person, unless that person is a big prospective client and wants to spend time with you.

  C. Spend too much time with other people from your firm.

  D. Set up private meetings at times scheduled for association events, unless you know the person well.

Formal networking groups can be valuable.

In many cities, groups of business people meet regularly with the unabashed purpose of helping each other get business. Some of these are branches of national or regional chains. Others are independent organizations. Most of the participants are small-business people: stationery suppliers, printers, travel agents, and the like. Almost all have a heavy representation from area professionals. Though participation by large firms is less common, a committed player from a large organization can do well. The case example at the beginning of this chapter describes the benefits that one professional has received from belonging to such a group. For the sole practitioner or member of a small firm, the structure, motivational support, and informal training these groups provide can be major attractions.

A little asking around will help you find groups in your area. Exhibit 9.3 provides a list of some of the national and regional chains. If you can't find one that is suitable, consider forming your own.

EXHIBIT 9.3 Formal Networking Groups

Formal networking groups exist in many cities. Most are unaffiliated with any other organization. The only way to find them is to ask area business people if they know of them. Chains of clubs are run by the following:

- Ali Lassen's Leads Club, PO Box 279-7797, Carlsbad, CA 92018 (roughly 300 chapters). Telephone: 800-783-3761; Web site: *www.leadsclub.com*
- Business Forums International, 1930 Century Park West, Los Angeles, CA 90067 (25 chapters). Telephone: 800-718-5634; Web site: *www.businessforumsinternational.com*
- Business Network International, 545 College Commerce Way, Upland, CA 91786 (roughly 4,500 chapters). Telephone: 800-825-8286 (outside Southern CA), 800-608-7575 (inside Southern CA); Web site: *www.bni.com*
- LeTip International, Inc. 8909 Complex Drive, San Diego, CA 92123 (roughly 650 chapters). Telephone: 800-255-3847; Web site: *www.letip.com*

Regional chains are run by Creative Referral Networks (Kansas City area), and The Business Resource Group (Dallas, TX).

These groups formalize many of the networking guidelines provided in the last chapter. Following are some of the common practices.

Members help each other.

This is the avowed purpose of the organization. To ensure that it happens, most have exclusivity rules: Only one member is allowed for a specific business, in order that intragroup competition for business, which would inhibit cooperation, may be avoided. Many devote a portion of each meeting to sharing leads. Small groups of members will sit around tables and offer or ask for help at specific companies. Many organizations use a form to track the number of leads provided by each member, and some require minimum quotas. At the good ones, if you don't contribute over the course of a year, the executive committee will ask you to leave. This preserves a sense of urgency and obligation.

Members recognize leads for others' services.

Formal networking groups expend a lot of effort helping the members learn about each others' services so that each will recognize leads for others when they hear them. At each meeting, at least one member will describe his services, his customers, and what he sees as a good business opportunity. Members are also expected to make house calls, one-on-one meetings between pairs of members that take place between regular meetings.

Members make a sincere effort.

Groups recognize that some individuals will be able to give more leads than others, and they accept that. They also recognize that Member A may be able to give leads to Member B, but that B will not have many opportunities to give to A. As long as B gives to someone else in the group, the one-way flow is accepted.

Members express gratitude.

At each meeting, each member has an opportunity to publicly thank those in the group who have helped him.

Membership is built on trust.

A serious networking group will quickly drop anyone who violates trusts. Trust is also developed through regular contact resulting from meetings and house calls and from seeing members help each other. Because all new members are referred by existing ones, trustworthy people tend to get admitted, if a group functions well.

Members make a time commitment.

Networking is time consuming. Groups usually meet semimonthly for breakfast for about two hours. Add to that travel time, house calls, phone calls, and time devoted to helping others, and the group will easily demand 5 percent of your available time. If you cannot commit that much time or would not find doing so worthwhile, don't join a formal group. On the other hand, if you have difficulty imposing the self-discipline that networking requires, the structure of a formal group may help you.

I have participated in three such organizations in my career and found all valuable. If you have a chance to join a formal networking group, ask yourself these questions before accepting:

- Do I have anything to give to these individuals? You have to give to get. You will want to ascertain that enough of the members sell to the same market you do for your contacts to be worthwhile.
- What is the probability that the return I will get from them is worth 5 percent of my time?
- Are the members serious, and do they understand networking?

If your answers to the preceding questions are no, consider starting your own group targeted at your market. Exhibit 9.4 provides some guidelines for getting started.

EXHIBIT 9.4 Guidelines for Establishing a Networking Group

1. **Determine the focus of the group.** A group will be more effective if it has a clearly defined focus, whether that be by industry, geography, or some other unifying affinity. Networks with high affinity produce more results.

2. **Identify a core group.** Invite two or three people you know and trust and who also sell to the identified market to discuss the potential for establishing a formal networking group. Explain the goal of such a group, which is to help each other get new business. Explain the ground rules. First, no two members may offer the same service, because if they did it would inhibit open discussion of opportunities. Second, no new members will be admitted without a majority vote of all active members. Third, no one is required to make a specific introduction. All members can choose who they want to introduce to whom, but everyone is admitted with the understanding that they will be willing to get to know the other members of the group and to introduce them when they can to their business contacts. Fourth, everything said within the group is confidential; violation of this confidence is a serious breach.

3. **Invite additional members.** Each core member should identify at least one potential additional member. Networks that grow produce more value than those that are stagnant or declining. At succeeding meetings, core members interview prospective members and vote in private on admissions. It is imperative that each potential member have clearly defined business space that does not overlap too seriously with any existing member.

4. **Spotlight one member per meeting.** At each meeting, allow one member to make a presentation on her services.

5. **Insist that members meet between meetings.** If the members only get together at formal group meetings, the network will not be effective. Everyone should be required to meet with at least one other member between meetings and to report that fact.

6. **Provide an opportunity to show gratitude.** At each meeting, members should have the opportunity to thank each other for help received since the last meeting. This is far more effective than having members boast of the help that they have given. The burden should be on the receiver to recognize help given.

7. **Keep the agenda varied.** If the group follows the same agenda at every meeting, the meetings will become tedious. Try changes of venue, guest speakers, and other variations. A good exercise is to have each member introduce the member seated to his right, explaining what she does. This forces members to practice describing their colleagues' services.

8. **Eliminate ineffective members, if you can.** Members who repeatedly miss meetings and other dead weight should be subject to termination from the group. This can be difficult to enforce, but if it isn't, the group's time will be increasingly taken up by non-contributors. That has been the undoing of many formal networking organizations.

9. **Let the group die.** If it ceases to be productive, simply stop calling meetings or resign from the group, rather than waste your time.

Internal networks also have value.

Many professionals work for large firms offering a variety of services, which are delivered by different business units. These units are usually called practices in accounting, consulting, and law firms, and studios in architectural firms. In such cases firms grow by cross-selling, that is, from staff members in one practice introducing their clients to staff members in another practice.

Firm management can encourage cross-selling through incentives and communications programs but can seldom mandate it. The client/professional relationship is too sensitive to permit strong-arm tactics. A partner at a large accounting and consulting firm struggling with this problem noted that cross-selling deteriorated markedly when several consulting assignments went sour at once. Reviving the effort, even after the consulting operation had been overhauled, proved difficult.

At large, multi-practice firms, the emerging marketer must make friends in other practices and induce them to help her get business. In short, she must network. While operating fundamentally on the same principles as external networks, internal networks deserve some comments of their own.

The professional who assumes that sales will be had more easily when working with an internal network than an external one will be quickly jolted out of her naiveté. The opportunity to cross-sell within a firm is easier than working an outside network in some ways and harder in others. On the positive side, it results in the following:

- **Clout:** Top management encourages cross-selling through incentives, communications programs, and occasionally threats because it is a way to increase revenues and profits.
- **Eased access:** Most professionals will extend the courtesy of meeting with another member of their firm on request. This isn't always the case when dealing with external contacts.
- **Exclusivity:** In external networks, exclusive relationships can be difficult to capture. The best sources of leads often want to spread their help among many contacts to earn good will from as many people as possible. They will give to your competitors as readily as they will to you. The potential for capturing an exclusive relationship is greater in an internal network.
- **Reflected good will:** If one practice has a good relationship with a client, he will be inclined to look favorably on buying other services from the same firm.

Against these benefits must be weighed the following negative aspects:

- **Resentment and distrust:** A noticeable percentage of professionals are distrustful of working with others outside their practices. They are not predisposed to network with anyone. This distrust is only increased when they feel a relationship is being forced on them.
- **Lowered perceived objectivity:** When you recommend another company, your recommendation will often be seen as objective. Proper networking means you will only refer the best. Clients will not perceive the same level of objectivity when you recommend another part of your own firm.
- **Increased downside risk:** If an external contact you have referred lets your client down, it can hurt your own relationship with the client. If the contact is internal, it will almost certainly do so. First, you and the contact share the same firm name. Second, your recommendation is likely to appear more self-serving and is therefore less likely to be seen as an honest mistake.

There are several rules to follow when dealing with internal networks.

Treat them the way you would any other network.

Do not expect others in the firm to refer you business just because management wants them to. They may not know enough about your services to recognize a lead for you. They may not want to risk a valued client relationship by bringing in someone who might spoil it. You must follow all of the guidelines for external networks. You must help your internal contacts, contact them frequently, show how your services will help them with the client, and do all the other things outlined in the preceding chapter on networking. That is how you will earn trust. Leave arm twisting to the senior management, which wants cross-marketing to occur.

The benefits of helping are different.

Internal contacts can benefit from helping you in ways that external contacts can't. They may receive a cash incentive for a referral, recognition within the firm, increased potential for promotion, and a deeper relationship with their own clients. These are the benefits you have to sell.

Of particular importance is recognition. When someone else in your company helps you make a sale, do everything you can to make sure her help is recognized. You can do any of the following:

- *Send her a thank-you note.* Make sure you also send a copy to her boss and her boss's boss. It will go into her personnel file.
- *Have your boss send a letter to her boss.* Often, the higher up the recognition comes from, the more it is valued.
- *Submit her name for an award.* Many firms have awards programs. Look into them to see whether any offers an appropriate means of showing appreciation for help received. If none exists, consider creating your own and publicizing it.
- *Thank her in a public forum.* Don't just say thanks. Make it clear exactly what she did for you and how valuable it was to the firm and to you, personally.
- *Make sure she is mentioned for her help in the firm newsletter.*

Internal contacts are judged by different standards.

You will eventually drop an external contact who gives you no leads. When dealing with internal networks, you must adopt different standards. You must ask what the individual does for the firm. If the work you help her get adds significant revenues and profits to the firm, you should continue to extend help, even if you receive no direct return. You must hope that you are judged in the same way.

Expect moderately increased collections problems.

In many large firms, the individual responsible for a major account must approve all billing to it. This individual looks at two issues that you might not before approving a bill: the good of the firm, and his own skin. This means that if the client is unhappy with your service, the account rep is less likely to take a strong collections approach than you might because he wants to guard a larger relationship. This is a cost of the lowered perceived objectivity cited previously. Once in a while an account rep will make a freebie of your service in order to mollify a client unhappy with the rep's own work.

If you understand that the structure of internal networks makes such events inevitable, though infrequent, they will anger you less. Judge each case on its own merits and either drop it or appeal to a higher authority. Get on with life as quickly as you can.

Conclusion

Organizations provide a structure for networking. They permit you to make many new contacts in a short time and to build relationships that can be the source of new business. Any beginning networker should consider working through one.

10 Increasing Network Quality
by Mimi Spangler and Gary Pines

The size of a rainmaker's network varies with the nature of her practice, personal preferences, and age. I know of one rainmaker, a recruiter, who cuts his network back to 2,500 at the beginning of each year. Recruiters need big networks, and he is a social person. Some rainmakers claim to work networks of under 100. When I have explored the number with them, I have always found that they underestimate the quantity of contacts they have. Most leave out colleagues from their own firms, for example. As a crude estimate, assume you need to have between 200 and 300 people in your network to have the depth you will need to ensure a good lead flow. Much larger networks are commonplace.

Most professionals, and especially younger ones, need to focus on adding people to their networks to have a reasonable chance of finding opportunities to make introductions and pass information. Once you have bulked your network up to between 100 and 200 people, you can start making adjustments. So, for example, many developing rainmakers grow their networks for a year or two. They then shrink them for a while around the more valuable contacts with a purge before starting to grow them once again. People with large networks pay more attention to contact quality than do beginners. The number of leads you are able to generate, the percentage of them you are able to convert into paid work, and the speed with which you are able to do so depend, in part, on the richness of your network. Spend time with the right people, and new business flows more easily.

A network can be rich in several dimensions, including these:

- **Purchasing power:** A network with a high percentage of people who can hire you is likely to produce high returns. Networks made up of CEOs and other senior executives are the epitome of this class of network.

- **Access and influence:** People with access to decision makers and influence with them are also valuable contacts and are called connectors. Some rainmakers focus on connectors rather than on decision makers. This is especially true of those whose services are rarely needed, so that finding a decision maker who needs their services *now* is like looking for a needle in a hay stack. An accountant, the founder of a successful, mid-sized firm, told me that he doesn't network with potential buyers because people so rarely change accounting firms. Rather, he networks with bankers and other financial advisors who hear from their clients when they are dissatisfied with their accountants and can refer him in at that time.
- **Affinity:** The greater the affinity—by industry, interest, function, or geography—your network has, the greater chance you have of getting business from it. Some rainmakers also devote a part of their networking to a subset based on gender, race, or religion.

Networks need to be built with the above three criteria in mind.

Buying power is a critical factor.

Example: Senior Executives

Senior executives have two clear advantages as network members: purchasing authority and influence. They are the ultimate decision makers. The professional they want is usually the one who gets hired. This afternoon I met with a consultant who had just lost an engagement that he had pursued for six months and been told he had won. A division chief overruled a lower-level decision to hire him, insisting that his subordinate retain someone else. My friend had no hope of appeal.

Even when senior execs choose not to exercise their authority, they exert great influence. This happens even when they have no intention of doing so. Years ago, when John Nevin took over as head of Zenith Corporation, he replaced a Cadillac the company supplied with a Lincoln because he had previously worked at Ford and still felt loyalty to his former employer. Though he never said a word about it to anyone, within two years every car in the company's executive fleet was a Lincoln. Each time a Zenith executive was told that it was time to replace his leased limo, he followed the boss's lead and picked a Ford product.

It is often the same when decisions are made to hire a professional. A firm that has the CEO's unofficial stamp of approval often becomes popular elsewhere in the organization. If the CEO employs an executive coach from Firm X, there is a good chance that others will soon, too.

Senior executives' influence extends well beyond their own organizations. They sit on each other's boards, are members of the same clubs, and live in the same communities. They see each other at charity, cultural, and civic functions. Like the rest of us, they find it helpful to exchange ideas with people who share the same problems that they have, which, in their case, means with other senior execs. Idea exchanges inevitably result in the passing of referrals.

An architect got to know two senior executives, one at a finance company and the other at a pharmaceutical company. These relationships helped his firm win major design projects at both companies, including both companies' corporate headquarters. And they also helped win many other projects at other companies, colleges, and institutions where the senior execs had influence. These two relationships were the cornerstones of much of the explosive growth that this firm enjoyed.

It is no surprise, then, that senior executives are coveted network contacts. But they are hard to get. They are the busiest of people, with little time for schmoozing with professionals on the make. Few of us can just call up a CEO to pass the time of day. They have skilled gatekeepers who make sure that such callers don't get through. Getting on their calendars is hard, even when you have something important to say.

Also, there is a lot of competition for relationships with senior executives. If an exec already has a strong relationship with a mergers and acquisitions attorney, it will be that much harder for you to get access to her, no matter how great your skills in this same area.

There is often an imbalance in power between a professional and an executive that makes networking difficult. Networking is based on mutual help. It's obvious what the exec can do for you, but what can you do for the exec, over and above selling him your services? Often a senior executive is much older than an up-and-coming rainmaker, who may be an age peer of the executive's children. The executive has far more people reporting up to him, often heading up an organization with thousands of employees; most professionals have but a handful of people reporting to them. And the executive is much wealthier. This imbalance can make the prospect of approaching an executive intimidating.

Here are some suggestions for developing relationships with senior executives.

Start early and catch a rising star.

The strongest relationships take years to develop. This is true of relationships with senior executives, too. If you work with a client who is competent and ambitious, maintain the relationship after your work is completed. The client will likely end up in a senior position somewhere, and when she does, you will have a senior executive relationship much stronger than it would have been if you had let the relationship go cold for several intervening years. Here's how one rainmaker describes it.

> Some of the people you meet go in the A bucket. They are interesting and are probably going places, and you like them. The Bs you are not so sure about. The Cs I tend not to do much with. But stay in touch with the As. Send them an e-mail from time to time, asking how they are doing. People can be afraid to reach out and talk to someone else unless they have something deep and rich to say. But that isn't always necessary. If you are twenty-five years old, start building a network now.
>
> [The CEO of a consumer products company] is an example of someone I have kept in touch with that way. I first met him in 1985 when we were doing work for [a large food producer]. I met [John] during the project, when he was in his mid thirties. He was a really good guy, and I stayed in touch over the years. He wasn't a big user of our services and could be difficult, but I really liked him. When he resigned from [the food producer], I wrote him a note.
>
> When he surfaced at [another food producer], I called and suggested that we get together, and we met one night for a drink and he liked what I said and brought me in. When that company was acquired in a hostile takeover, he was out. I called him and suggested that he join us in a buyout company. That progressed through the planning stages. Then I got a call one day saying he had joined [the consumer products company] where he is now. We had two meetings before he started work that began our relationship there. We've done huge amounts of work there, since then.

Note that this relationship began twenty years ago, long before the client in question was a CEO.

The same has proved true for our own firm, Harding & Company. After ten years of coaching professionals on business development, some of the people we had coached started arriving at senior positions in their firms. It has been a pleasure to see good people doing so well, and these new senior execs have created a flow of new business for us.

Be patient, and try multiple avenues.

These relationships are tough to get and will take time to develop. You may have to try a variety of approaches to gain access and begin the relationship. And you must earn the right to proceed at each step. The following story illustrates how hard a management consultant, Tom Saporito of RHR International, worked to start just one such relationship and how patient he was.

It helps when you can get to know an executive from a number of different directions. A client asked me to join the board of a local charity. The chairman of the board of this organization was a top executive at a large company based in our region. I got to know him through the charity work but didn't push our services because it wouldn't have been appropriate in that environment. Still, now I knew him, and he was eventually promoted to the chairmanship of his company.

But that wasn't the only way I approached him. We do a lot of work for companies in the same industry as the company in question. So when the relevant industry association had its meeting in our city we went, knowing that the chairman was likely to be there. I went up to the chairman—he was acting as a local host—at this event and reminded him of how we knew each other. This was a business forum, and he asked what kind of business I was in. I gave a brief description and said I would like to meet with him some time. Because he knew me from the charity work, he said fine.

We were also working this account from a third direction. We had worked with one of the human resources people there when she was with a different company. She suggested that the head of human resources meet with me. When I met with the head of HR, we talked and he said he wanted to introduce me to the chairman. I said fine, that I already knew him and was supposed to set up a meeting with him anyway. The head of HR thought this was great. So it all came together at once.

We had three meetings with the chairman before we sold any work. The first was pure chemistry check, the second was about backgrounds, and the third was about a specific issue and his needs. At the final meeting, we laid out a strategy, and we got the go-ahead to get started. If I had gone for the kill in the first meeting, we wouldn't have gotten the work.

Go where you can find senior executives.

If you want to meet them, you must go where they are. For some, this means picking the right communities to live in, while others join the same clubs or select activities where they will meet senior execs. Here are some examples:

- **From a management consultant:** "I've lived in Greenwich, Connecticut for fifteen years. There must be fifty CEOs who live there, plus all the Wall Street guys. It's an exceptional community that way. And, my wife and I bought a house in [an exclusive area] in Florida and were sponsored into the club there by [an investment banker]. A lot of interesting people belong there. I met the chairman of [a restaurant chain] there. It's a $10 billion company, so I'll follow up with that one. I met [the CEO of a large financial institution] at a cocktail party in my neighborhood. We got to talking about what we do, and he gave me his card and said to call him."

- **From William Wolf:** "I know that [James McKinsey, founder of McKinsey & Company] moved into an apartment house in Chicago on Lake Shore Drive for one reason. The apartment house had two units on each floor. When you got off the elevator there were two doors. McKinsey wanted to meet the man behind the other door, so he rented the apartment next to his.[1]

- **From a mechanical engineer:** "Like many of the leaders in the real estate community in New York, he is philanthropic. He learned early on that this was a good way to meet people. Once he got to know them, he would see them also at cultural events. His relationships with property owners and managers goes back years now. They have worked together in tandem on these charities and got to know each other there. This solidified their relationships."

When you have an opportunity to advance a relationship, take it.

Opportunities to meet and spend time with senior executives don't come often. You must take full advantage of them when they do. David Nadler, the founder of Mercer Delta Consulting, tells this story.

> I was asked to give a speech at a conference for a lot of senior executives at the Homestead resort in Virginia. I went down to breakfast the morning of the speech, went through the buffet line and sat down at a table with other people attending the meeting. We all introduced ourselves, and I found out that I was eating breakfast with six very senior executives. After we finished eating and got up to go, I realized that it would be a long time before such an opportunity came again. So, I went back through the buffet line and sat down at another table. I had three breakfasts that morning and probably put on pounds, but it was worth it.

Find ways to provide value.

In the end, developing a relationship with a senior executive depends on providing value. Because of the imbalance of power, this is hard to do, but it's not as hard as it may seem. Among the things you can do for a senior executive are the following:

- *Provide information about his own organization.* Your work for a client will often give you insights into the organization valuable to a senior executive. You bring an outsider's fresh perspective and are in a position to compare the client organization to others. Information coming up through the ranks to an exec is always filtered. Yours won't be.

- *Offer introductions.* All senior executives have people they would like to meet. These include other senior executives, potential employees, and suppliers of professional services. Many also appreciate the chance to meet senior government officials and celebrities. If you are in the position to make such an introduction, offer to do so.
- *Offer congratulations and condolences.* Senior executives appreciate recognition of personal triumphs and losses as much as the rest of us do.

Use one senior executive to meet another.

Rainmakers use their relationships with one senior executive to meet others. At appropriate times they ask for introductions:

- *The managing partner of a large strategy consulting firm's German office was renowned for the many relationships he had with senior executives.* He had a specific method for getting them. He was highly athletic and liked extreme sports and would identify executives who had similar interests. Once a year he would set up an extreme sporting event, such as climbing a mountain. Usually, the idea for the event came from a conversation with a senior exec who became the first participant. Once he had one acceptance, he could leverage that person's name to line up others because senior executives like to spend time with each other. Sometimes an exec would suggest other people who might be interested in coming. Once you have bicycled across Germany with someone, you have a relationship.
- *When a large corporation ran into trouble, the chairman of a consulting firm knew there was an opportunity.* Several top executives, including the CEO, had been indicted, and a new management team had been brought in. The consultant thought the new CEO would need some outside help cleaning the place up and turning it around. He didn't know him, so he did some research on him and the company. It turned out that one of his old clients had just been appointed to the board. He called the former client, who said he would be glad to introduce the consultant. That's how his firm got in front of the CEO.

Connectors are just as critical as execs.

Some people know everyone in an industry, a functional area, or a city. They know not only the right people but also the latest news on what is going on. These people are called connectors.[2] They will also enrich your network. Want to know the background of the newly appointed executive at a target company? Ask a connector. Want to know the history of a rivalry between two people in a market? Ask a connector. Want an introduction to the decision maker? Again, ask a connector.

Anyone with a large Rolodex and the right mindset can be a connector, and certain jobs predispose people for the role. Auditors learn about all sorts of needs that a company has with which it may want help. So do corporate attorneys. Real estate brokers come in at the initial stages of facilities projects that run for years and require many kinds of professionals. This gives them an opportunity to introduce other professionals to the client. Relationships with such people are much sought after and pose their own special problems.

These problems are captured in a story my partner, Mimi Spangler, tells about her first days developing business for a large architectural firm.

> A big real estate brokerage firm was in a position to know about many opportunities for architects. I mustered my courage and invited the head of the regional office to lunch, and he accepted. There I was, twenty-something, with this high-producer in his early fifties. I started describing the kinds of projects our firm worked on, when he interrupted me. "Who do you know?" he asked. I said we had worked for Company X and Company Y, and again he asked, "Yes, but who do you know at these companies?" I said that our company knew people in all of them, and he asked, "Yes, but who do you know?" He wasn't being unkind; he was simply telling me that I didn't have much to offer unless I had contacts of my own. It was a lesson I needed to learn.

When someone says to a connector, "I think our two organizations might have a lot to offer each other," all too often he means, "I want you to help me get business." Connectors are all too used to people who want them to make introductions and who have little to offer in return. Here are some ways to be of benefit to a connector:

- *Start a relationship with a connector by offering help.* This will be a refreshing change for the connector and will set you apart from others seeking her help. Note that the offer will not seem genuine if it is a veiled attempt to help yourself. The connector may see your offer to provide a small pro bono service to her client as a savvy way to meet someone who might hire you for a million-dollar matter. She is unlikely to see it as much of a gift to her, even if she gets to offer the free service for her client.
- *Be sure that the connector perceives what you are offering as help.* The connector often trades in a currency different from yours, and you must deal in that currency if you want to be helpful. When in doubt, ask if the offer is seen as helpful and then listen carefully to the response. If you offer to

introduce an executive recruiter to a friend, even an accomplished friend, who is looking for a job, the recruiter is likely to say, "Well, send his resume along and I'll get it into our system." This is a far cry from, "Great! That would be a big help." Rather, the subtext of her words reads, "Good grief! Another one who has no concept of my business! "

- *Ask who the connector would like to meet.* Connectors are connectors because they appreciate the value of knowing a lot of people. There are always additional people they would like to know. Ask a connector for a description of the kinds of people she would like to meet.
- *Build your network.* The larger your network, the more attractive you will be to a connector. Connectors especially like meeting other connectors. Act like one.
- *Show appreciation for help received.* Connectors like helping people and are good at it. They would like a new contact to pass some business their way, but they often help people unlikely to be able to do so.

This last point is an important one to remember. Connectors don't like being taken for granted. Here is how one connector describes it:

One of my colleagues introduced me to someone who competes with us. I met with him, and he made out as if he were an experienced networker. I liked him, so when we were offered some business that we couldn't take, because there would have been a conflict with one of our clients, I referred the business to him and left him a message telling him to expect the call. That's the last I heard of it. No thank you or update from this guy, so I thought the client had never called him.

Then I got a call from a second company where we were conflicted. I figured we might as well try again and so referred the same guy. I know these people, so I called them to see if they had talked with him. Yes, they had and they liked him. But I got not so much as a thank you.

One of our people ran into him at the airport, and he told her that he owed me a call. But I know this type. He won't call. Not unless his business dries up. He's the kind of person who's there for you when he needs you. He doesn't even realize that, himself. But it's the way he operates.

Look through your contact list now and see how many connectors you can identify. When did you last talk with them? Is it time to catch up with them? Do you know what kinds of help you might be able to provide them? If not, consider arranging time with them to ask the questions in Exhibit 8.2 (on page 87). When you know the answers to these questions, you will be in a better position to help them. And helping a connector is a good thing to do.

Look for networks with affinity.

Example: Women's Networks

A network with high affinity will provide you with more benefits than a highly diversified one. For example, say that a client loses his job as CIO of a large medical center in Richmond. You will be well equipped to help him find a new one if your network contains many people in health-care facilities in the region (be it Virginia or Surrey) or many people in technology positions. It will be far more difficult if your network consists of a stockbroker in New York, a matador in Seville, an outsourcer in Hyderbad, a tool-and-die maker in Taipei, and other people who have little in common with each.

Affinity is possible on many dimensions. As an example, we will look at women's networks.

Women above a certain age either preceded the women's movement or were in its first wave. Many of them didn't see much value in networking with other women. There weren't enough other women to build a significant network and, in what was clearly a man's world, networking with other women was seen as emphasizing a woman's exclusion rather than helping to overcome it.

As the number of women has grown in the professions, circumstances have changed, followed rapidly by changes in attitudes. Women's organizations have exploded in number and size and make no apologies for their gender orientation. These include standalone organizations—NEWIRE (New England Women in Real Estate), Women in Finance, The Chicago Network—as well as special-interest groups of larger organizations, like the American Bar Association's National Association of Women Lawyers, and the women's organizations started within many professional firms, with the goal of making those firms more accepting of and attractive to women.

Unlike male-dominated organizations, where men network largely with other men because they are comfortable doing so, women in women's organizations network with each other out of a sense of mission. Whether this is another phase of the integration of women into the workplace or a permanent fixture remains to be seen. Here are some of the guidelines that today's women rainmakers follow, often implicitly, to get the most out of gender affinity:

- *Make no excuses.* The women we interviewed recognized that their gender made some aspects of networking more difficult—sports outings were a frequently cited example. They had also found that gender had compensating advantages. As a group, they were far more focused on finding and exploiting the advantages than picking over the difficulties.

- *Recognize the advantage of being a woman.* The women rainmakers found it easy to develop relationships with other women. As one rainmaker put it, "Women in leadership roles connect to other women in leadership, largely because there are so few of us." She has found her gender an advantage when meeting women executives at client companies.
  - ■ The gender difference can also help a woman network with men. A rainmaker who attended an industry function observed, "Women were rare there. I stuck out like a sore thumb and people remembered me." Another tells a similar story.

I was the only woman in our firm's leadership group. We all went to a CEO conference, where everyone else was an old white guy. At first, I was uncomfortable, because I didn't feel that I fit in. But it turned out to be easy because I was different. I gave up any attempt to fit in and took advantage of the recognition that came from being different and just met lots of people.

- *Find or create a peer group.* As they discovered the benefits of working with other women, the women rainmakers soon sought to formalize the interaction with other women by joining or creating an organization. A partner at a multinational human resources consulting firm found herself isolated as a working woman and mother of small children at her male-dominated firm. She found it helpful to talk to a woman from another firm who faced similar frustrations. They started to meet regularly at the local Starbucks. From this simple beginning, an organization with thirty-five members has evolved, which includes women from both professional firms and client organizations. The group meets every six weeks and is an excellent place to build relationships and look for leads for new business.
- *Plan events that you enjoy.* Some of the women rainmakers play golf or tennis, but many didn't. They found themselves excluded from male-oriented events. Most have overcome this obstacle by planning events that are oriented towards women. One turnaround specialist says this.

I'm organizing a spa event in New York and inviting a group of twenty to thirty women, who are either clients or referral sources. The idea came up over a lunch with a client who has lots of women partners. We were talking about how we could get our teams together to expose them to each other. This would typically occur over a dinner, but when the idea of a spa event came up, she loved it.

- *Target local clients.* Many of the women rainmakers noted that pressure to do more selling coincided with the years when their children were small. They needed to avoid the heavy travel associated with many professional careers. To do so, they needed to develop strong local networks and to target local clients.

Another network based on affinity is composed of people at the same client company. That network is so important that we devote Chapter 13 to it.

11

How Markets Structure Networks

The underlying logic of networking is simple and the same for all networks: Identify the right people to know. Find ways to meet them. Stay in front of them by being helpful. Remind them of what you do in low-key ways. When appropriate, ask for favors, such as introductions. Leads for new business will follow.

How this simple logic is applied depends on the network you want to enter because the structure of networks varies. There are well-established networks, around for generations. In such cases, the challenge is to break in. In other fields, there is no established network, or only one that is diffused, and the challenge is to create or solidify one.

Less obviously, I believe that most referral networks form power curves. A power curve occurs when a few players gain a disproportionate share of the value derived from participation. It is known that many kinds of networks have this characteristic, with one well-studied example being linkages among Internet sites. A few sites, like Google, have millions of linkages; most have only a few.[1] Many years of working with and observing referral networks has made me believe that they form power curves, too.

A power curve is shown in Exhibit 11.1. In any given referral network, a small number of people occupy the lower right end of the curve, deriving a disproportionate share of the value. If value is defined in terms of, say, the number of leads for new business, they get a preponderance of the leads. Most people fall to the left side of the graph, receiving few leads for their efforts. Some may be happy with the small return. Some may be looking for things other than leads, and some may be miserable with their lot. Whatever their feelings, they get few leads. The challenge is to move to the right end of the curve.

EXHIBIT 11.1 Power Curve

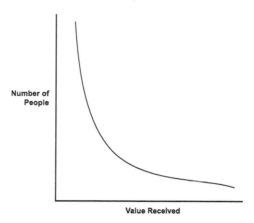

Research into other kinds of networks shows that two factors are critical to moving to the right. First is time in the network.[2] The longer you participate in a network relative to others in it, the greater the return you are likely to get. With a large, long-established network, business development gets easier over time. Rainmakers know this. Read these words spoken by accountant Richard Eisner.

> Marketing is like an inverse pyramid; it gets easier and easier over time. It was extremely difficult when I started. I hadn't developed the quality of relationships I have now and we didn't have the reputation yet.

Fortunately, time is not the only determinant of success. The second is something called "fitness."[3] Even though it isn't the oldest search engine, Google has more links than those that predate it. Users discovered that it was simply better at finding things on the Web. It was fitter. The definition of fitness varies depending on the network.

In referral networks, our subject here, fitness has several parameters. One is delivering high-quality work to your clients so that people want to refer business to you.

Another is dogged persistence: showing up at events, meeting people, staying in touch with them and following up on opportunities. As noted in Chapter 9, along with two colleagues, I once founded a networking group for people who sold to professional service firms. After several years we did an analysis of who got the most leads from it. One of the other founders and I did particularly well. We had the founders' advantage of more time in the network, and we also gave the most leads. The third person who did well in the group was Dallas Kersey, then a marketing communications consultant. He was a relative latecomer to the group and so didn't have founders' advantage. Dallas did well because he was fitter than others. When you gave Dallas a lead, he would relentlessly track it down and turn it into business. Others would meet a little resistance, like a few unreturned phone calls, then give up. But Dallas never gave up.

Other characteristics of fitness vary depending upon the way specific networks function. To see this, let's look at five examples of well-established networks: the distressed-company network, the pension-and-benefits advisory network, the office-move network, the municipal water-and-wastewater network, and the high-net-worth advisory network.

Access to people guarding a secret is key for the distressed-company network.

A lot of people make their living from a company tottering at the brink of failure. This is true whether the company ultimately survives or dies. Owners struggling to salvage their investment through a turnaround or sale and creditors scrambling to recover cents on each dollar they are owed create opportunities for those who specialize in dealing with such crises. These specialists know how to deal with legal and financial complexities of companies on the edge, improving the outcome for their clients and often for other stakeholders at the same time.

There is a well-established network of people who work with distressed companies and their creditors, and that network has been evolving for a long time. In the 1970s, Harvey Miller, at the time working at Weil, Gotshal & Manges, built the firm's bankruptcy practice from three to 300 attorneys. While doing it, he brought bankruptcy law into the mainstream of large, prestigious law firms. He is seen today as the dean of bankruptcy attorneys and is credited with seeding the creation of today's turnaround and bankruptcy industry. He and a few others certainly revolutionized how troubled companies are dealt with. But even earlier, many professionals built their practices by helping clients in crisis.

For example, like many turnaround specialists today, James O. McKinsey, the founder of the consulting firm McKinsey & Company, was an accountant and he did a lot of turnaround work. (He died at age forty-eight of pneumonia caught while overworking himself trying to turn around the department store, Marshall Field & Company.) Back in the 1930s, he obtained business just the way many restructuring specialists do today, by getting bankers to refer him to their distressed commercial customers.[4] Even earlier, Frederick Winslow Taylor, famous for his time-and-motion analyses, built a reputation as a turnaround manager.[5]

Like all markets, the one serving distressed companies has peculiarities that derive from its fundamental aspects. Three such aspects stand out. First, few senior executives in the corporate world are ever in such desperate straits that they need restructuring services, and of those that do, most need it once in a career.

Second, when a company runs into trouble, management seldom advertises the fact for fear of spooking customers and creditors. Identifying and getting access to a prospective client in this environment is hard. There is usually a brief window of opportunity when professionals get hired. Miss that window, and you are out of luck. In this field, early warning of an impending case provides a significant advantage to influence who will get hired before competitors can move in.

Third, there are many sides to every case, with different sides requiring different degrees of professional support. The sides frequently include the debtor, bank lenders, trade creditors, public noteholders, shareholders, and so-called "vulture" investors. Each side needs legal and financial advisors. Each has different goals and planning horizons. Most stand to lose money.

Infrequent, major events; secrecy; corporate management in denial; many players with a stake in the outcome—this is an environment bound to be filled with gossip and cliques. It provides rich ground for the establishment of networks.

Exhibit 11.2 provides a diagram of such a network. The first thing that strikes you is its complexity. But there is good reason for that complexity and there is structure within it.

EXHIBIT 11.2 Distressed Company Referral Network

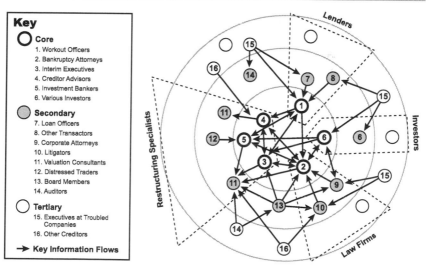

Key

○ **Core**
1. Workout Officers
2. Bankruptcy Attorneys
3. Interim Executives
4. Creditor Advisors
5. Investment Bankers
6. Various Investors

◐ **Secondary**
7. Loan Officers
8. Other Transactors
9. Corporate Attorneys
10. Litigators
11. Valuation Consultants
12. Distressed Traders
13. Board Members
14. Auditors

○ **Tertiary**
15. Executives at Troubled Companies
16. Other Creditors

→ **Key Information Flows**

Look first at the innermost of the diagram's three large concentric circles, which shows only the core network. It consists of those that make their living off of companies in distress. There are the workout specialists at major lenders, most commonly at banks. There are bankruptcy attorneys. And, there are restructuring specialists, who include interim executives (also called turnaround specialists) and creditor advisors. Some people do either of these jobs, depending on the case; some just one or the other. Restructuring firms often offer several of these services. Investment bankers compete in this space, too, and so are shown in the same trapezoid.

Entering this space from the right (in the block arrow) is a mix of other investors, including private equity investors, hedge fund managers, and venture capitalists. This group was not a major player in the distressed company market in the 1990s and is only now entering the core of the network.

Notably absent from this core network are the executives at troubled companies. Executives at healthy companies see no reason to hobnob with those specializing in failures. Those at troubled companies are often in denial. When an executive is forced to admit there is risk of failure, she seldom has a network of specialists to turn to. She has had no reason to know these people before. In short, those core network members who get hired by such executives don't have direct access to prospective clients. They need intermediaries, connectors in the language of network analysis, to get that access.

Now look at the whole diagram of the distressed company referral network. The secondary network consists mostly of connectors and people with money at stake, those who work with healthy companies but who sometimes have clients or other business associates who run into trouble. Note that the different core members tend to have different kinds of connectors. The workout officers at banks are fed by loan officers, asset-based lenders, and other transactors. Bankruptcy attorneys are fed by corporate attorneys, accountants, and distress investors. Feeders for restructuring specialists are more diverse. The turnaround managers are fed by workout officers at banks and bankruptcy attorneys, and, more recently, by auditors, who are no longer able to refer restructuring work to in-house specialists. Creditor restructuring specialists are referred by distress investors and bankruptcy attorneys. It is to gain access to information and leads from each others' connectors that the core members network with each other.

Serving many of these players are the valuation consultants who determine the value of assets that may be carved from the distressed company.

As the exhibit shows, executives at troubled companies are peripheral to this network. (They are central to each case, of course, but peripheral to the referral network.)

In this environment, where success depends on getting early information and access, referral networks are key to success, and established players with long-established relationships and a track record of good work have a huge advantage. In other words, they are ways up the power curve. In each of the professions working the field, there are a few star players who get the best shot at the biggest and most attractive cases. These star players work in loose and changing cliques.

The neophyte must work hard to make a place for himself. He can do this by doing excellent work on cases and building relationships with potential players at other firms in the process. He must take advantage of opportunities to help other network members. For example, immediately after a client files for bankruptcy, but before news of the filing is generally known, a restructuring specialist can ethically share this now-public information with a few people who would benefit from having this knowledge ahead of the pack. He can build relationships with other up-and-comers. He can work on cases where those with stronger relationships are conflicted out. But it will take time before he can run with the big dogs.

The diagram makes clear one aspect of fitness in this environment: Core players need relationships with connectors to executives at distressed companies and to investors with a troubled investment. While working on a case, one young restructuring specialist I know impressed an investor. The investor started referring him to other opportunities. As the first advisor to these companies, he was able to recommend other specialists like bankruptcy attorneys and valuation consultants. More referrals started to come back to him from people he had helped. This single connector provided the starting point for the young man's success in the network.

It is doubtful that a two-dimensional diagram can capture the true complexity of such a dynamic network. In reality, communications flows are even more complex than the diagram suggests. But the diagram does give a sense of the structure of the network.

Clients are central in the pension-and-benefits advisory network.

Compare the former network to the pension-and-benefits advisory network, shown in Exhibit 11.3. This network operates in a market with different conditions, so the network is different, too.

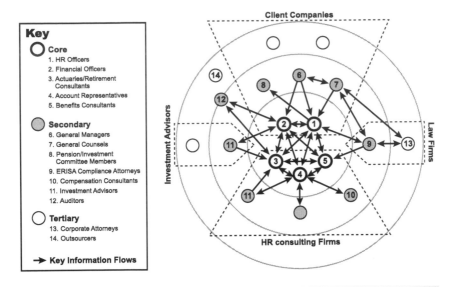

EXHIBIT 11.3   Pension & Benefits Advisory Network

Client companies always need pension-and-benefits advice. There is no secret about it. To the contrary, corporations employ full-time pension-and-benefits administrators to deal with these issues. Pensions and benefits have human resource, financial, legal, and general business implications, so people from many different departments get involved in the issues from time to time. Unlike the distressed company referral world, clients are central to this network.

The corporate pension-and-benefits administrators must spend a lot of time with their professional advisors. These advisors generally come from human resources consulting firms. Primary among them are retirement consultants, who are usually actuaries, and benefits consultants, also sometimes actuaries. In many cases, but by no means all, the consulting firms also assign their clients a separate account representative. The consultants, in particular, have deep technical knowledge.

There are annual cycles of activity, as well as periodic needs for services as a result of new labor regulations, ideas about how to provide better services, the need to reduce program costs, or a corporate event like an acquisition or layoff. The annual cycle of activities provides the incumbent consultant with regular opportunities to meet with the client team, learn about their needs, and develop strong relationships. (See Exhibit 11.4.) The smart ones maintain the core pension advisory work and seek out and sell special projects. Through years of work, they know a lot of details about the client's pension-and-benefits programs, things that the clients don't know themselves.

EXHIBIT 11.4   The Incumbent Actuary's Advantage

(Assumes client plan year = client fiscal year = calendar year)

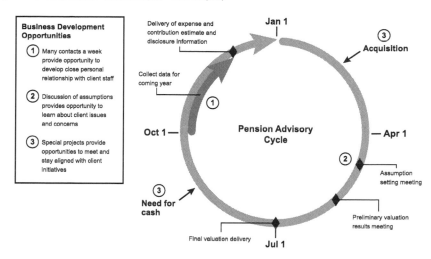

This environment breeds a close relationship between client and consultant. A client organization is likely to use the same advisors for years. As a result, turnover of accounts is infrequent and fiercely contested by the HR consulting firms when it happens. Low account turnover also creates an incentive for the HR firms to sell additional services into their loyal accounts.

As shown in Exhibit 11.3, then, the core network is composed of two kinds of people on the client side. First, there are the human resource officers, starting with the pension-and-benefits administrators and rising to the head of the department. Hardly less important are the financial officers, who must use the information provided by the consultants in their financial planning and reporting. In some companies, the human resource staff has more influence over the relationship with the consultants, but in others the financial people have more influence. The core members of the network in the consulting firms work hard to maintain deep relationships with both groups, and especially with the dominant one. A mistake in this area can be terminal.

The secondary network members, then, include specialized personnel at the HR consulting firms. The core members bring these people to their clients in order to bring the client more value and to sell additional services. (Most of these people are in profit centers of their own and must also generate business. As such, they are core members of their own, somewhat different networks.)

Secondary networks in client organizations are made up of people who have periodic needs for pension-and-benefits information and who make requests of the HR and financial officers for changes in pensions and benefits. Most notably these include general managers, investment committee members, and general counsels. Access to these people can help the consultants anticipate the needs of the HR and financial officers they work with most closely. External information sources sometimes help in the same way. They include labor attorneys (especially those specializing in ERISA compliance), auditors, and investment advisors.

In this network, it is not just the referral sources but also the clients who have entrenched relationships. Breaking in is hard. One way for a pension or benefits consultant to do it is to inherit a client from a colleague who retires. That is a slow process. Otherwise, success depends on meeting and staying in front of prospective clients and being fitter than your competitor. Fitness often means bringing the client better and more timely information.

For example, a Fortune 500 corporation had been the client of one HR consulting firm for decades. The consultants were entrenched with the financial officers, who at this company had always controlled the hiring of the pension-and-benefits advisors. An account developer at a competing HR consulting firm noticed that the corporation had hired a number of new high-powered HR officers. Visiting them, he learned that they had a mandate to make major changes in the way the company handled pensions and benefits. Sensing a change in the power relationships within the account, he cultivated the HR staff, giving them access to his firm's thought leaders in a variety of fields. When the company's contract with its existing actuaries expired, the HR staff had heavy influence over who was to be hired and replaced the incumbents with the second consulting firm.

In markets characterized by long-term relationships between a client and a professional, following migrating executives as they move to new employers is a major source of new business. The head of an office at one large HR consulting firm noted he could attribute every new client his office had won over the past year to migrating executives. In this environment, maintaining relationships with rising stars can deliver a big payoff.

Who gets early access to the client counts in the office-move network.

When a tenant decides to lease new office space, it triggers an event that feeds dozens of firms, including real estate brokers, building managers and developers, real estate attorneys, interior architects, mechanical and electrical engineers, furniture dealers, movers, construction managers, telecommunications equipment vendors, printers, and others. With so many different players standing to benefit, the market that has grown up around leasing new space is highly networked. (Of course, the same can be said about the related but somewhat different market that serves clients who build a new building.) In this case, it is valuable to contrast the flow of events with the flow of information through the network.

The flow of events (shown in Exhibit 11.5) is quite linear and creates a food chain. A general manager of the tenant decides she needs new space because of an impending lease expiration, growth that exceeds existing space, the need for a new branch office, or some other reason. If a long-distance move is contemplated, she may retain a location consultant, who specializes in analyzing labor markets, employee retention rates in the event of a move, and other geographic variables. More typically, she asks her real estate manager to find new space. The real estate manager hires a real estate broker to do so, who then contacts building owners and managers to confirm what he already knows is available. Once a short-list of buildings is selected, an interior architect is hired to confirm the tenant's requirements and block out its operations in the new space to give the tenant a sense of how the organization would fit into each one. A building is selected, and real estate attorneys for the tenant and building owner prepare a lease.

EXHIBIT 11.5 Office Move Timeline

Showing approximate timing of involvement in work of different participants. Assumes leased space, rather than a new building.

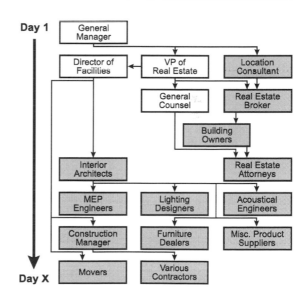

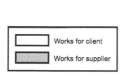

At about this time, interior architects are asked to submit proposals for designing the fit-out for the chosen building. They, in turn, add mechanical and electrical engineers, as well as other design consultants, to their teams. Once an architect is chosen, she designs the interiors, recommending specific finishing, covering, and furniture.

Soon a construction manager is hired to build out the space and he, in turn, hires a variety of subcontractors. Finally, a mover is retained to move the tenant in. It's all pretty straightforward.

But the communications flows (shown in Exhibit 11.6) aren't. Competition for participation in the deal is intense. There are usually dozens of brokers, attorneys, building owners, architects, engineers, construction managers, furniture dealers, and movers who want the business. Only one from each category will get the opportunity, with the exception of real estate attorneys, in which case there will be two: one representing the tenant and the other the building owner. When a tenant's plans to lease new space become public, all these competing firms are likely to swarm the real estate and facilities managers and even the general manager, all seeking to make a pitch for their services. This can be so disruptive that the tenant usually erects a wall, refusing to talk with any of them, except in a highly structured process that tends to equalize the frequency, quantity, and type of information coming in from the vending firms. Each firm, of course, tries to avoid getting stuck in this limiting process; that's where the network comes in.

EXIBIT 11.6 Office Move Network

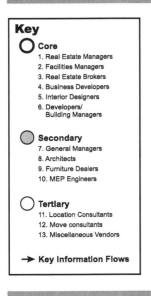
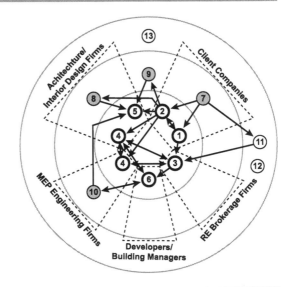

There are two ways to beat the system. One is to get early warning about the impending move, so that you can get in to talk with the tenants before the wall goes up. The other is to have so close a relationship with the real estate manager or, better still, the general manager, that you get special treatment. The next best thing is to have a relationship with someone who has one of these advantages and who is willing to use her relationship to help you. Also, players higher in the food chain may influence who gets hired among firms lower in the chain. You want their help. These things are what a good network gets you.

Networks are developed in the context of current projects, on the golf course, at charity events, at association meetings, and in all the other ways we have talked about. From their networks, different players look for different kinds of information to give them advantage. The tenant may prefer one or two architects, for example. An engineer who knows this is in a better position to get on the right teams than one who doesn't.

The smart players, then, seek to develop relationships with the tenants and with others higher in the food chain than they are. Offering help in the form of information about a client's concerns, needs, or preferences is one way to do that. Intervening in behalf of someone else is another.

For example, an architect was pursuing a large office project with a major financial institution. The head of the firm suspected that the real estate manager at the company would lobby against his firm because the architect had gone over his head to his boss to win an earlier project. A friendly construction manager who had previously worked at the financial company and knew the real estate manager was able to confirm that this was true and brokered reconciliation. The architect won the project, and the construction manager could count on his support to win future ones for his construction firm.

Displacing an incumbent is hard in the municipal water- and-wastewater network.

Civil and environmental consulting engineering is a highly fragmented industry with many small and intermediate-sized players who compete intensely for municipal and other projects, most of which must go through a defined and public bidding process. As many as twenty-five firms may respond to a town's request for proposals for a project. (See Exhibit 11.7.)

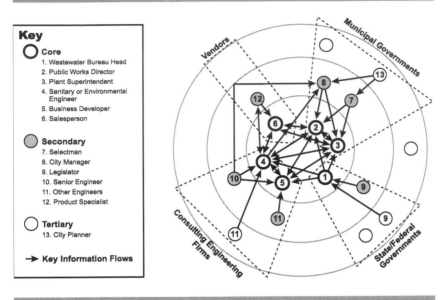

EXHIBIT 11.7 Municipal Wastewater Network

Key

○ **Core**
1. Wastewater Bureau Head
2. Public Works Director
3. Plant Superintendent
4. Sanitary or Environmental Engineer
5. Business Developer
6. Salesperson

● **Secondary**
7. Selectman
8. City Manager
9. Legislator
10. Senior Engineer
11. Other Engineers
12. Product Specialist

○ **Tertiary**
13. City Planner

→ **Key Information Flows**

But much routine work isn't open to regular competition. Each town's public works department employs an outside firm for help on day-to-day operations of its water treatment and distribution and its wastewater collection, treatment, and discharge. Though this is often under a formal, on-call services agreement, in some cases the relationship is informal and traditional. In either case, the day-to-day work provides the incumbent engineers with many opportunities to get to know members of the public works department, elected officials, and other key community leaders. By doing the work, they gain detailed knowledge of the community's operations, often giving them advanced warning about additional needs and helping them astutely pursue projects not covered in their service agreement. These tend to be long-term relationships, in some cases running for twenty years or more and in most for more than five years. Competing firms find it difficult to unseat an incumbent.

But it happens. This is a political environment, and the incumbent engineering firm can get caught on the wrong side of a political controversy. This may happen, for example, if state regulators threaten a town with a sewage-treatment violation. That results in a special project outside the purview of the incumbent's contract. That the violation occurred on the incumbent's watch can also provide a reason to use another firm to address it, particularly if the violation is recurring and attracts intense attention from state regulators and if the other firm moves quickly.

A firm that does well on clearing up a violation can help a community avoid or limit big fines. By doing so, it can sometimes position itself to replace the incumbent when the incumbent's contract is up. At the same time, the incumbent is at risk of being blamed, rightly or wrongly, for the problem. The political opposition in the city council may choose to characterize the incumbents as the pets of the current administration. In such cases, the administration will often seek to distance itself from its one-time friends, so placing the incumbent's relationship at risk.

Getting the job to address the violation is, then, critically important, both in its own right as important work and as a vehicle to breaking into a new account. Early warning of an impending state action against a community gives a firm the opportunity to gather intelligence and position itself to win the resulting consulting engineering contract. The civil or sanitary engineer or his firm's business developer can get early warning of a violation issue from several sources in addition to his contacts in a town's public works department. If he has a close relationship with the state wastewater bureau personnel, one of them may provide a tip. Word could also come from a city manager or member of the town council interested in helping him get the work. The vendors of sewage treatment equipment the town uses may also know information of value.

A violation is not the only event that puts the incumbent at risk. Others include a disagreement over billing, a botched presentation to a board, which places a pet administration project in jeopardy, or the arrival of a new head of the public works department. In all these cases, long-term relationships between the engineers and the public works department can sour quickly. Then the competitor with the best ties to key players in the community has a good chance of replacing the traditional service provider.

Networking in this environment is intense. At a regional level, each firm has its established, long-term clients. While working hard to maintain these relationships, the firms also meet regularly with state agency personnel, other engineers, equipment suppliers, city managers, planners, public works employees, elected officials, and anyone else who might give them gossip about a possible falling out between a competitor and one of its clients. They meet at trade association events, social gatherings, lunches, and anywhere else that those in the know might gather.

A power curve applies in this network, too. The engineer with long-established ties to many players has a clear advantage. But a diligent newcomer can come up the curve in a few years by working hard at developing contacts and being helpful to them.

The high-net-worth advisory network is filled with many categories of professional.

An active network of professionals and other service providers help rich people deal with the legal, financial and administrative burdens caused by wealth. They service old money, new money, entertainment and other celebrity money, and anyone else who has a fortune, small or large.

Core members (shown in Exhibit 11.8) include tax, estate and trust attorneys; tax accountants; and private bankers, stock brokers, insurance agents, and other investment advisors. Also playing in this space are celebrity business managers and other managers employed by the rich to handle their affairs. All of these people are following the money, making a good living by protecting and enhancing the wealth of their clients. Also active in the network are some of the wealthy, themselves, who like to refer their rich friends to good service providers.

EXHIBIT 11.8   High-Net-Worth Referral Network

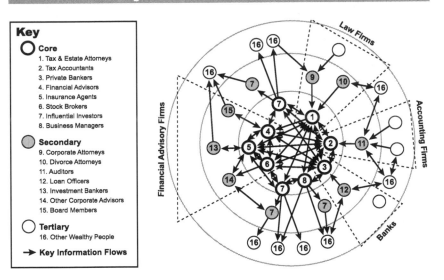

The new entrant into this market will have difficulty breaking into the established relationships. Anyone who has been rich for a while already has a lawyer, an accountant, a banker, and investment advisors. Core network members also have established relationships. Every established tax and estate attorney has her preferred relationships with tax accountants, private bankers, and other core group members. She makes the referrals she has to these people, and so is unlikely to refer a client to a newcomer. This is especially true if the newcomer has few clients yet to refer in return. So it is with the established tax accountant, the established private banker, the established insurance broker, the established financial advisor, and the established business manager.

These relationships shift gradually over time as people retire, change jobs, and fall in or out with each other, or as the business environment changes. For example, accountants and insurance agents used to refer each other business in these networks. This is far less true today because many accounting firms now sell insurance themselves.

Each of the core members also has a feeder system that gives her special access to clients. The tax and estate attorney is fed by corporate, divorce, and other attorneys in her firm. The tax accountant is fed by auditors (though this referral relationship has been altered by the Sarbanes-Oxley Act in some cases), consultants, and other partners in the firm. The private banker is fed by corporate loan officers. These referrers often have closer ties to the clients than do the core members of the networks.

The power curve is clearly evident in this network, with a few players in each field gaining the lion's share of the business in each geographic or specialty market by referring each other business. The newcomer, lacking the advantage of time in the network, must be more fit. In this market, this means working harder to build referral relationships, but a frontal assault on established ones is unlikely to work.

The newcomer to the network has several options. One is to disintermediate a core member by establishing a direct relationship with a referral source. So the young tax accountant might establish a direct relationship with a corporate loan officer who knows few tax accountants and is in a position to refer a client for accounting work to the tax accountant at the same time he refers the client to the private banker for financial advice. The tax accountant risks alienating the private banker by doing so, cutting him out of the chance to make a referral needed to maintain his own network. If she is wise, she will go out of her way to do good work and support the banker's relationships with the client, earning his trust and, perhaps, a position in his network over time.

Another possibility is to go after an underserved market. This usually, but not always, means new wealth, since old money is already well served by a cadre of advisors. New money includes the suddenly wealthy. An accountant built a practice serving hip-hop artists when this genre emerged. An attorney developed a specialty helping lottery winners protect their newfound wealth.

New money also includes those on a slower but reasonably assured track to wealth. Young professionals can develop relationships with age-peers in high-income professions like investment banking, serving these people well when their incomes are below those of interest to established players, then maintaining the relationships as the clients' incomes rise. This is called *catching a rising star.* Or they might seek to serve the younger members of a wealthy family who are in line to inherit wealth but are not yet wealthy.

The professional may also develop a special relationship with one wealthy person who is willing to use his influence to refer other high-net-worth friends. An attorney did a special assignment for a wealthy client and the pleased client, the member of a tightly knit religious group, referred several rich friends to him. The lawyer eventually became the professional of choice for this group.

Finally, the new entrant may develop special expertise that allows her to break into established networks. One Washington-based attorney analyzed a new tax code, picking out issues of special concern to high-net-worth people, wrote articles and gave speeches on these subjects, and began to receive referrals from less-knowledgeable attorneys from across the country. Others have developed specialties in complex wealth transfer strategies for closely held business owners, free transaction planning prior to the sale of the business, the issues of corporate executives owning large amounts stock in their publicly traded companies, money-management issues of professional athletes, and other arcane subjects.

For the new entrant, the best strategy is one that gives her special access to high-net-worth people, avoiding a frontal assault on the relationships among established players who have been in the market working together for many years. Her success in doing so will greatly influence how quickly she is able to develop her practice.

As she develops clients of her own, she will meet the other professionals serving them. She can then broker introductions among these advisors, behaving like the more advanced networker she has become. This behavior will further enhance her reputation and bring her additional opportunities, moving her up the power curve. That is often the way a professional in this market builds a practice.

Structured networks share commonalities.

As different as these networks are, there are some lessons that apply to all of them. First, there is a correlation between the complexity of a professional's network and her success at winning business. A network that contains only core members or only a few kinds of members isn't as effective as one that has many members of various types. The small, simple network cuts you off from information and introductions, which may be key to winning business. Complex networks can only be built over time. Only people who see potential in relationships with lots of kinds of players are likely to build them.

Second, if you can disintermediate another core member of a network by developing a relationship with the people who provide him information and opportunities, you can often capture advantage. The architect who has a relationship with the general manager in addition to ones with the real estate and facilities managers has an advantage, as does the environmental or sanitary engineer who hobnobs with city council members as well as the head of public works. Balancing both relationships can be hard because the lower-level contact may resent your relationship with his boss. But if you can pull it off, your network will be more effective.

Changes of personnel in client organizations often disrupt established networks and create opportunities for new entrants. This is especially true of networks typified by long-term relationships between clients and professional service providers. New people also bring new mandates, which can generate the need for additional services. For this reason, several astute rainmakers that we know review the want ads to see what potential client organizations are advertising for help. One determinant of a networker's fitness is the degree to which he follows contacts when they change jobs.

A final determinant of fitness is the networker's ability to become known as an expert in some area of value to her network. A reputation for expertise in a niche can give a new player an advantage over a more established one with clients who want best-in-class advice. For information on increasing your fitness this way, see Chapters 1, 2, 5, and 27.

We have found that professionals often find it helpful to diagram their networks. When they do, they understand them better and sometimes see opportunities they are missing.

From Networks to Leads

Of course, you network to generate leads. A lead is an opportunity to sit face-to-face with a prospective client to talk about a problem that he or she has that you might be able to solve for money. In short, it's an invitation to a sales meeting. Rainmakers spend a lot of time just getting to the table to have such conversations.

Professionals beginning to develop business usually want to know how they can speed up lead generation from their networks. The hard truth is it takes time. If you are attentive to the members of your network, listen for their needs, wants, and dissatisfactions, and respond with help when you can, the leads will follow. For reasons explained in my earlier book, *Creating Rainmakers,* helping your contacts and generating leads get easier and easier as your network grows.[1]

But there are things you can do to speed things up. It's a two-step process. First, you must surface a lead, and then you must shift from relationship-building mode to selling mode in a way that that the client finds acceptable.

Bring leads to the surface.

You can generate leads directly from clients or through referral sources. These two different audiences require different techniques. Let referral sources know that you are interested in finding new clients. If you don't, they may not think to help you. If they sound interested in doing so, make it easy for them to help you by providing them with a description of clients you work with. List some of the indicators that identify a company as a good candidate for your services.

Techniques you can use with clients include the following:

1. *Asking directly:* You will quickly wear out your welcome with clients if you are seen as always pushing for more business. This is especially true if

you are in the midst of an assignment and the client has not yet seen the results of your labor. It is best to wait until the client is happy with you, either because of the good work you have done or for some other reason. Whenever someone is happy with you, you are in a position to ask a favor. If you have done many favors for a prospective client, at the right moment you might say, "Are we ever going to do business together?" If you have worked with a client for a while and it is near the end of the year, you might say, "We want to continue to support you next year as well as we have this year. It would help us ensure that we have resources in place for you, if we knew a little about your plans. Do you have a sense of what you might be wanting from us next year?" Such a direct approach is not always feasible.

2. *Asking indirectly:* A major purpose of all your relationship-building calls to your clients is to ask some version of the question, "How are things going with you?" Rainmakers are sincerely interested in how the other person is doing. This question helps surface the clients' needs, wants, and dissatisfactions, uncovering opportunities to be helpful. It can also turn up leads. The question has many versions. Among them are these:
   - "The last time we talked, you were wrestling with _____. How is that going now?"
   - "I saw the news about your company in the paper this morning. How is the change likely to affect you?"
   - "You seem a little distracted today. Is everything okay?"
   - "What is taking you out to the West Coast?"

3. *Offering intellectual capital as bait:* Rainmakers will often offer their clients the results of research and analysis, hoping to elicit a request for their services. Having accepted the opportunity for some free education, the client may feel misused if she discovers that she has been lured into a disguised sales meeting. Converting such a meeting into a sales call requires tact and technique.

Shift into sales mode.

Just because a client mentions a problem that you can help with doesn't mean he wants to listen to a sales pitch. If you move into sales mode too quickly, you may ruin any chance you have of making a sale. This is especially true if the client has been talking with you as a disinterested advisor. In that case, moving into sales mode too quickly can damage a relationship. Rainmakers are sensitive to this fact and will sometimes forego a chance to make a sale for this reason. If they do move into sales mode, they do it cautiously and tactfully. Here are some techniques they employ:

1. *Asking permission:* They will acknowledge that the client isn't looking for a sales pitch and ask permission to proceed with one. They will use words like "Actually, that is something we could help you with. I know you didn't expect a sales meeting today, but I would be happy to talk a little about how we might help you, if you are interested." Alternatively, they might say, "Would it be all right if I put my sales hat on for a while, because that's something we could help you with?" If the client agrees, then proceed. But if the client shows any hesitancy, drop the subject immediately.

2. *Telling an anecdote:* Sometimes asking permission would be too forward. In that case, a rainmaker will sometimes use an anecdote to demonstrate familiarity with the issue the client is concerned about. The anecdote must not be a lengthy advertisement for the professional with a lengthy description of how he solved another client's problem. In a sentence or two, the professional simply shows that he has seen this kind of problem before. For example, a client might mention to an accountant how difficult it is to estimate the value on a specific piece of intellectual capital. This is a clear opportunity for the accounting firm's valuation practice. So the accountant might say that this is a common problem and then cite an even more complicated example. He might even choose not to tell how the problem was resolved, in hopes that the client will ask.

3. *Flagging an issue:* If an anecdote fails to pique the client's curiosity, a rainmaker will often drop the issue for a while, coming back to it the next time he sees the client. He will then ask the client how the issue is progressing. After showing concern several times this way, the client may ask for advice, or the moment may come when the professional feels that it is all right to ask permission to sell.

Building Client Relationships That Last

Much of what has been said about networks and networking in previous chapters applies to developing an account. As with all networks, you must meet the right people, stay in front of them by being helpful, and remind them of what you do, and opportunities will come to you. Of course, an account where you have a foothold through a paid assignment is far easier to scale than one that offers no purchase. Your position as a service provider gives you license to do many things that an outsider can't.

Rainmakers know this and use a small portal assignment to get in the door and, while doing the work for it, build out their networks at the account. In my third book, *Cross-Selling Success*,[1] we looked at the ways rainmakers do this, conducting over 100 interviews with professionals who are adept at cross-selling. In brief, here is what they do.

Enter an account through portal services.

Many rainmakers and many professional firms use carefully designed portal services to enter an account. To work effectively as a portal, a service must have all or most of the following characteristics:

1. *Be in the client's best interests and provide clear value:* The client will not believe your claims of providing value on future assignments if he sees none in the current one.
2. *Be affordable:* You don't want the price of this initial service to get in the way of the client trying you out. An affordable service will help you gain the advantages of working from within the client company, while competitors are stuck on the outside, trying to get in.
3. *Provide access to many of the people in the client organization:* This small project, which won't return much profit, is worth it to you because it allows you to know many key players in the client organization.

4. *Answer a question that the client needs answered now:* Perhaps what you and your contact believe the client company needs will cost a million dollars in fees—a million dollars she can't get her bosses boss to authorize just yet. The portal engagement might be diagnostic to confirm (or not) that the expenditure is necessary.
5. *Does not require displacement of another firm:* That gets you in the door without having to go up against entrenched competition.
6. *Lie at the intersection of two functional areas or business units:* When no one inside the client company has clear responsibility for an issue, the company is more likely to hire someone from the outside to deal with it.

Portal services often take the form of audits (of firm governance, of the company's cost structure, or of the accessibility of company-owned facilities to the handicapped) or diagnostics (the company's worker compensation payments are high; is the company paying more taxes than it needs to?) and feasibility studies (can parking be added at the client's office without building a second parking facility? is there case law that can be used to justify suing a competitor for use of others' intellectual property?).

Employ BEST Selling™techniques.

Once they are working within the client organization, rainmakers make certain that the work done is excellent. At the same time, they work a deliberate process to entrench themselves in the client company. The process, which we call BEST Selling and which is shown in Exhibit 13.1, requires working with four variables simultaneously:

EXHIBIT 13.1 BEST Selling™ Model

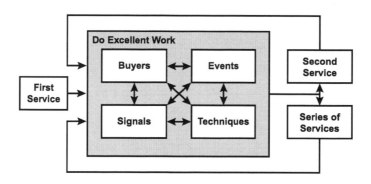

- **Buyers:** These are people who can either authorize the purchase of your services or can influence someone who has that authority.
- **Events:** These are meetings with buyers. They can either be a part of the project, like a fact-finding meeting, or apart from it, like a golf outing. A list of common kinds of events is provided in Exhibit 13.2.

EXHIBIT 13.2 Events Checklist

Relationships are begun and developed at meetings. Meetings with buyers are also the best places to identify signals that a client may need additional services and to increase the client's commitment to using you to provide those services. Review this checklist when you need to meet with a buyer but are unsure how. It summarizes the most common kinds of events available to you.

Event	Description
Fact finding	A meeting to learn about the client's issues and needs; can be a part of a larger service or larger sales process. This is a good place to start or further develop a relationship and to identify signals from clients for more needed services.
Update and review	A meeting to inform the client about recently completed work and plans for coming weeks and to receive the client's feedback.
Strategizing and planning	A meeting to determine a course of action, weighing its strengths and weaknesses.
Idea generation and consensus building	A meeting to generate ideas by brainstorming (or some other technique) or to obtain a group's commitment to a course of action.
Negotiating	A meeting to negotiate something on behalf of the client. The client must be present for this kind of event if it is to help you with cross-selling.
Travel	A trip with a client to conduct a site visit, interview people, or negotiate with them as required by the work you have been hired to do.
Client education	A meeting or workshop to inform clients about something they would benefit from knowing.
Celebrations	An event marking the successful completion of a major task.

(Events Checklist *continued*)

Event	Description
Sales	A casual meeting with a client made simply because you are going to be in the area on other business.
	Meeting to advance or make a sale. These can be initiated either by you or by the client. They range from cold calls to introducing yourself and your services to responding to a client's request for help with a specific issue.
Social and service	A gathering to have fun or to make a social contribution.
Professional	An association meeting to stay abreast of issues of importance to a profession or industry and to network.

- **Signals:** Signals are indications that a buyer has a need for your services. They can be macro signals, like a merger, indicating the need for many services. Or they can be micro signals, indicating the need for only one service, such as information from interviews with former sales personnel indicating that the firm's compensation system is ineffective. You obtain signals from buyers at events. Furthermore, signals provide an indication of what buyers you need to meet with next and maybe even the kind of event required.
- **Techniques:** These are sales methods used with buyers at events to get future events or signals from buyers. They include such simple techniques as asking for sponsorship, for instance, asking the head of the business unit you have been working with to introduce you to the CFO. A list of common kinds of techniques is provided in Exhibit 13.3.

EXHIBIT 13.3 Techniques Checklist

Professionals use techniques to obtain events with clients, identify signals, and advance sales. Review this checklist when you need to do one of these things but are unsure how. It summarizes some of the techniques available to you.

Technique	Description
Asking for sponsorship	Asking a contact to introduce you to someone else you want to meet, or to advocate for your firm to do a specific assignment

Technique	Description
Pedestal selling	Talking about colleagues' abilities as if you were putting them on a pedestal to increase the client's desire to meet and work with them
Presumptive selling	Acting as if it is presumed that something will happen, such as a meeting with a contact you want to get to know, as a part of a current assignment
Questioning	Asking clients questions that help them better understand the issues they face and help build their commitment to taking action on those issues
Seeding ideas	Stimulating a client's thinking by introducing an idea
Bridging	Helping a client understand issues that cut across functional or business lines within his or her own organization
Business case	Showing why a line of action makes sense from a business perspective, often but not always supported by a simple financial model
Benchmarking	Showing how a client compares to other firms and showing opportunities for improvement
Selling a vision	Helping a client see a desired future state and how to obtain it

As Exhibit 13.1 shows, the four elements of the BEST-selling model are closely interrelated. You first obtain events from buyers, and you meet buyers at events. You then obtain signals from buyers at events, and the signals indicate which events, with which buyers, you might want to arrange in the future. You use the techniques with buyers at events to obtain signals and to obtain future events. The buyers you are working with and the signals you obtain from them suggest what techniques to use to advance the sale.

If you have enough events with enough buyers, and you obtain enough signals using the right techniques, additional work is likely to follow. Once you obtain a second assignment or series of assignments, the process begins all over again. That is how cross-selling is done.

Here is an example of BEST Selling as one environmental engineer applied it.

> We had tried to get into [a large plant of a major automobile supplier] for over two years. We had made presentation after presentation and submitted proposal after proposal, but always came in fourth or fifth. Finally, we started asking what kinds of problems they were having (at an event, presumably a sales call). The plant engineer (buyer) told us they were having problems with lab analyses of their wastewater discharge. Whenever they sent samples to Indiana for analysis, the results kept coming back late. We told them of our lab capabilities, and soon they visited our lab (event). We pointed out that because we were so close to them, they wouldn't have to ship samples to us, as we could easily pick them up.
>
> After that visit they gave us our first job (portal project), a small analysis worth about $2,500. We gave them really good service, and from then on the lab analysis work grew until we were getting most of it.
>
> The plant engineer was authorized to buy services for up to $15,000. If a project cost more than that, he needed the approval of the plant manager (buyer). We knew we would have to get to him, but first we worked hard to develop the relationship with the plant engineer because we needed his to support to get more work. He said he really appreciated the service he was getting.
>
> I would stop by and meet with him (events), and sometimes we would go to the cafeteria for lunch (events). I would ask him what was going on (questioning technique). One day he mentioned that they were "being killed" by the EPA and the local municipal wastewater treatment authority (single). The city's rates for treating wastewater at the municipal treatment facility included a surcharge if the strength of the company's wastewater exceeded an agreed-upon level, which it often did.
>
> I mentioned that we had helped an industrial client with a similar problem in Detroit (technique). He asked to hear more about what we had done. I said I could bring in the people who had done that work and who could tell him more about it (technique) and he agreed. We had the meeting (events), and he liked what he heard. Then we assessed how we could treat his wastewater to avoid surcharges, how much the company would save, and what the payback would be on the investment required to fix the problem (technique). After that he asked for a proposal.

Of course, he couldn't authorize a project of this size by himself, so he helped us get a meeting (event) with the plant manager. Several other people had to buy into the project, too, and the plant engineer helped us get meetings with them as well (events). After that, we were delighted to be hired on a sole-source basis (second service).

We proceeded to design an air-flotation treatment system, which our client was really pleased with. The oil their new system recovered from their wastewater was of such high quality they could use it for fuel to heat the building. The payback was even faster than we had estimated.

We continued meeting (events) with their people (buyers) during this project, getting to know them really well. At one of the meetings, they revealed that they were putting in a new overhead crane (signal) and needed help with the structural work. It was a small retrofit, but it demonstrated yet another one of our services (third service).

PART III

Sales Tactics: How Professionals Advance and Close a Sale

For the purposes of this book, a lead is defined as an opportunity to sit with a client and talk about a problem she has that you might be able to solve for money. The first two sections of this book describe ways to get you to the table to have that conversation with a client who, if possible, is predisposed to hiring you. It's taken a lot of work just to get this far. Now that you have a lead, you want the best chance possible to convert it into business for your firm. That requires sales skills, and these skills are the subject of this part of the book.

"Selling" is still a dirty word to many professionals, though not to as many as it was when I started my career so long ago. I use the word because it is the simplest, most commonly understood word to label what I am writing about. To me it doesn't have negative connotations. It is not about tricking or pressuring people. Rather, it is a conversation, or series thereof, designed to help the client better understand the problem she is facing, and, if you can help her with it, to persuade her to hire you by presenting your offering as compellingly as possible in the fairest terms that are consistent with honesty.

Many professionals lose opportunities strictly as a result of poor selling skills. This is true even though today, more professionals have had sales training than at any time in the past. Most of the losses occur because *these professionals act as if the meeting is about them, rather than about the client*. They feel compelled to show the client how smart and experienced they are by interjecting stories and facts about themselves as the client tries to explain her problem. Some will repeatedly finish a client's sentences for her, a loathsome habit.

Once you are in a sales meeting, you want the client's business. You need to manage the meeting to get it. To achieve that objective, I suggest you want the client to do the following:

- **Open up:** You want the client to talk about the needs her organization has that you might be able to address. That way her time and yours will be well spent. You need to get a clear understanding of each issue's importance to the client because that will determine the client's urgency to buy and the desirability of the work.
- **Trust you:** The client must trust you enough to share sensitive information that might affect your approach to the problem. This may include personal ambitions and fears.
- **Be clear:** You want the client to describe the barriers she sees to getting the job done. It is in overcoming these barriers that you provide value.
- **Set a goal:** You want the client to articulate a desired outcome so that you have a clear idea of her objectives.

With this information you can take the following actions:

- *Understand the client's problem as she sees it including any errors or mental filters she may have.*
- *Determine whether you want the work.* If not, you can avoid wasting her time and your own by moving on, perhaps referring her to someone who can help her.
- *Design a solution to her issue that is technically correct but that also addresses her non-technical concerns.* A solution that addresses her political concerns or personal aspirations will capture her attention.
- *Describe how you can help, and do so concisely and compellingly.*

Getting all this accomplished requires a structured process. The process must be adaptable to the diversity of selling situations a professional is likely to face. These include the informal discussion with the buyer, the formal presentation, the chemistry-check meeting, the fact-finding meeting, the unexpected sales meeting when a client brings up an issue you can help with in a meeting being held for another purpose, the order-taking meeting that simply confirms the agreement and then starts the project, and many others.

All of these are sales meetings, but each situation is so different that to expect one process to work for all of them is unrealistic. Many people in the professions see situations analogous to each one of these examples each year. What are they to do?

The following five chapters describe a sales process that is flexible and so can be adapted to different selling situations. It is designed around components that, like Lego blocks, can be reassembled in many ways, allowing you to address the myriad of different selling situations you will face. Subsequent chapters address other aspects of selling an engagement, such as writing a proposal and quoting a fee.

The Sales Meeting:
The First Five Minutes

The first few minutes often determine the direction of an entire sales meeting. Getting them right is as important as getting the foundation right in building a house. Get them right, and the rest of the structure goes up a lot more easily; get them wrong, and you will have to work a lot harder—and even if you do, your chances of success have been reduced. So plan those first few minutes carefully.

We call this portion of the meeting *rapport building*, and it should last five minutes, perhaps ten at the outside. You have a lot to accomplish in a short time, so you and your team members had better have a clear idea of what you are going to say before you walk into the room. Components to use in constructing a rapport-building sequence, depending on the specifics of the meeting, include these:

1. Personal link
2. Agenda statement
3. Positioning statement
4. Stage-setting anecdotes
5. The big question

We will discuss each component in turn and how it should be used in different kinds of sales meetings.

Make a personal link.

Some sales books recommend against starting a meeting with personal small talk. They say that an all-business approach is more professional and more likely to win a sale. Many disagree, including me. Done right, such a conversation is not really small talk; it's a brief emotional linking with the buyer.

The final decision on which professional to hire comes down to emotion. The client recognizes that several firms can do the work and hires the one he likes, justifying his decision with logic after the fact. An all-business start reduces the chance that a client and you will link at an emotional level. In some countries, this need is more clearly recognized than in the United States, and business meetings start with a lengthy personal conversation. Moving to business too quickly is considered rude as well as ineffective.

Buyers will acknowledge the importance of emotion in the process, though they seldom use that word. It is what they mean when they speak of *chemistry.* You want to establish good chemistry, and often this is best started before you get down to hard business. Still, in most business meetings in the United States, the opening conversation should be kept short. Generally, the less you know the contact, the briefer you should keep the personal linking. You must create a personal link quickly. Methods for doing that include the following:

- **Identifying a mutual friend:** A brief exchange about a respected friend whom you both know shows that you associate with the right kind of people. "I understand that you know Molly Smith" is a good lead.
- **Identifying a shared experience:** If you both worked for the same company in the past, or if the client's former employer is a former client of yours, and you are free to reveal the names of your clients, mention it.
- **An interest in the client's company:** If the company has been in the news or you know something of importance about it, that topic can be the basis for an observation or a question that will start a short conversation. For example, "I've always admired how this company has survived and made money in an industry that has seen such a series of shake outs."
- **Something you observe in the client's office:** This should be a last resort, but can be effective, especially if what you see reveals a shared interest. A prominently displayed photograph of the client's children is worth a question, especially if you have children of your own.

But keep this personal conversation brief. Remember, most clients are busy and don't want a lengthy social conversation. Be prepared to dispense with it altogether if the client replies tersely to your probes.

Set the agenda.
You should start the business portion of every sales meeting—of every sales meeting—with a concise statement of what you propose to accomplish and a request for the client's agreement. Here is an example of what a tax accountant might say at the beginning of a meeting he requested with a prospective client.

I would like to briefly describe our firm, so that you get a sense of who we are, and then share with you some of the ways that we see other companies are adapting to the new tax laws and then hear what issues are of greatest concern to you. We should be done in about forty-five minutes. Is that agreeable to you?

This short statement indicates clearly that the speaker will talk briefly first, that he then expects the client to talk, and that he asks for his agreement to do so. If he agrees, the chances that he will talk are high. It advises the client to prepare himself to communicate important issues. It states that the meeting is about adapting to new tax laws, rather than something else, and asks for agreement on that. If the client wants to talk about something else, this gives him an opportunity to say so early in the meeting. (And if he does want to talk about something else, now is the time to find out.) This also reminds the client what the meeting is about, in case he has forgotten. Finally, it says that the speaker expects the meeting to run for a certain length of time. If the client's plans have changed and he has less time than expected, it is better to know now rather than five minutes before he has to leave.

Here is another agenda-setting statement, this one from a public relations specialist who is responding to a call from a friend of a client.

Jim mentioned that you are expecting some good publicity around your new product and want to make the most of it. Let me give you a short description of our firm, so you know who you are talking to. Then, I would like you to describe the new product and the expected publicity and what you want to accomplish. If we can help you, I will describe what we might do. If not, perhaps I can refer you to someone who can. I've budgeted an hour, but this sounded urgent, and I can stay longer if need be. Is that our contract?

Once again, it sets a clear understanding that the professional will talk briefly first, but then the client will talk. It asks for confirmation of the subject and duration of the meeting. This time the request for the client's agreement has a more formal tone, asking for a verbal contract.

Here's one final example. In this case, an attorney is responding to a call from a former client about a matter similar to one he has handled for the client in the past.

You mentioned that you are downsizing and need to get out of a lease, as you did in Jacksonville. Maybe you could describe the specifics of this case, then if I think we can help you, we'll talk about what we can do. Does this sound about right to you?

Because the client knows the attorney and has worked with him on similar issues, the attorney skips the opportunity to talk about himself and suggests that the client start talking immediately.

Every sales meeting should start with an agenda-setting statement of this kind. After you make your statement, stop and look at the client expectantly until he either agrees to the agenda or suggests a modification. Failing to start a meeting with a statement like this is a rooky mistake.

I did this about a year ago. We were completing a pilot project at a big firm, when the day-to-day contact from the client called me to say that the big boss wanted to meet. I asked why, and my contact told me that the boss wanted to hear how the pilot had gone, but that I should save a little time at the end to talk about a rollout to more people.

At the meeting I followed this advice and jumped right into a description of the pilot without making an agenda-setting statement. The big boss listened politely but wasn't really engaged. About five minutes before the meeting was to end, I asked if he wanted to talk about a possible rollout. He immediately became enthusiastic and talkative. It was obvious that that was what he had wanted to talk about all along. He had politely deferred to my agenda. But we were out of time and had to schedule another meeting to talk about the rollout.

Due to several cancellations and reschedulings, it took six months to get in front of him again—a six-month delay that neither he nor I wanted! I could have avoided it if I had just asked for his agreement to an agenda at the beginning of the meeting.

Position wisely.

Most agenda-setting statements are followed by positioning statements. The positioning statement reminds the client of who you are and establishes the credibility needed to get him to open up and talk with you about his problems. If you are selling a repeat service to an old client, you may not need one, but in many cases you do.

Most people are reluctant to share their problems with just anyone. The issues are sensitive, and we are all pressed for time. But most will talk, if they feel that they may get help in return. If I know that you are a psychiatrist who specializes in extreme mental disorders, I might share with you my concerns about a mentally ill relative. I certainly wouldn't with a podiatrist, who deals with the other end of the body. The positioning statement identifies you as a person worth opening up to.

A short reminder of who you are also allows the client to refocus on this meeting, in case she is still reflecting on whatever she was dealing with before you entered the room. It starts to stimulate her thinking about the issue you are there to discuss, so that when you ask her to talk, she is ready.

Positioning statements vary greatly depending on the context of the meeting. For example, a recruiter introducing his firm for the first time to the new head of human resources at an insurance company might provide a brief overview, stressing work done for insurance companies.

> We help our clients recruit top talent for senior positions. We have extensive experience recruiting senior investment and actuarial talent as well as other skills required by insurance companies. Among our clients are Prudential, Aetna, and The Hartford. At this company, we helped recruit the chief investment officer, Alan Prime, and at least ten actuaries over the past four years.

The positioning statement can be used to change a client's perception of your firm. Because his current perception is based on past work you did, it might be missing something important. Clients often associate you with the last service you provided. A consultant meeting with a client who in the past has hired her for strategy work might reposition the firm by describing its implementation expertise.

> You know us largely for our strategy consulting work. That is what we are best known for, but many of our clients want us to help them with implementation, which now accounts for 60 percent of our revenues. We provide implementation services on roughly 80 percent of our strategy projects. This exhibit diagrams the range of our implementation services, which include everything from plan development, to training, to providing temporary staffing for critical operations.

Sometimes we need to position a colleague we have brought with us as an expert. An accountant might focus on introducing a colleague who is a specialist in the issue of concern to the client.

> I brought Gary with me today because he heads up our valuation practice. Gary worked with Company X when it spun off its Latin American business, helping to value affected assets. Whenever one of my clients has a valuation issue, he is the one I go to. I thought we could start by letting him say just a few words about the issues he sees companies facing in valuing intellectual property.

If a graphic or two can help summarize your positioning, use it. But keep this statement brief. You don't want it to interfere with your main goal, which is to get the client talking.

Because many professionals go astray on the positioning statement, turning it into a boring, irrelevant, and time-consuming mini-presentation, let's review a few things that should *not* go into it:

- **A history of your firm:** The client doesn't care. The client doesn't care! And always remember, this meeting is about the client, not about you!
  - Always make clear why information about your firm is relevant to the client. If you find that hard to do, prune what you have to say until its importance to the client can be stated clearly and simply. If it is important for the client to know that you are a well-established firm with values, say so as briefly as possible. If the client needs to know that you can serve his company internationally, make the point succinctly without a history of your expansion.
  - If the client may know the firm under an earlier name, say so with a minimum of history. "A lot of people still remember our old firm, Dank Engineering, which merged with Ropus Wells three years ago."
- **A description of your firm's organizational structure:** As a client, I'm only interested in ways your organization will affect the service you provide me. If I work for a utility company, why would I want to know *anything* about the work you do for banks? Focus the meeting on me, the client, not on you and your firm! Tell me that you know *my* industry or *my* functional area. "Our utility practice is one of the firm's largest. We've worked with six of the largest ten investor-owned power companies."
- **A list of your services:** Please, oh please don't bore me with a recital of your services! I will most likely pass out after the first sentence. If I remain awake, there is a high chance I mentally ticked off every single service you listed as one I didn't need. In that case, you just hurt yourself!
- **Extensive proof of your experience or brilliance:** This is not the time for a presentation on your brilliant success with your last client. Yes, if you take this approach, you may wow me with your brilliance, catch me at a moment when I am open to your idea, persuade me with your logic, and get me to sign for a large project. If you are very smart and very lucky, I'll give you a 3 percent chance of doing so. But what about the other 97 percent of the time? It's the client's view of things that counts in this game of selling. If you want to learn what she thinks, you have to shut up and let her talk. That is, if you really care what she thinks.

The goal of the positioning statement is to establish enough credibility that the client will feel comfortable opening up to you. That's all. It is not a pitch to hire you. It should be short and simple.

Use stage setters.

You may have offered to provide me some insights into my company or industry as an enticement to get me to meet with you. You have to give me something. I expect it. Or the positioning statement may not give me, the client, as much information as I want about your services.

If so, tell me one or two anecdotes that illustrate what other companies are doing or the kinds of issues you work on. These are called *stage setters*. Stage setters offer the client and you several advantages. First, they are interesting. Please take no offense, but as a client I find stories about me or people like me much more interesting than I find you and your services. This means, of course, that the stage setters must be told from the clients' perspective.

Second, when carefully selected, they help stimulate my thinking and so help me get ready to talk when my turn comes. So, if I am in the facilities department of a university and you are an architect who specializes in dormitory design, based on your pre-meeting research, you might tell me two stage setters, each addressing a different issue you know I am concerned about. The first might show how a new dorm was able to compete effectively against off-campus housing, both solving financial problems that unoccupied dorm rooms had created and improving community relations. The second might show how a properly designed dorm greatly reduced long-term maintenance costs, in spite of the students' sometimes hard use of the building. Facing these problems myself, your stories remind me of my concerns and get me ready to talk about them.

Third, they show the kinds of issues you help clients with, without a lot of detail on what you did. Too much detail on what you did isn't desirable yet. The client probably isn't ready to hear it, and also each client situation is different. What you did for a former client probably won't match exactly what you want to do for the current one.

Also, stage setters provide an indirect way to raise an issue that you suspect may be important to the client. That lets you avoid telling him what his problems are or what he needs, which would be presumptuous.

Finally, stories are memorable. They stick to a client after you are gone far better than a list of your services will. This is especially true if they are told from the client's perspective.

Here is an example of a stage setter told by a management consultant.

Sometimes a company must address both the cost and revenue sides of its business at the same time. An insurance subsidiary of one of the world's largest financial institutions had seen the volume of its business decline 50 percent due to severe price competition. To meet the parent company's ROE requirements and avoid being sold off, the president had to cut the cost of delivering its traditional product, while simultaneously identifying and launching new, higher-margin products. She was deeply concerned that her entire workforce, from management levels on down, had habits that were too entrenched to make this possible. Nevertheless, she publicly committed herself to making it happen. Over eighteen months, with some help from us, she achieved a competitive cost structure and introduced several radically new products successfully, all with the existing workforce and with minimal turnover.

This stage setter has all the components of a good anecdote.[1] It has *a plot*, which is a threat or an opportunity that creates urgency. In this case, it is the threat of being sold off. The threat or opportunity should be similar to one you believe the listener is facing.

It has a *character*, a person for the client to identify with. Any listener will find a story about a person much more interesting than one about an abstraction, like a corporation. That is particularly true if the story is about someone like her. Thus, the story isn't about the professional; it's about the client. In the example, the consultant barely appears. *Let the client be the hero!*

When telling the same anecdote to different people, you may want to change the character to increase its relevance to each listener. A recruiter had prepared the following anecdote for a meeting at a troubled technology company. Reminded that he would be speaking with the head of human resources, not the CEO, he inserted an additional detail:

A $500 million technology company had made some bad technological bets and was rapidly losing market share and had recently fallen into the red. The new CEO quickly realized that to return the company to profitability and growth, he would have to change out much of the senior management team. He made his case for doing so before the board, promising to do so without further damage to the company's financials. *Upon returning from the board meeting, he dumped the problem in the lap of the VPHR.* Within nine months, a new management team was in place, and the company had returned to a break-even basis and a strong expectation of future profitability.

The small change, shown in italics, greatly increased the anecdote's interest to his listener.

Each stage setter should have *an action*. This is a physical action, usually of somebody doing something. The listener can visualize the action, and that picture makes the anecdote memorable. Actions are the toughest elements to add to our anecdotes because often our work doesn't lend itself to them. In the preceding stories by the management consultant and the recruiter, the chief executives make public commitments, clearly to the board in the latter case. It is even better if the action is stronger. Take this stage setter, told by an attorney.

> A large pharmaceutical company was being sued for race discrimination. Activists had picked up the cause and were demonstrating in front of the company's headquarters every day, attracting media attention. The CEO had called the general counsel into his office and instructed him to get the problem fixed. A review of the cases found one bad one, which was settled. Three went to trial, which the company won, and the remainder of the employees either came back to work or left the company under negotiated terms. The demonstrations stopped, and the general counsel could report that there had been minimal cost or damage to the company's reputation.

We can all visualize the picketers in front of the company's offices and the general council in the CEO's office, getting his marching orders.

Finally, each stage setter has *an outcome*. The threat is mitigated or the opportunity is captured.

Note how little the anecdotes tell about the actual work done by the professionals. Sometimes, when talking with a technical buyer, a little more is required—but not much. This story, told by a structural engineer, has about as much detail on how a problem was solved as an anecdote can bear:

> The head of business operations for a major-league football team had been charged with developing a new 700,000-square-foot stadium, the largest project he had undertaken in his career. In addition to meeting aesthetic requirements expected of a major public arena, he had been asked to deliver it under a tight budget and schedule. If the project could not be completed in twenty-one months, the organization would lose a season's revenue from ticket sales. The head of operations promised the owners to have the building completed on time. The facility was built with a tied-arch truss design, which saved the owner about $300 a ton on the total cost of the roof and made possible fast-track construction by allowing the roof erection time to overlap superstructure work. The new stadium was completed on budget and in time for the fall season.

Note that each of these stage setters is short, none requiring more than six sentences. You aren't making a case for hiring you or proving that you are the best professional in your field. Remember your goals in telling these short anecdotes: to give the client enough information about you to be comfortable talking to you about his issues and to stimulate his thinking, so he is ready to talk. The sooner you can get him to talk, the better. Don't burn up time with long stories about you and your services.

Not every meeting needs a stage setter. If the meeting were set up at the client's request, because he had a problem to talk about, I probably wouldn't use one. But they are an effective way to give the client information he wants without boring him or lapsing into a presentation or presuming to know his problem.

Ask the Big Question.

All of what you have said up to now is simply a lead-in to the big question. This is a broad question that gets the client talking about a subject of importance to him that you might be able to help with. In short, it gets you to a subject that both of you can benefit from talking about. That's what we call the Productive Zone (shown in Exhibit 14.1). The more time you spend in the Productive Zone, the more value both the client and you will receive from the meeting.

EXHIBIT 14.1 Spend Your Time in the Productive Zone

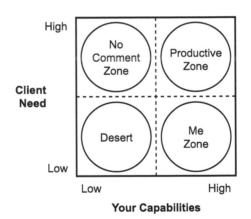

- **Both the client and you will get more out of the meeting, if you do.**

- **The Big Question should get you there quickly**

Getting there is easy when a client calls you in to discuss a problem. The Big Question then becomes some version of the words, *Why did you call?* It's much tougher when you asked for the meeting to introduce your firm. Then you face two risks. If you let the discussion roam too freely, you are likely to end up in the No-Comment Zone, talking about a subject that is of great concern to the client but one where you can't offer any help. That's what's wrong with the hackneyed question, *What's keeping you awake at night?* If you spend much time in the No-Comment Zone, the client will learn how little you have to offer. It's a waste of time for both of you.

But if you focus the discussion too narrowly, you risk ending up in the Me Zone, talking about an area where you have great proficiency but where the client has little need. Again, you have wasted his time and probably sounded self-centered, to boot.

A good question helps you avoid both of these traps and gets you efficiently into the Productive Zone. Examples include questions like these:

- These are some of the environmental (or tax, litigation, compensation, etc.) issues we see others in your industry facing. What issues are of greatest concern to you?
- Are there any issues of importance to this company's (or division's or department's) success where your people aren't getting the traction you would like to see?
- What projects are you contemplating for the coming year that you feel you may not have the resources in place to handle?
- You agreed to this meeting to talk about making acquisitions effectively. Are there any aspects of that process that you would like to focus on today?
- With that brief introduction, perhaps you could tell us why you called us.

Remember, the goal of the Big Question is to get to a subject of mutual interest as quickly as possible. Choose your words for it carefully.

Done well, the rapport-building portion of the meeting lasts five or six minutes. Done well, it tees the client up to talk and talk about something of importance to him, something that you may be able to help him with. Keep that goal clearly in mind because if the client does pour out his heart to you on an issue, the sale is half made.

15 The Sales Meeting: Questioning and Listening

The Big Question shifts the focus of the conversation from you to the client. During the portion of the sales meeting that this shift initiates, the client will do most of the talking while you ask questions and listen intently. Your job during this portion of the meeting is to understand the client's issue as the client, herself, sees it. Her thinking may develop as she talks with you. That is a byproduct of responding to good questions. But it is still her view, not yours.

You may not agree with her view. That's your prerogative. But you will not argue with her or try to show her the error in her thinking or show her how brilliant or well informed you are. At least not now, while she is absorbed in discussing her issue. That would take the spotlight off her, and this is her time to be in the spotlight. This is her time to shine, and she is likely to find interruptions from you distracting or even annoying. At the very least they disrupt her thinking, creating the risk that you will miss learning about something important to her.

Your ability to get good information on the client's issue depends on your skill at questioning. Most professionals think they are skilled questioners, and for many this is a dangerous arrogance. Often they are applying questioning skills appropriate to other areas of their work (grilling a witness comes to mind) but not to selling. Their questions are sometimes designed to make the client see the issue as they do—in other words, to show how smart they are and to sell a specific solution. Sometimes they fail to ask a key question because they think they should already know the answer, and so they miss critical information. These mistakes are easy to make and can cost you a sale.

Questioning and listening, then, comprise a crucial second stage in your sale, regardless of how the sales process is structured. In a one-meeting sale, questioning and listening will take up a large part of your time with a prospect. If the prospect expects a formal presentation, questioning and listing may have to take place at a separate meeting or meetings before the presentation.

Selling is more listening than talking. The most skilled rainmakers will talk only 20 to 30 percent of the time. They listen well, then make a few words tell.

At times, the untrained seller's compulsion to talk verges on rudeness. I could cite many cases, including some from my own early years in consulting, before I received professional sales training. One will suffice.

After months of work, I arranged a meeting for the firm where I was working with the representatives of a Fortune 500 company. Prior to the meeting we all agreed that it would be best to ask the prospects about their needs before describing our services. After introductions, I began the meeting by saying that although I had had an opportunity to talk with our guests, the others on our team had not. Since it is always best to hear things from the source, would they mind describing their situation again?

The prospects were delighted by this chance—most people would rather talk than listen. The senior representative began, "As you are probably aware from the press, our company is shrinking its work force, including our department. At the same time we are under increasing pressure to deliver new projects quickly . . ."

While the prospect's mouth was still open to complete his sentence, the senior member of our team, a principal of the firm with over twenty years of experience, jumped in with an anecdote demonstrating our ability to deliver fast-track projects like no other firm. A short way into this story the prospect closed his mouth, hardly to open it again during the entire meeting. The principal was oblivious to what he had done.

This man is not unusual. In my experience, many professionals interrupt their prospects to score points and are unaware that they do so. *Never* interrupt a prospect! Watch yourself to see whether you are doing it. Ask others to catch you if you do. During this stage of the sales meeting, listen; if you must talk, talk with a question that will keep the prospect talking. Keep the questions short. Take good notes. You can tell your story and make your points later, when you know more.

Think of selling as fishing. Lures are the questions you choose to engage the prospect and develop his interest.[1] Casting is your skill at asking them. Fishing requires patience. You have to cast many times before you get a nibble. Once you get the prospect on the line, you must play him with more questions, or he will snap the line and get away. Only when he is tired of talking can you reel him in with your presentation.

Don't think of selling as a game of basketball in which you score points. Too much aggressiveness and you will find you are scoring points against your prospect.

Eliciting information on a prospect's needs requires good questioning and listening technique because prospects don't talk freely. They are inhibited from giving you a full understanding of their situation by factors such as the following:

- **Time constraints:** The prospect is busy and probably doesn't have time to tell you everything you would like to know.
- **Self-esteem:** Giving you a full story might embarrass the prospect. He may be reluctant to admit how little influence he has on the buying decision or that he is ignorant of certain facts. He will almost certainly not admit that he finds hiring a professional threatening. Yet any of these things may be true.
- **Self-interest:** The prospect may feel that telling you too much could hurt him. He may be afraid of word getting back to others in the company if he shares negative opinions. He may fear that your price will go up if he shows how much he needs you or that you will decline to bid on the project if he tells you that he favors a competitor. Prospects often feel that sensitive information should be kept from you until you are actually hired.
- **Etiquette:** All buyers view it as bad manners to pass on certain kinds of information. This sometimes applies to information that would seem too self-laudatory. A story of a feud between department heads is another example. The prospect is unlikely to fight for airspace with you if you interrupt him. He will never tell you he doesn't like you.
- **Confusion:** The buyer may not understand his own needs. This is extremely common in some professions. In such cases the buyer simply draws the wrong conclusions from the facts at his disposal.
- **Unconscious behavior:** Everyone who has sold knows that some buyers sound optimistic and others pessimistic. Two people reporting the same situation can give it quite different spins, depending upon their personalities.

A commonly heard phrase among professional salespeople is that buyers are liars. I detest this view because it suggests that buyers should meet a standard no one else does. Buyers, like other human beings, are incapable of being completely open and forthright. They need encouragement to talk more freely. This is also true of your boss, your peer, and your employee. Depending on how you work with the buyer, you can either raise or lower his inhibitions. When you lower them, the quality of the information you get improves.

You can encourage the buyer to give you information with the following:

- **Recognition:** People respond to positive feedback, such as "Your comments are very helpful." You must use recognition carefully, however, so that you neither sound like a toady nor unduly bias the information you get.
- **Empathy:** Showing interest in and sympathy for the buyer will generally improve the information you get. A comment like "That can't be easy for you" does this.
- **Rewards:** The buyer will give you more information if he understands how it will help him. This can include things like helping him hire the best professional, do his job better, or avoid specific problems.
- **Personal satisfaction:** The buyer may feel good about helping you if he likes you or feels an obligation to you. He may enjoy the mental stimulation or fun of talking with you.
- **Catharsis:** Occasionally a buyer may benefit from the opportunity to vent pent-up feelings to an outsider.[2]

Different buyers will respond to different kinds of encouragement. As the seller, you must lower the buyer's inhibitions about talking with you by effective encouragement. You have several tools to do this.

Ask a good question.

The most obvious tool is the question. You will get more information from answers to your questions than from any other source. The quality of that information will depend in part on how good your questions are.

Start by knowing what you want to learn before you talk with the client, whether face-to-face or by phone. Exhibit 15.1 provides a list of some of the things you might want to know. Review it before you go to a meeting, and set your information objectives according to the specifics of the situation. The first two columns list information you will want to know about the buyer's need and his process for hiring a professional. Borrowing from linguistics, I refer to the questions in the second column as "deep questions" because they are universal to all professions.

EXHIBIT 15.1 Question Planning Form

What the seller wants to know		What buyer can answer
SELLER'S OBJECTIVE	DEEP QUESTION	SURFACE QUESTIONS
1. To learn enough of client's issue to scope out a project		
A. To establish issues	What do you need?	Why did you call? Would you please elaborate on the issue you called us for?
B. To establish cause	What brought this on?	How did it start? How did it happen?
C. To establish scope	How big an issue is this?	How many . . . ? Over what area does . . . ? Does this affect all of . . . ?
D. To validate buyer's diagnosis	How do you know you have this issue?	What indications do you have that . . . ?
2. To establish impact or implications of the issue		
A. To determine financial impact	What is a solution worth?	What is this costing you? If you were able to do this, what would it be worth?
B. To determine other implications	Why is this so important to you?	How will this affect your customers? What are the legal ramifications? What will you employees do if . . . ?
C. To establish personal impact	How much is a solution worth to you personally?	If you didn't have to worry about this, what would you do with the extra time?
3. To learn what stands in the way of getting this fixed		
A. To determine need for your services	How badly do you need help?	Why wouldn't you do this in-house? Why not let your regular . . . ? What happened the last time you tried to fix this?

What the seller wants to know		What buyer can answer
SELLER'S OBJECTIVE	DEEP QUESTION	SURFACE QUESTIONS
4. To learn buyer's agendas and ideas for a solution		
A. To determine if client is ready to deal with the issue	What do you want to do now?	Where do we go from here? What is the first step to getting this fixed?
	What solution do you want?	What does success look like?
5. To learn about the process for hiring a professional		
A. To establish process	What are the steps in the process for hiring a professional?	What do you want from us? Will you need anything else?
B. To identify buyers	Who else will participate in the selection process?	Who else is on the committee? What will be that person's role in this?
C. To establish timing	When will you decide who to use?	When will you decide on a (consultant, accountant, actuary architect, engineer, lawyer, recruiter)?
D. To determine readiness to close	Are you ready to hire us?	How soon would you like us to start? Where do we go from here? What next?

Because you must place questions in context and couch them in words that will lower the buyer's inhibitions, you can seldom ask these questions directly. This results in "surface questions," those the buyer will understand and feel comfortable answering. Because the form of surface questions depends heavily on your specific profession and practice and the specific context in which you ask them, I cannot give you precise words to use. The best I, or anyone else, can do is give you a general idea of the kinds of surface questions that will elicit answers to your deep questions and leave it to you to come up with words that are suitable. Take out a sheet of paper, and as you review the previous exhibit, see if you can devise surface questions appropriate to your profession for every deep question. As an exercise, do so with a particular prospect in mind.

To make a sale, you will want an answer to every deep question listed. When answering one question, a buyer will sometimes volunteer an answer to a second. But if he doesn't, you must have a surface question ready to bring it out. Develop a question plan before you meet with the buyer.

There is no substitute for a clear knowledge of what you want to know. Some professionals take great pride in their ability to wing a sales meeting. The ability to do this can certainly be an advantage at times, given that the unpredictable often happens in sales. But to use this ability as a justification for ill-preparedness is as foolhardy as ignoring safety precautions with a gun because you happen to be a good marksman. Real professionals neither respect nor indulge in such vanities.

In constructing your surface questions, make use of the two basic question structures:

- **Open questions:** These encourage the buyer to talk at length by putting only the broadest parameters on what information you want. Such questions often begin with "why," "what," or "how," as in, "Why are you considering hiring a (specific type of professional)?" or "What gives you an interest in my firm?" Though technically not questions, polite demands can also be open: "Please describe (your problem)."
    - Open questions are particularly good for eliciting needs, opinions, values, priorities, and sensitivities. They permit you to explore a subject without presuming to know where the answer might lead. They give the prospect freedom to decide what it is important for you to learn.
- **Closed questions:** These require a narrow answer, such as a date, fact, or number. Questions that can be answered with a yes or no fall into this category. They usually begin with such words as "when," "how many," or "will."
    - Closed questions serve two purposes. They help you elicit specific facts about the client's issue that you need to know, such as its size and key deadlines. They also help you confirm what you have learned from open questions or by other means. ("Am I correct in understanding that you . . ?")

You must decide when to ask specific questions. The sequencing and timing of your questions will help determine the quality of the information you get back. Often a closed question confirming your prior knowledge is a good place to start. ("I understand you have a patent problem. Is that correct?") Next, ask several open questions to establish the prospect's concerns as fully as possible. ("Please tell me about your reason for asking me to meet with you. How did this problem arise? What responses have you considered? What help would you want to get from me?") Open questions are usually followed by a series of closed questions to gather facts and confirm what you have learned. ("How much is this problem costing you? When did it start? Would you consider a settlement that would allow him to license the patent?")

Once you have collected information in one area, you should move on to the next with a second set of open questions, followed by more closed questions. ("Where would you like to go from here? What is your process for hiring counsel? When do you plan to make a decision?")

Beyond this general framework for sequencing questions, you will want to save sensitive questions, if they must be asked, until you have talked with the prospect long enough to establish a rapport.

Listen closely to the answer.

How you listen affects both you and the buyer. You learn more if you listen well, and the buyer will judge your interest in him and his problem by how well he perceives you to be listening. To listen well, you must use your body, voice, ears, and eyes.

Body techniques include sitting with pen poised to take notes, looking at the seller with interest, waiting for a response to your question. Note taking implies interest in what you are hearing and helps your memory later. It will also inhibit your own tendency to talk.

At times you should listen without taking notes. If you are waiting for the answer to a sensitive question, you might wish to gaze at the seller with your pen conspicuously laid on your pad, showing you understand that the topic is a sensitive one.

The most potent listening technique is simply not talking. Don't talk about yourself or your firm during this portion of the meeting. Don't relate interesting stories of your own, even if they are relevant. Don't interrupt with another question. Don't talk! When you don't, the buyer will usually fill the void. When the buyer seems to have finished answering a question, especially an open one, wait for several seconds before asking another and continue to look at him intently. The silence and encouragement your posture gives will often stimulate him to talk more.

Some verbal encouragement is necessary, of course. But you must keep clear the distinction between verbal encouragement and all other kinds of talk. Verbal encouragement does not sell; it helps overcome the buyer's inhibitions about talking. It is brief. It is focused on the buyer. When you say, "This is extremely helpful" or "How interesting!" you encourage the *buyer* to keep talking. If he gives insufficient information on a subject, you can encourage him by saying, "Tell me more about that." The one-word question, "Really?" almost always keeps the client talking. "What else?" is another useful probe.

In different situations, a buyer will be more comfortable talking with either an insider or outsider. If you sense this, a few words of encouragement can keep him talking. If, for example, he briefly volunteers some sensitive information, you may choose to take the role of an insider by saying, "Yes. I'm aware. What do you think about it?" Understanding that you are in the know will probably encourage him to give more information. Sometimes an insider is one who has seen such a situation before. You might say, "Yes, that often happens in situations like this. This is helpful. Tell me more." You might say, "We found the same thing at XYZ Company. Tell me more." At this point you should avoid relating an elaborate story of a past project that shows your inside knowledge. There will be time for that later.

At other times, you will sense that the role of an outsider will get you better information. A comment like, "Obviously, I won't get that deeply involved in your personnel issues, but I can do my job better if I understand the sensitivities. What role do you think he will have in the project?" may keep a buyer talking.

When you are not talking, use your ears. Your understanding of what you hear depends on three things:

- **What is said:** The words the buyer uses when answering your questions are your principal source of information. You can learn about his concerns and opinions. You can learn his view of the facts. All of this is valuable, though it must be treated with caution. If you ask about the decision process for hiring a professional and the buyer tells you that she will make the choice, that is valuable information. She may be the decision maker. She certainly either thinks she is or wants you to think so.
- **How it is said:** The buyer's choice of words also informs you. Small contradictions or qualifiers and the use of vague or evasive language ("That will be decided some time in the fall." By whom?) are all indicators that the buyer may feel inhibited about telling you something. If, after telling you that she will make the hiring choice, she says that she will just want to run her decision by a couple of people to keep everyone in the loop, she is telling you that the decision may not really be hers to make after all.
- **What is not said:** The absence of information also informs you. In our example the sudden appearance of "a couple of people" who are involved in the choice of a professional and about whom you know nothing is a

sign that the buyer feels inhibited about telling you something. It also informs you of a potentially serious gap in your information. A few open probes may overcome inhibitions and fill this gap. ("That's great. If there are other people interested in the process, we want them to be happy with the choice as much as you do. Could you tell me a little about them?")

Finally, observe the buyer carefully. This is listening with your eyes. The buyer's level of eye contact, his gestures, and his posture all provide information about the buyer and what he is telling you. You want to watch for signals that he is uncomfortable with what he is saying: Hesitation, avoidance of eye contact, shifting posture, and running a hand through his hair may all be signals. This is especially true if such body language is combined with verbal signals.

When this occurs, you have a choice. You may want to try to open up the issue with an open probe. ("You just said . . . Tell me a little more about that.") You may choose to encourage the response by providing recognition ("That's very perceptive. Tell me more."); by showing empathy ("That could put you in a tough spot," with a pause as you wait for a response); or by offering a reward before you probe ("I know what kind of difficulties that can create. I think we can help there. Tell me more."). You may feel that the issue is so sensitive that pursuing it would antagonize or embarrass the buyer. If so, make a note of it so that you can try to find out about it later by other means.

Visible changes in the buyer's intensity and emotions also provide clues about personal concerns and priorities, which may be distinct from those of the company.

Ask the right person.

Long ago I was pursuing a project at a division of a large conglomerate. I had worked for other divisions and for the parent, and I knew the COO; I was pretty sure I would win the job. When it went to a competitor, I called the COO. "I would have liked to see you get the job," he told me, "but the people in the division wanted the other guy. They showed me your credentials and his, and he didn't look bad, so I let them hire him. They're the ones who have to live with the result. Between you and me, they may have liked the fact that he didn't know me." In fact, I had relied too much on my relationship with the COO and not devoted enough attention to learning about the people who ran the division.

Often, several people are involved in hiring a professional, and they are involved in different ways. Governments and universities often use committees to make hiring decisions, and some committees have no dominating member. But for most sales there is a single individual who will ultimately decide who is hired. This individual works with others to arrive at a decision. Responsibilities she may give to others include these:

- **Screening:** The decision maker may want to avoid the time required to evaluate every possible contender for the work. She may ask someone to select the best candidates, then choose from among this smaller group.
- **Advising:** She will want experts to advise her about the alternative firms. Experts can come from inside or outside the company and are often accountants, attorneys, engineers, purchasing agents, or other specialists. The decision maker may also seek advice from those within the company who will have to work closely with the professional and live with the results of his work. By seeking their advice, she often hopes to increase their acceptance of the professional's work later. These people will then have input on needs and selection criteria.
- **Recommending:** She may ask these same people whom she should hire. She may not be obliged to accept their recommendations, but she will pay a price if she ignores recommendations too often.
- **Deciding:** She may delegate the decision to someone else. This may occur if she is satisfied that all of the professionals under consideration can do the work or when she is particularly anxious to support the individual to whom she delegates the decision.

Your chances of making a sale will be greatly enhanced if you can talk directly with all those involved in hiring, ask questions, listen, and develop a relationship. Sometimes you will be introduced to all the involved parties without having to ask. When you aren't, you must proceed carefully; a buyer will sometimes feel threatened by a request to meet others in the organization. If you ask to see others in the firm, always tie it to one or both of the following:

- **Need for specific information:** The more you can legitimize your need to talk with additional people by a real need for information that they can best provide, the less resistance you will get from the initial contact.
- **Need to develop buy-in:** If group buy-in on the results of your work is crucial to project success, you can request to meet key participants in order to develop rapport prior to being hired.

Some professionals insist on meeting all participants in the buying decision as a precondition to submitting a proposal. You must decide whether the risks of such a demand outweigh the potential benefits.

Once you have gathered information on your prospect, you are in a position to present how you can help meet his needs.

16

The Sales Meeting: Offering Your Solution

To do interesting work, you must first convince the prospect that you should be the one to do it. All the effort to generate a lead and the hours spent developing a relationship and collecting information on a prospect will only produce work for your firm if you can persuade the prospect to hire you. When you ask a client for her ideas for a solution and the role she might want you to play, you send a signal that it is time to talk about solutions. The buyer will expect to hear your solutions.

This chapter describes ways to present your solution compellingly.

Link to high-level need.

When the time has come for you to tell the client how you can help her, your first few words have disproportionate impact. In her mind, all of her talking up until now has been to help you understand her problem to prepare you for this moment. Now she is looking for a return on this investment. You probably have her undivided attention, a state that may not last. Your first few words set the tone for everything that follows, so they had better be good. This is true whether your response is in the context of an informal discussion, a stand-up presentation, or a proposal.

A construction management firm we know was asked to present its capabilities for the construction of a building dedicated to a specific field of medical research at a major university. Construction contracts of this sort are always competitively bid. The same cast of five or six major national firms and one or two strong regional firms are asked for qualifications. On the basis of their submittals, three or four firms are short-listed and asked to present to a selection committee.

All of the short-listed firms have strong credentials and can do the work. In this environment, the bologna of differentiation gets sliced pretty thin. This was the situation the construction management firm faced. Additionally, times were tough and the regional office in question desperately needed the work.

Later, as the selection committee deliberated on the presentations it had heard, it came back again and again to the opening statement made by the head of the regional office of the firm in question. As the chair of the selection committee later said, this brief statement convinced the committee that "yours was the only firm that understood what a university is all about, and that can't be rehearsed." The firm got hired.

Of course, the regional office head had honed and rehearsed his opening statement repeatedly. It went something like this.

Ladies and gentlemen of the selection committee, my name is Karl _____ and I am with XYZ Construction Company. As we understand it, this university is at the leading edge of the [area of medical research in question]. The contributions you have made in this area, both to knowledge and the public good, are the kind of thing that make this such a preeminent institution.

To maintain this leading-edge position, you need to attract faculty members, those best minds in this field, from wherever they are located across the world. If you attract the best faculty, you will attract the best students and together, the faculty and students will win the research dollars that will keep you out in front.

We want to build you a laboratory that is so right for this kind of research, and so appealing, that prospective faculty members who see it say, "That's where I want to work!"

That simple statement proved a major differentiator and is what we call a high-level opener because it links the professional's services to the client's high-level goal. Such statements do the following:

- *They show that you are focused on the client, rather than on yourself.* And, have no doubt, clients are much more interested in themselves and their needs than they are in you and your services. You and your services are but a means to an end. If you want to capture their attention, talk about them before you talk about yourself. What a different tone the construction manager would have set, if he had led with talk about XYZ Construction!
- *They show that your interests are aligned with the client's.* If you truly understand my goals and are aligned with them, the chance that you will make good decisions in my absence goes up. A sense of alignment can be decisive when clients pick whom they are going to hire. When you finish your opening, you want the client to say to herself, "He nailed it! He understands exactly what I want."

- *They demonstrate that you share the client's passion.* Most clients feel passionately about the work they do, though most disguise their passion in their day-to-day work. Remember, you are talking about people's careers and aspirations and about the contribution they will make during the short time they have on this planet. They want to hire a professional who shares their passion. Note how the following high-level openers capture the clients' passions:
    - *A recruiter speaking to the founder of a biotechnology firm:* This company is at a turning point. You have done a wonderful job of developing a treatment for [a truly horrible disease]. Now you must get this treatment to those who suffer from that disease. As you have stated, many successful drugs never make it to the people who need them. For yours to do so requires that the company become commercially successful, and that will require the talents of an executive skilled at taking biotechnology startups to the next level. We want to help you find that executive.
    - *A management consultant speaking to the head of a family-owned firm:* Your grandfather and father built a company that has served this community for three generations, while providing amply for the needs of this family for sixty years. But the world has changed, and there are strong indications that the model they developed won't work in the future. The task falls to you, then, to reinvent this company so that you can leave it as strong for the next generation as it was left for you, and we want to help you do it.
- *They give dignity to sometimes mundane efforts.* Even if what a client does seems mundane to others, it doesn't seem so to her. She prefers to work with someone who recognizes the importance of what she does and sees dignity in it. Take this example of a high-level opener, made by an engineer.

This company is experiencing hard times. To turn the situation around, management is investing heavily in the redevelopment of your products. That redevelopment requires large amounts of cash, and every department must do its part to help free up money. You want to reduce energy consumption in the buildings in this complex as a part of your contribution, and we want to help you do it.

- *They allow you to synthesize a client's complex problem into the essence of its importance.* Refocusing the client from the nitty-gritty of a problem with all its details and side lines helps clarify what is needed. This can be an important role for a professional. Take these words from a labor attorney.

This company has been accused in a dozen cases of employment discrimination, all claiming that you have discriminated against minority employees. This, of course, poses a financial threat, but I hear a frustration and anger in your description that shows you are concerned equally with the damage the claims make to the reputation you have carefully built for integrity and fair dealing.

You want these cases dealt with quickly. If wrong has been done, you are prepared to do what you can to make amends. In cases where no wrong has been done, you want that understood. But, most importantly you want this situation dealt with quickly and in a way that will be the best for the reputation of the company. That's what we want to help you do.

A high-level opener gets the case for hiring you off to a strong start. Here is some guidance on preparing one.

First, you must determine the client's high-level goal or need. Usually, you do that by asking, sometimes several times, why a client wants to do something, as demonstrated in the following hypothetical exchange between an engineer and a client.

Engineer: Why are you interested in reducing energy consumption on this site? I can think of several good reasons, but what stands out in your mind?

Client: Our department has a goal of cutting $3 million out of the facilities budget over the next year, and we believe a chunk of that can come from savings in energy costs.

Engineer: Saving money is always a good thing. Is there any reason why doing so is particularly important now?

Client: The company isn't doing so well, and every department is expected to find a way to cut back. We want to do our part.

What you learn by asking can be supplemented by reviewing the client's Web site, conducting a media search, and asking knowledgeable third parties.

Once you understand the high-level goal, you can construct an opener. For practice, start with the words, "As we understand it, . . ." They will help get you going in the right direction. Until you gain skill at creating compelling openers, consider using one of the following common themes:

- You have a rare opportunity (to accomplish something, gain a competitive advantage, leave a legacy . . .).
- You want to contribute to the important mission of this organization.
- Your organization is at a turning point. It has done well in the past, but you recognize that what worked well then won't do so now and that your organization must change.
- You have something of special value that is important to preserve.

Remember, the opener is largely about the client. You only link yourself to the high-level goal briefly at the end. Once you have given your opener, confirm that you have done it correctly by asking the client, "Have we understood your basic concern?" If she agrees that you have, she has moved a little closer to hiring you by saying so. If you haven't, she will tell you. Better that you find out now.

Stress the benefits.

Once you have shown how your services link to a high-level goal, you can tell the client what you will do for them. As a young consultant I presented to Vernon Loucks, the president and later chairman of Baxter International. During the presentation he interrupted me three times to ask, "Why is this important to my company?" He taught me a lesson I have never forgotten: At all times, the presenter owes it to his audience to make it clear why he should be listening. In a sales presentation, this means focusing on benefits.

Benefits are what clients get from you that help them meet their needs. Benefits include such things as reduced risk, commitment of the management team to action, reduced operating costs, or any other thing that meets a specific need. You provide benefits through the features of your firm and its services. Features include such things as the experience of your professional staff, your methodologies, proprietary databases, and your industry or functional knowledge.

You are far more likely to make a sale if you stress benefits. When doing so, you should always describe the benefits you will provide before you describe the features of your services. This is basic sales knowledge, but each generation of professionals must learn it, and too many professionals still don't understand it.

Professionals often talk about the features of their services before they describe the benefits they will provide. But your features are of no interest to the client except as a source of benefits. He doesn't want to hear about them until he understands and believes in the benefits he will get from you. Think about it. No one wants a database or a contract or blueprints of a building's plumbing for its own sake. Such things are only of value as a means to an end. The same is true of the experience of your staff, or its industry knowledge, or the location of your offices, or your methodologies. Start by describing the client's needs, proceed to the benefits you will provide to address these needs, and only then list your firm's features. Once you have described your features, you can provide proof of their effectiveness.

Of course, this means you must know what benefits to stress. Each of us has a tendency to define benefits in terms of the most obvious outcomes of our work and to overlook benefits that the prospect may desperately want and that we can provide. An example is issue resolution. A benefit derived from the work of many professionals is getting an issue resolved so that a client can get on with his business. Clients will pay good money for help of this kind, especially if conflicting views have obstructed progress. Some professionals fail to recognize this need when they hear it and so fail to stress the issue-resolving benefits of their services.

Exhibit 16.1 provides a list of benefits that professionals provide. It is not definitive, nor are the categories discrete, but it has stimulated the thinking of many professionals about the broad range of benefits they actually provide. Review it, and see whether you can cite a case in which you provided each benefit to a client. It will be good practice.

EXHIBIT 16.1 Benefits Checklist

(For idea generation only. This is not a definitive list, nor are categories discrete.)

Better decisions
- ❏ Issue clarification/diagnosis
- ❏ Better information
- ❏ Reduced uncertainty/risk
- ❏ Faster information
- ❏ Better analysis
- ❏ Objectivity
- ❏ Lack of fear

Increased revenues
- ❏ Increased market share
- ❏ More sales
- ❏ More loyal customers
    - Better product availability
    - Better selection
    - Better pricing
    - Better service
- ❏ Cash awards

Issue Resolution/Change
- ❏ Information
- ❏ Validation
- ❏ Issue clarification/diagnosis
- ❏ Consensus development
- ❏ Generating commitment
- ❏ Awareness building
- ❏ Perceived objectivity

Cost reduction
- ❏ Staff
- ❏ Equipment
- ❏ Facilities
- ❏ Inventory
- ❏ Utilities
- ❏ Raw materials/parts/product
    for resale

Cost avoidance
- ❏ Financial stewardship
- ❏ Better vendor selection
- ❏ Lower prices
- ❏ Negotiation skill
- ❏ Lower fees or fines

Increased productivity
- ❏ Better organization
- ❏ Better employees
- ❏ More efficient systems
- ❏ Better work flow
- ❏ Better equipment
- ❏ Fewer errors

Management support

- ❑ Manpower/adjunct staff
- ❑ Specialized expertise
- ❑ Sleep insurance
- ❑ Financial stewardship
- ❑ Objectivity

Problem avoidance

- ❑ Experience/knowledge
- ❑ Due diligence
- ❑ Risk identification
- ❑ Avoided litigation
- ❑ Confidentiality

Speed

- ❑ Faster decisions
- ❑ Faster inventory turns
- ❑ Faster production
- ❑ Faster product development
- ❑ Faster delivery

Personal satisfaction

- ❑ Prestige of working with you
- ❑ Mental stimulation
- ❑ Increased job security
- ❑ Avoidance of pain/suffering
- ❑ Friendship

Avoid the temptation to present newly discovered benefits to every client. Remember that benefit is defined by the buyer, just as need is. Stressing something that the buyer sees no need for at best wastes valuable presentation time and at worst shows you weren't listening.

But what about the features of your firm? Does all this mean that you should ignore them? No. Use them as proof of your ability to provide benefits. If they don't support a benefit mentioned by the prospect, however, you should probably leave them out. Exhibit 16.2 lists several benefits of a professional service firm. As an exercise in relating features to benefits, list one or more features or other proofs that support them in the space provided.

EXHIBIT 16.2 Supporting Benefits with Features

Identify at least one feature that helps create each benefit.

Benefit	Feature
A. Accurate diagnosis. *We can identify the crux of your problem.*	
B. Issue resolution *We will help your management achieve consensus*	
C. Cost Avoidance *We will save you money.*	
D. Increased Productivity *We will increase your employees' effectiveness.*	

Answers:
There is no single right answer. Sample right answers might include:

A. Specialized industry and functional experience of firm and team members.
   Methodology used for diagnosing
B. Facilitation techniques.
C. Cost reduction methodology.
D. Methodology used to increase productivity.
   Relevant degrees of certifications of staff working on assignment.
   Increased productivity
   We will increase your employees' effectiveness

Get a sense of the flow of a professional's description of his offering from the following example from a turnaround management firm. As is often the case with such firms, the client's high-level goal is survival, or more prosaically, avoidance of bankruptcy. The high-level opener went something like this.

You have built this company up over the last twenty years into a leader in your industry. Now you have hit a bad patch that puts all your hard work at risk. Most immediately, your control of your own destiny is being threatened by creditors who have lost confidence in the company's ability to meet its financial obligations. It is imperative that you regain their confidence and get this company back on track quickly, so you can refocus on what you do best, which is growing a business. That's what we want to help you do.

The turnaround executive then turned to the two most urgent needs that the client would have to address:

- **Finding cash to pay creditors:** The company needed to reallocate its cash outflows to spend as much as possible to pay off creditors and buy time for a restructuring. To do this, the turnaround specialists would rapidly identify sources of cash (benefit), which it could do because of the extensive experience of its asset valuation team (feature). It could rapidly turn selected assets into cash by selling them (benefit), because of its knowledge and access to buyers of the kinds of assets in question (feature). Finally, it could quickly reduce cash outflows (benefit), by applying its proven cost control procedures (feature). The turnaround specialist then offered references for his effectiveness at cash generation (proof).
- **Gain creditor acceptance of a restructuring plan:** To be allowed to reinvent the company, management would have to gain creditor acceptance

of a restructuring plan. Before accepting it, the creditors would have to believe that the plan would result in a smaller loss than would immediate foreclosure. The turnaround specialist offered its strong credibility with creditors (benefit), which was based on its prior track record (feature), proven creditor communications process (feature), and negotiating skill (feature). He told a story about another case in which he had won over skeptical creditors (proof).

Now it's your turn. Think of a specific business opportunity that you are pursuing, and develop a concise description of your offering. Use the form in Exhibit 16.3 if it helps. Start with a high-level linking statement, followed by descriptions of benefits you will provide and features you will use to provide them. Prepare your words to your client by listing her needs in order of importance to her. Order is important; the client will feel that you understand her needs clearly if you rank them the way she would.

EXHIBIT 16.3 Presentation Planning Form

Client: _____ Date: _____
High-Level-Need: _____

Needs	Benefits	Features	Proof

For each need, next list the benefits you will provide. Try to reduce each benefit to a two- or three-word phrase (for example, increased market share, reduced risk, reduced staff turnover, lower maintenance costs, increased customer loyalty). That will help ensure that what you are providing is clear in your mind, even if you use more words when you describe it to the client. If it's not clear to you, you will have a hard time making it clear to the client. Next, list the features that are the source of each benefit (facilitation skill, knowledge of the client's facilities or the court system in question or of anything else that results in value for the client, proximity of your offices, global reach of your firm, your methodology). Then list any proof you will offer, such as a relevant anecdote, data, references, a tour of another client's operations, or bios of your team members. Finally, confirm that the client agrees with your approach. You can do this in many ways: "How does this sound?" "Are you comfortable with this approach?" "Are we missing anything?"

Once completed, use this document as an outline for the words you will say and for your proposal. Exhibit 16.4 provides one structure that you can use to describe your approach to the client's problem.

EXHIBIT 16.4 **Structure for Giving Information**

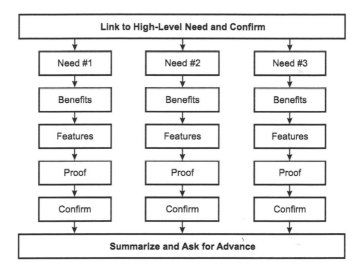

Ask for the business.

Now express your interest in the client's business. You can do this in many ways, but make sure that client understands your personal interest in her issue. Wording you might use includes the following:

- "I would very much like to be your attorney on this matter." "I would very much like to be your accountant (or consultant or architect)." "I would very much like to do this search for you."
- "We would very much like to be a part of this exciting project." "This is exactly the kind of project I want to work on."

Finally, ask for an advance, the next logical step to getting the business. Asking for the advance helps keep the sale moving and avoids having it go into the limbo of unreturned telephone calls or telephone tag. Typical advances include the following:

- **Another meeting:** For most professional services, more than one meeting is required to make a sale. There are often additional members of the client's team you must meet or information to gather or a more detailed approach to prepare. If you ask for another meeting, make it clear who is responsible for what. ("We would like to come back next week and meet with your boss and the CFO. Can you arrange that? I will bring the head of our practice and the project manager I mentioned, who has done so much of this kind of work.") If it is possible, schedule the next meeting before you leave. ("If it's okay, on the way out I will talk with your secretary about scheduling the next meeting.") If the client resists, remind her how important the issue is to her. ("I'm sorry. I didn't mean to push, but this sounded like a top priority for you, so I didn't want things to drag out.")
- **Authorization to proceed:** The best advance is, of course, agreement to hire you. If you sense the client is ready to do so, ask. ("I sense you're ready to go ahead with this. Am I right?") If you are less certain but still think the client is ready, you can ask the same question less directly. ("Where do we go from here?")

When the client agrees to an advance, leave as quickly as is polite. Your job for the day is done. If you keep talking, the best you can do from that point on is take up your client's and your own valuable time. The worst you can do is say something that will cause the client to reconsider. Between those two points there is no good ground.

The Sales Meeting: Formal Presentations

Many clients ask professionals to give a formal, stand-up presentation, usually as a final step in deciding whom to hire. When required, the presentation is the climax of a sale, the single most visible point of success or failure. Present well, and negotiations on fee are a manageable finale; present poorly, and the music ends abruptly. Professionals who say, "We won (or lost) it in the presentation" seldom use such language for the proposal or information-gathering portions of the sale.

Prospects also see presentations as the culminating event in their selection of a professional. From debriefings on lost projects, I learned long ago that when proposals are submitted simultaneously with presentations, prospects place overwhelming weight on the presentation. When asked about both, they could barely recall the proposals but could cite many details about presentations.

For these reasons, I devote this chapter to formal presentations. Note, however, that all of Chapter 16 applies to formal presentations, too. If you haven't read it, you should do so now.

There are many ways to conduct a formal presentation. You may present by using slides before a committee or by chatting across a table with one or two buyers. Whatever the format, your formal presentation will be better if you do the following.

The presentation is a small part of the sale.
Your presentation will be better if you recognize that it is only a small part of a sale. If you have gathered good information on the prospect, her needs, and the competition, and you have developed a relationship with some or all of the buyers, the presentation itself will go better.

Those who have turned to this book for guidance shortly before they must present should review Chapter 15, with its emphasis on questioning and listening. It may not be too late to gather information that will make the difference between a good presentation and one that is off-target. I once coached a group of interior designers on a presentation they were preparing for one of the largest banks in the country. Early in our planning it became apparent that the team lacked knowledge about the prospect's needs. I recommended postponing the rehearsal until the afternoon to give the team a chance to call the buyer with questions. When we reconvened, the presentation was completely overhauled on the basis of the information that had been collected in a single phone call. The designers won the project.

Planning for every presentation should begin with a review of the following:

- Background on the prospect company
- Background on the people you will be presenting to
- Background on the situation the client faces
- Background on client needs
- Background on special needs of the people you will present to
- A review of any formal requirements for the presentation requested by the buyer (length, content, etc.)
- Background on the competition and its strengths and weaknesses

This is all information you should try to collect prior to the presentation.

Plan your presentation from the buyer's perspective.

With this background information, you can plan your presentation from the buyer's perspective. This means that you must consider what it is like to sit and listen to several presentations in a row. You can be reasonably assured that the experience is all of the following:

- **Confusing:** Unless the presentation is very clear, the buyer will have to make inferences about the importance of what is being said. Sometimes those inferences will differ from the ones the presenter wants him to make.
- **Repetitious:** All of the presenters will claim to be the best. They will all claim to be good listeners, to be responsive, to be the oldest and the biggest. They will all claim that their top people will work on the engagement. This will make it hard to differentiate among them.
- **Boring:** Because it is repetitious, and because many who present will do so poorly, the process won't be much fun.
- **Hard to remember:** Because the presentations will be boring and repetitious, and because everyone's mind wanders during presentations, the content will be hard to remember. It may also be hard to remember which competitor said what.

- **Cold:** One-way communications predominate in many presentations. Most one-way communications are cold, and it is distasteful to hire someone you feel cold about.

The more competitors are asked to present, the more formal the presentation format, the more compact the schedule for the presentations, and the more confusing, repetitious, boring, hard to remember, and cold the process will be. Though informal one-on-one presentations are easier on the buyer, you are safest assuming that the same concerns apply.

To overcome these obstacles, your presentation must achieve the following goals:

- *It must be persuasive.* It must clearly and logically explain why you are the right one to get the job.
- *It must be memorable.* A day or a week after the presentation, the buyer must be able to remember you and your message.
- *It must create an emotional link with the prospect.* It must show that you care about the prospect and will be good to work with.

Differentiate your firm through the consistent use of a theme.

Every formal presentation should have a theme. Akin to the angle you use when planning an article, the theme ensures the focus and clarity of your message. Develop it around the most compelling reason that yours is the right firm to do the job. Very possibly this can be derived from the exercise you have completed to tie your services to the prospect company's core objectives. The theme should differentiate your firm in one of two ways:

- **More is better:** This approach assumes that others offer fundamentally the same services you do, but that you offer a higher quality or quantity. Unless you dominate a market, this approach is risky. Prospects seek a floor level for most attributes and discount the benefits of levels above that floor. Thus, having done twenty projects similar to the one you are being considered for when a competitor has done only three may give you specialized knowledge that translates into shorter learning curves, better diagnostic ability, and better solutions. But having done seventy similar projects when a competitor has done forty may not be perceived as a great advantage and is difficult to verify. You probably don't know what claims your competitors are making. Proving the value of having more of an attribute is often difficult and sometimes impossible.
- **Different bundle of benefits:** You can also suggest that you offer a different set of benefits. Yes, you offer *a*, *b*, and c, as other firms do, but you

also offer *d*, which no one else does. If *d* is something valued by the prospect, this is a powerful argument. Examples of this kind of differentiation include the following.

- *People:* A consulting firm hired the top quality expert from a company with an internationally acclaimed quality program to head up its total quality management practice.
- *Methodology:* A university professor developed a methodology to assist lawyers in jury selection and developed a large consulting practice around it.
- *Range of services:* A consulting firm gained significant advantage by offering one-stop shopping for a full range of services associated with a particular kind of project, when competitors dealt only with pieces.
- *Relationships:* A civil engineering firm stressed its special relationship with planning and zoning boards in its state when competing for work from developers seeking to do business there.
- *Knowledge:* Attorneys at a large law firm wrote a book on U.S. securities law for European companies and used it to demonstrate knowledge specialized to the needs of that market. This became its sales theme.
- *Responsiveness:* An executive search firm located offices in intermediate-sized metropolitan areas to provide it with an advantage when competing against large firms with offices based in major metropolitan areas. It sold its services to firms located near to its offices by promising responsiveness based on proximity.
- *Reputation:* In each field, there are firms that have developed strong reputations that have helped them sell business because buying from them seems low-risk. McKinsey is the best example in consulting.

If you can choose among several differentiators in developing a theme, remember to select the one of most importance to the prospect. Do not expect to pick one differentiator and use it forever; if it works, others will soon imitate you. As one rainmaker said to me, "I knew we were becoming a factor in our market when versions of our slides started appearing in competitors' presentations."

You should be able to express your theme in one sentence, just as you do an angle. Try completing the following sentence with a specific prospect in mind: "We are the firm best able to help you because . . ." Try different endings until you find one that you think the prospect will find compelling. Examples of alternative endings include these:

- . . . we have specialized methods and databases that will ensure rapid project completion and reduce your costs without damaging product quality.
- . . . we have an unequaled track record of defending corporations in employee-initiated suits in this court system.
- . . . we have specialized knowledge of the accounting practices in your industry and so can help you defer and reduce taxes.
- . . . we are the one firm that combines high-quality medical facility design with internationally acclaimed aesthetic design.

Once you have a theme, you can build your presentation around it.

Outline the case you want to make.

Next, create a clear, logical, and concise outline of the case that will demonstrate that yours is the best firm for the job. Note any statistics or other proofs that you may want to use to support your argument. Make sure that each point supports your main theme.

If it helps you to write a draft of the presentation, do so, but do not use it to rehearse from. You write only to ensure that your reasoning is sound. Memorizing opening and closing lines can help you to get started and to end. The rest of your presentation should not be memorized.

Use examples to make your services more tangible.

In a weak economy, my firm hungry for work, I flew to Cincinnati to call on a small metal fabricator thinking of building a branch plant. At first, the prospect seemed promising; the president was determined to lower his labor costs by establishing a branch plant and wanted help deciding where in the South to locate it. That was my specialty.

Then he told me the size of the plant: twenty people. Because it was my business, I knew instantaneously that the additional overhead of the branch plant would eat up any labor savings. There would never be a payoff on the initial investment.

When the time came for me to present, I began with a story. I told him of a well-known metal fabricator I had worked with that also wanted to lower labor costs. Instead of moving to the Sun Belt, the company located its twenty-person plant in a small town in Wisconsin within a three-hour drive of its Chicago-area headquarters. Labor costs were as low as anywhere in the South, and overhead was limited to one foreman-cum-plant manager. Whenever human resource, engineering, or other help was needed, someone from headquarters got in a car and drove up to the plant. This would have been impossible at a distant location.

Largely on the basis of this story, the client hired me. It had showed him the following things about me:

- I understood his core objective to become a low-cost producer.
- My experience had value to him.
- I would be creative in addressing his problem.
- I would save him money.

Better still, it did so in a way that was more persuasive and memorable than if I had spoken in abstractions. That's a lot to get from one short anecdote.

The value of a good anecdote was summarized to me by another prospect who had hired a competitor. He said, "We saw our problem in the story they told." Now that must have been a good story! It had made a service, which the buyer could not experience until after a professional was hired, seem tangible. Ever since I have sought to make my stories meet this standard.

The heavy use of anecdotes is one of the primary differences between selling professional services and selling products. In part, this is because professional services are so abstract; in part, it is because professionals must sell themselves. This is a very different proposition from selling a widget. The statements "This is a great widget!" and "I am a great accountant (or actuary or architect or consultant or lawyer)!" have quite different impacts on the listener.

Exhibit 17.1 lists some of the characteristics that buyers typically like to find in the professionals they hire. How do you claim such attributes without seeming immodest? Through the artful use of anecdotes.

EXHIBIT 17.1 Adjectives Used to Describe a Good Professional

• Experienced	• Knowledgeable
• Smart	• Expensive but worth it
• Insightful	• Attentive
• Empathetic	• Analytical
• Objective	• Creative
• Trustworthy	• Innovative
• Client-focused	• Sensitive
• Professional	• Persuasive
• Wise	• Ethical
• Savvy	• Practical
• Interesting	• Tactful
• Conscientious	• Energetic
• Self-controlled	• Concerned

A good anecdote has the following characteristics:

- *It is relevant.* The prospect must be able to identify with the protagonist in the story. Build relevance by describing those characteristics of the past client that most resemble the prospect, be it industry, location, size of company, or similarity of need. It is hard to use a story about a casino operator with a publisher of Bibles. If the prospect doesn't see the relevance, he will discount the message, however apt.
- *It is benefits-oriented.* A good anecdote highlights the benefits of working with you by showing either the good things accruing to someone who did or the bad things besetting someone who didn't.
- *It is brief.* An anecdote that gets too long ceases to be one. If a story gets too long it becomes a distraction from the main theme of your presentation instead of a reinforcement. The anecdote should run five sentences at most. Three are better.
- *It is made up of four key elements.* Just like a stage setter in the rapport-building part of the meeting, it must have a plot (need to lower labor costs, for example), a character (a metal fabricator), action (driving to Wisconsin), and an outcome (bigger success than a Sun Belt plant would have made possible). If it also has humor, so much the better.

Some professionals become so proficient at telling anecdotes that they overuse them. Often this results from a shortage of other selling skills. Do not fall into this trap. Professionals who have an anecdote showing how great they are for every sentence spoken by a prospect are annoying and lose jobs. Use this tool sparingly when it counts the most. Just one story closed my sale to the metal fabricator.

What people see is as important as what you say.

I once lost several sales in a row to a competitor. In debriefings with the prospects, two said that he had a better database than I did and so could complete the project more quickly and accurately. From an employee who had formerly worked for the competitor, I knew this was not true. A few weeks later I sat in on a presentation he gave at a trade association meeting. He put up a slide that struck me like a rock. This single image is what had convinced my prospects of his superiority. With beautiful simplicity it created the impression of a wealth of useful data. I developed a knock-off exhibit and stopped losing jobs to him.

I have always remembered this lesson in the value of superior presentation graphics and have striven ever since for the same combination of simplicity and substance that my competitor had found in that one exhibit. What your prospects see is as important as what you say.

What you do is as important as what you say.

A joint-venture team of architects and engineers lost a project because the architects and the engineers unwittingly sat at opposite ends of the table during the presentation, destroying the image of unity. In debriefings, all three members of the selection committee commented on disparity between what they heard about teamwork versus what they saw.

The next time this team presented, not only did they sit together, they all wore maroon suspenders. It was done subtly (not everyone removed his jacket, for example), but the client got the message. After sitting through five back-to-back presentations, the selection committee could still recall the words of the "red suspenders *team*" (emphasis added). The team got the job.

I listen well. I'm enthusiastic about your project. I care about you. I know what I am talking about. We are a team. These and many other messages are delivered more by how you act than by what you say. This means that your presentation must be structured to demonstrate key attributes that cannot be communicated with words.

Like the team in the preceding story, you must decide what aspects of your presentation require reinforcement from your behavior then plan to act accordingly. Here are some things you can emphasize:

- **Enthusiasm:** Physical animation communicates enthusiasm. Smiling, holding your hands open in front of you while making a point, and moving deliberately closer to your audience as you speak all create the sense of enthusiasm.
- **Interest and caring:** Strong eye contact communicates interest and caring. Many presenters let their eyes wander aimlessly during a presentation, or, worse, look frequently at their boss. Maintain eye contact with your audience.
- **Listening ability:** Ask a question during the presentation, and then listen carefully to the response, looking intently at the speaker. Make a *short* comment at the end that shows you understand what he has said. Be careful to ask a question that is thoughtful but unthreatening.
- **Confidence and knowledge:** Standing with your feet set slightly apart and arms at your sides communicates confidence in what you are saying. Avoid rocking from foot to foot, holding your hands in the fig leaf position (hands clasped at groin), or putting hands in your pockets or behind your back.

Some presenters find standing with their arms at their sides unnatural. It does not appear so to the observer, and his opinion is the one that counts. If the discomfort is acute, try holding a pointer or a pen in your hand, but don't fiddle with it.

How you say it is as important as what you say.

Take the three words, "Oh, it's you." Depending upon tone, volume, rate, pitch, and accent, you can communicate many different messages with them, including: "I love you," "I hate you," "I expected someone else," "It's good to see you," and "I'm bored." You can do this naturally without any training in theater or communications. Try it. I mean it. Close the door to your room and try it out loud.

Your voice will communicate underlying messages, called "subtexts," during your presentation, and you can control these underlying messages as naturally as you did when saying "Oh, it's you." Before speaking, repeat to yourself the underlying message that you would like to give. It will come out in your voice when you begin to present. Here are a few examples of underlying messages:

- **Interest, caring, emotional linkage:** "I care about you."
- **Enthusiasm:** "It's great to be here!"
- **Confidence:** "I can help you."

Practice the statement that communicates your subtext aloud to a friendly critic until you can say it convincingly, then go right into a rehearsal of your presentation. Ask the critic if the message is coming through. You may feel awkward doing this at first, but it works.

The words you choose for your message are also important. Don't talk about "I" and "we" and "our clients"; it sounds self-absorbed. Talk about the prospect, using "you." Instead of talking about "our methodology," talk about "how we will help you." Always ask yourself, "Is what I am saying focused on this prospect, or could I be saying the same words to any prospect?" If it's the latter, fix it.

Rehearse!

I have known many professionals who claim that they do better without rehearsing, that they are more natural and that the words are more fluid. This claim is preposterous. Politicians rehearse, actors and musicians rehearse, professional athletes practice. They do it because it makes them better, even though it takes time and can be painful. Professionals don't wing it.

The real reason most avoid rehearsing is to avoid the embarrassment. People who take this position don't realize that they will embarrass themselves anyway if they don't, although the prospect will be too polite to say so. That they feel better in a presentation than in a rehearsal doesn't make them better. It just means they have more adrenaline in their bloodstream.

Embarrassment at rehearsals often derives from ineffective critiquing, which destroys confidence in how a professional presents but doesn't show a better way. If this is your problem, be sure to rehearse with a sympathetic critic of your choosing who has read the following critiquing guidelines:

- *There is only one coach.* Ideally this will be someone who will not attend the presentation. No one else is allowed to make comments, except on technical issues the coach doesn't understand. Having more than one critic is destructive.
- *The coach represents the prospect.* The presentation is made to her.
- *Everyone must rehearse.* No one is excused. You can't build a fluid presentation if some team members don't participate, and you can't build team morale. Each must try speaking as if this were the real presentation.
- *Everyone must actually rehearse.* General discussion of roles and subjects is planning, not rehearsing.
- *No one is allowed to rehearse or present from a written script.* If you do, you will look at it often. This breaks eye contact with the listener and creates the impression of lack of confidence. Write a script to get your thoughts in order, if it helps you. Then list the four or five major points, plus a statistic or two you might forget, on a five-by-seven card. That is all you should use when you speak.
- *If someone is having special difficulty, the coach should work with him alone.* The coach can work with him later to avoid taking the entire team's time.
- *Only criticism that can be acted on is allowed.* Saying that I am confusing or boring or cold does not help me, because I cannot act on it. I certainly am not being any of those things intentionally. Tell me what to do with my voice, my body, my hands. Tell me how to change the graphics I am using or how to shorten my anecdote. Tell me to increase my eye contact. Tell me to talk directly to you, using the word "you." Tell me to use simple language, avoiding professional argot. If you can't do these things, don't coach. If I can't act on what you say, it isn't coaching, it's complaining. Many people can coach, but it takes concentration.
- *The coach will not correct specific words unless they are objectionable to the prospect.* The goal is to obtain fluency with subject matter, not to memorize a speech. Presenters will use somewhat different words when they actually present. Now they are working on ideas, sequence, and delivery.
- *If the coach cannot answer the question, "Why is what the presenter saying important to me and my company?" she will stop the presenter.* And she will help him reformulate his words to make this clear. The audience always needs to know why it should be listening.
- *The coach will observe herself as a listener.* If her attention wanders, it is a sign that something is wrong with the presentation, not with her listening. The coach must figure out what is wrong and recommend a fix.

Unless she is experienced, the coach should read this chapter before the rehearsal so she will understand the large issues of what constitutes a good presentation.

Exhibit 17.2 provides a checklist the coach can use while rehearsing a presenter.

EXHIBIT 17.2 Coach's Checklist

Content

- ❏ Is it clear? (*Solutions:* Reword, reorder, state reason for listening, shorten, delete tangential content, avoid tangential language and argot)
- ❏ Is it concise? (*Solutions:* Fewer words, fewer subjects, fewer or shorter examples)
- ❏ Is it persuasive? (*Solutions:* Stress benefits, work on delivery, use anecdotes, provide proof)
- ❏ Does it engage me? (*Solutions:* Stress benefits, use "you" instead of "I"; customize it to prospect's situation, use anecdotes)

Delivery

- ❏ Posture (*Solutions:* Stand straight, don't rock, hands at sides, shoulders back, feet slightly apart)
- ❏ Gestures (*Solutions:* Sufficient movement at key points, clear and decisive)
- ❏ Eye contact (*Solutions:* Look at coach; don't look at notes or visuals or boss; if you must refer to notes or visuals, pause while you do so and begin to speak again when eye contact is reestablished)
- ❏ Volume (*Solution:* Use more resonance)
- ❏ Emotional impact (*Solution:* Work on subtexts)

During your presentation or after it, the prospect will want to talk. Actually, I prefer to seed the presentation with a few questions of my own to create a dialogue. These are often confirming questions or questions offering simple choices, which we can then follow up on. Dealing with the prospect's questions is the subject of the following chapter.

18 The Sales Meeting: Handling Questions and Concerns

Throughout the sales process, your prospect will ask questions. The way you deal with them will influence whether you get his business. He will use your answers not only to judge your capabilities and approach but also to decide what you would be like to work with.

Often the most satisfactory answer is given before a question is asked. Telling your mother that you won't be able to call her on Mother's Day because you will be traveling in Indonesia is better than answering the question, "Why didn't you call me?"

Michael Graves, the famous architect, beautifully preempted a critical question when he presented his credentials to design a college library. The selection committee had announced that it was most concerned about meeting schedules and budgets. Because famous designers are perceived as unconcerned with both, it was easy to predict that the committee would want to grill him in this area.

His opening words to the committee were, "During this presentation, I'm not going to say a word about either schedules or budgets!" This stunned the committee and grabbed its attention. He went on to describe a library he had designed at another college. As he completed his description his project manager jumped up and quoted the words on a sign she held: "Delivered on budget and two months ahead of schedule." Graves went on to describe another project, and another. Each time the project manager interjected the same kind of commentary. He won the job. The committee never asked about his ability to meet schedules and budgets.

Before any meeting with a client, and especially before a presentation, review your knowledge of the company, its issues, and the people you will be meeting with. What concerns about you are they most likely to have? Answer their questions before they come up, and your answers will be more persuasive. The more sensitive the issue, the more important it is for you to be the one to bring it up.

Chapter 15, with its emphasis on questioning and listening, tells you how to elicit a prospect's concerns. The foundation you have built by questioning and listening helps you preempt a prospect's questions later. Use this information before the questions start, and you will have less need for the rest of the guidance in this chapter. When a prospect does ask a question, do the following.

Determine why he is asking it.

Prospects ask questions for several reasons. Knowing the reasons will influence the way you answer. A question can be inspired by one or more of the following desires:

- **To gather information:** This is the most obvious reason, and sometimes it is the only one. If a prospect is confused or needs information you have not provided, he will ask a question.
- **To gain recognition:** A prospect can show how smart he is or regain attention from a speaker by asking a question. He may be seeking recognition from you or, more likely, from others in his company who are present.
- **To advance the conversation:** The prospect may have accepted or rejected what you have said to this point and wants to move the conversation ahead.
- **To express skepticism about what you are saying:** A question can be a polite way of saying, "I don't believe you."
- **To test you:** A question may be asked simply to see how you handle it.

Use some standard techniques for all questions.

There are three common techniques in responding to all of these five kinds of questions. First, if you don't understand a question or are uncertain about why it is being asked, ask the questioner to clarify it or to elaborate. Answering a question you don't understand can get you in trouble.

Second, encourage the questioner by acknowledging that his question is welcome. This can be done with a smile and a nod or with a brief statement that summarizes or amplifies it. Avoid the sophomoric habit of responding, "That's a good question," every time you are asked one. The objective is to make the prospect feel good about asking the questions and show that you welcome the dialogue. This will ensure that your response doesn't sound defensive. Defensiveness or the appearance of defensiveness can hurt you. Prospects prefer not to work with someone who will react defensively every time they are asked a question. The appearance of defensiveness now will lower your prospect's opinion of you. It may also deter him from asking further questions, and it is through his questions that you learn about concerns that could keep you from getting the job. You want him to ask questions.

During a presentation, you can encourage questions by asking one yourself. Say, "We are about to change subjects. Do you have any questions up to this point?"

Third, keep answers short. I have seen many professionals get themselves into trouble by giving long answers when short ones would have served. Long answers risk creating new concerns or boring the prospect. A prospect seldom wants a long answer. You will sound more confident and businesslike if you give a short one. Professionals violate this rule so often that it bears repeating: Keep answers short!

If your firm has several people at a meeting, avoid letting every person respond to every question. Prospects find this irritating. Let the senior person on your team direct each question to the single appropriate respondent.

Answer directly, concisely, and at the right time.

These questions seek information that the prospect clearly needs but that you haven't yet provided. "Can you meet with my boss next Monday?" "What kind of documentation do you provide?" "How many of our people will you interview?" All these questions probably express a sincere desire for information and can be answered directly in a few words.

Sometimes a prospect will seek information prematurely. The most obvious example of this is asking about your fee before a project's scope has been determined. Usually it is best to postpone answering such questions by saying, "I can't answer that quite yet. Let's talk a little more about your situation, and then I can tell you." If you do this, make a note of the unanswered question and answer it at the appropriate time. You will appear attentive to the prospect if you remember to deal with his postponed concern without being prompted.

Often it will be important to learn a prospect's reaction to your answer to an information question. After answering, ask the open question, "How does that seem to you?"

Answer with an appropriate level of recognition.

When someone seeks recognition, she often does so by disguising a statement as a question. Questions beginning with, "Don't you think that . . ." or "Isn't it true that . . ." are usually of this type. So are very smart questions asked in a way that calls attention to their smartness. The way the question is posed seems to beg the response, "Gee, that's a good question." Recognition questions are sometimes deliberately oblique, requiring you to ask the questioner what she means. That gives her the chance she seeks to speak. If someone asks, "Are you taking into account the Ishtabibbel factor?" count on its being a recognition question. Sometimes a client will pose a question in hopes that you will bounce it back to them. "What role does the head of human resources typically play in one of your projects?" asks the EVP for human resources. I would place a large bet that rather than an answer from you, he wants you to hear his views on the subject.

In a one-on-one meeting, you may want to explore the questioner's opinions for a time until you sense she is satisfied with your recognition of her knowledge. In a larger meeting, unless the senior representative of the prospect team is seeking recognition, keep the response short and move on. A simple "Yes I can see you've dealt with this kind of issue before" is probably sufficient.

It becomes more awkward when you disagree with the statement disguised as a question. When this occurs, the questioner has unintentionally asked a test question, because others present will judge your tact, honesty, and ability to deal with difficult situations by how you answer. Before answering, ask yourself whether you really understand the question. If not, ask for clarification. When you respond, use non-argumentative language. Rather than disagreeing yourself, provide evidence based on the experience of others. "That may be true, but many companies have found that . . ." takes the onus of disagreeing off you and allows the questioner to back down gracefully.

Establish why a prospect is advancing the conversation.

When a prospect asks an advancing question, he is deliberately shifting the conversation to the next subject. Information questions can have the same effect, but they do not have the same intent. The two types can be distinguished by timing. Prospects usually ask advancing questions after a subject has been discussed. These questions could logically be preceded by, "Now that I understand that subject, let's move on to the next one." An information question that could advance a conversation comes earlier in a discussion and is, in effect, an aside, which could be introduced with "By the way . . ."

An advancing question signals that the prospect is ready to move on. Sometimes this is favorable ("How soon can you start?" and other words we like to hear), but don't assume so unless it is obvious. Questions that change the subject may mean that the prospect has decided he doesn't want to hire you and wants to get the conversation over with. If the advancing question is other than an obvious buying signal, establish the stage of the sale before answering it. Use an open question like, "Yes, we need to talk about timing next, but before we leave this subject, what is your sense of how our service responds to your situation?" If he raises a concern, explore it fully with follow-up questions before responding. A hasty, inappropriate response will simply increase his resistance.

If the reaction is favorable, move on to the next subject.

Supply proof.

No salesperson, even if he is a professional, is totally disinterested; when it comes right down to it, he wants to get hired. Prospects know this and will sometimes use questions to show their skepticism about what you are saying. When a prospect asks a senior professional, "How much will you, yourself, actually work on this project?" she may be seeking information. More likely she suspects a bait-and-switch, with the senior professional being replaced by a junior once the firm is hired.

You can best answer skeptical questions by offering proof. You might ask, "If the president of the firm sent you a letter committing 30 percent of my time to your account, would that make you feel more comfortable?" You might acknowledge her reasons for feeling skeptical—"Yes, I know everyone promises you he'll give you his personal attention; I can understand why you ask"—and then offer to provide her with references who can testify to the level of attention you give. Each time you are asked such a question, ask yourself what evidence you could provide that would prove the claim being questioned. Here are your choices:

- **Statistics:** These are useful when past performance is quantifiable.
- **Testimony:** A good reference from a past client can reassure a prospect on subjective issues. Sometimes you can use a testimonial letter, but a direct conversation between the prospect and the past client is more convincing.
- **Documents:** Examples of deliverables and documentation of methodologies can help dispel concerns about what a client is going to get and how it is going to be provided.
- **Assurances and certifications:** These help address skepticism about commitment or credentials. To say, "If you are concerned about that, I would be happy to include a commitment to it in our contract," is usually compelling. The strongest assurance is some form of guarantee.
- **An anecdote:** Sometimes an anecdote that shows how you handled a previous client's concern can reduce skepticism. This is especially true if the prospect is expressing skepticism about you or a member of your team, that is, if she is concerned about one of the attributes listed in Exhibit 17.1.

Answer after figuring out the test.

Many years ago, I made a presentation to the senior management of a defense supplier. I had had five previous meetings at the company and had been told bluntly that I had to be vetted before I would be allowed to present to the president, whom everyone feared. Now I had the chance to present to him while all his understrappers watched.

Three-quarters of the way through my presentation, he said, "What you're suggesting is going to cost a lot of money. Why should we spend so much? I think we should . . ." He then suggested a childish solution that would have eliminated the need for my services. I had the flu, I had had four hours' sleep the night before and driven three hours to get to the meeting. All my work to sell the engagement was about to go down the drain. I reflected for a moment and realized his words were a challenge. As kindly as I could I said, "Frankly, I think you're being naive, if you think that will work." No one spoke. All the understrappers looked up at the ceiling or down at their notes. I waited for a reaction. The boss smiled at me and said, "I think we should get started" and left the room. I had been approved, and I never had a moment's difficulty with this man again. He had wanted to know if I would stand up to him and give him honest advice, and I had proved I would.

Any professional who has sold for years has stories analogous to this one.

Prospects often ask professionals test questions, though the context is usually less dramatic than in the preceding story. If you buy a copier, you test it for resolution, speed, and ease of use. When you test-drive a car, you floor it to see how it accelerates, take a few turns, and try the brakes. You test a professional with questions.

You can recognize a test question because it does the following:

- **Challenges you personally:** This is a test of your personal honesty, tact, courage, objectivity, creativity, or other personal characteristics listed in Exhibit 17.1. It has nothing to do with your firm or features of your services, although it may be disguised to appear as if it does.
- **Feels more like a test than other questions:** You will sense that there are right and wrong answers already framed in the questioner's mind.
- **Comes as a surprise:** A test question does not fit with the favorable tone of preceding conversations. This occurs when the prospect decides to test a favorable opinion of you. He has suddenly become concerned that you may be just a good salesperson.

A prospect will seldom tell you what you are being tested on, so figuring it out is part of the test. Exhibit 18.1 presents several test questions prospects have asked me. Suggest reasons why a prospect might ask them and then, with a specific prospect in mind, try to answer them.

EXHIBIT 18.1 Sample Test Questions

These are all questions prospects have asked. Why did they ask them? How would you respond?

A. Why is this engagement important to you personally?
B. What can you tell me about yourself that is personal and that no one else knows?
C. What is the quickest way to get this sheet of paper out the door?
D. Why not just do it this way?
E. Now that you've talked to all my people, what have you learned about me?

Reasons for test questions:

A. To determine motivation and, therefore, commitment to engagement. To determine whether it would get personal attention.
B. To determine willingness to work closely with prospect and be open with him. Willingness to commit to him, personally, and not just his company.
C. To test creativity. (The fastest way was to wad up the sheet and throw it.)
D. To determine savvy and tact.
E. To test courage, tact, and honesty.

Test questions require that you provide a proof. The proof may be in the way you answer, as in the preceding example. It may be an anecdote that reveals somzething about you. It may be a reference who will testify to your personal attributes.

Position any reference you give.

References testify that you are as good as you say you are. Because they are perceived as more objective than you are, what they say will weigh heavily. Of course, you want to select your references carefully, but you want to do more than that.

Call each reference and ask permission to use his name. First, this is common courtesy and warns the reference that a call is coming. Second, most people will feel a stronger obligation to take the call and respond favorably if they have agreed with you directly to provide one. Third, it gives you a chance to prime the reference for probable questions. If you say, "I think they are likely to be concerned about our ability to work in a fragmented organization and achieve consensus. I'd like to give your name as a reference because there were aspects of that in our work for you," the reference is likely to volunteer information about this particular ability before being asked. At least he will be more prepared for the question when it comes. His remarks will be more persuasive.

Reconfirm your responses in writing after the meeting.

After any meeting with a prospect, it is courteous to send a note to show you are interested in his business. Follow-up e-mails are a good way to acknowledge major concerns again and reiterate your response. This is particularly true when you want to give an assurance or offer an additional proof.

Follow up by phone to confirm resolution of concerns.

A follow-up call after a meeting provides an informal opportunity to determine how successful you have been at responding to a prospect's concerns. If you say, "There were some questions about our ability to meet your schedule. Do you feel everyone is satisfied that we can?" the answer will help you decide whether you need to provide more evidence.

You should also ask a few open questions to make sure that no new concerns have come up. "What other questions came up after we left?" is a good one to start with.

Team Selling

The most profitable business is usually for work that addresses a client's most difficult issues. Often that difficulty results from complexity, size, and urgency, and addressing issues with these characteristics requires a team. Most rainmakers, then, must sell in teams. Of course the material on selling in the preceding five chapters is also relevant to selling in teams. If you haven't read them yet, you should do so now.

Selling in teams is more complicated than selling alone. Too often, planning is limited to a few short minutes on the way to the client site. The team members aren't coordinated, coming to the sales meeting without clear roles and responsibilities. As a result, they trip over each other in the meeting. Alternatively, one team member dominates the discussion, reducing the value of having a team. And that person isn't always the most effective salesperson in the group, though he often thinks he is. These problems sometimes tempt a professional to make the sale alone.

Yet when the members are skilled, a good team can outsell an individual any day. The client's problem is big and complex, and he derives comfort from knowing the key members of the team he is hiring to fix it. Specialists can address specific concerns the client raises that one generalist cannot. By differentiating roles, team members can reinforce the message that the firm brings breadth and depth to the client's problem.

In these circumstances, the ability to rapidly assemble a team that sells effectively provides a competitive advantage. Here are questions team members should be able to answer to sell effectively together.

Does your firm or practice have a shared approach to handling sales meetings?

If you have a shared approach, planning a meeting becomes much easier and less time consuming. If everyone knows, for example, that there will be an agenda-setting statement at the beginning of the meeting, they can immediately focus on what it should be and who should say it. The team can talk about the questions it needs answers to and who will ask them. The most effective teams share an understanding of how a sales meeting should be run.

Who owns the pursuit?

When the client's problem is complex, there will often be several meetings with different people in the client organization before a sale is made. In such cases, a sale becomes a formal pursuit, and someone must own it. The owner decides what gets done and by whom. She decides what meetings to ask for and who gets to go. She decides who gets to be on the team and what role each one is to play in the pursuit.

Some owners have a collaborative style, while others are more directive. Usually the owner is a senior member of the firm. But this role can also be held by someone more junior with delegated authority and responsibility. The owner can change during the pursuit, but someone must own this role at all times.

Obvious candidates for the position include the person who generated the lead in the first place, someone with knowledge of and responsibility for an account, or the senior person in a practice.

Note that I am not saying that someone owns a relationship or a client. No, just the pursuit.

Are sales meetings planned and rehearsed?

For the team to work effectively together, it must plan and rehearse. The pursuit owner should schedule and invite people to these meetings, and the team members should feel obliged to attend. Missing a planning session should be viewed as a serious breach of commitment. Anyone who consistently misses planning sessions should be disbarred from future sales efforts. (I know, I know . . . but they should be. They should at least get a firm talking to by the boss.) It is especially important for senior professionals to set an example for younger ones by participating enthusiastically in rehearsals. At the planning meeting, roles and responsibilities should be allocated, and the members should rehearse what they will do at the sales meeting.

There is always someone who balks at having to rehearse in front of colleagues. Here are some common reasons given for not rehearsing and appropriate responses:

- *I don't do well in rehearsals because they aren't realistic.* No one does as well in a rehearsal as he does in front of the client, so you won't be alone in that. But by rehearsing we do better when we are in front of the client than we would otherwise.

- *I don't need it.* Maybe not, but some of your team members do, and we must work together. Other team members will do better if they have a clear understanding of what you are going to say because they can adjust their comments accordingly. Hearing you actually say it is far more effective than hearing you talk generally about what you are going to say. We need you to support the team.
- *I feel it's demeaning.* We certainly don't mean it to be. We view it as one aspect of being a professional. How would you feel about a professional athlete who refused to go to practice or a professional actor who refused to rehearse?

If you are presenting as a team, you must rehearse as a team. Each team member needs to hear what the others will say so that content can be coordinated. For presentation coaching guidelines, see Chapter 17.

Does everyone know his role and its responsibilities?

Everyone who attends a sales meeting has a role, and with that role come responsibilities. They should be clear to all team members. Common roles include these:

- **The godfather:** This is a senior person who will not be involved with the actual work but who is there to show the importance of the matter to the firm and to commit the resources of the firm to the client. Unless this role is combined with others, the godfather usually makes a brief opening statement in which he commits the firm, compliments the team, and introduces the client partner. He then maintains a low profile during the rest of the meeting. He should make it clear to the most senior person on the client team that he wants to be called, if he is ever needed.
- **The client partner or project partner:** This person has overall responsibility for the work to be done. It is imperative that she look in control, so she runs the meeting, introducing other team members, asking questions, and presenting the firm's approach. With the client, she decides when to move from getting information to giving it. No one else has the authority to offer a solution until she does. If the client asks a question, the client partner either answers it or hands it off to someone else. At the end of the meeting, she asks for the advance.
- **Day-to-day lead:** This person has day-to-day responsibility for the work and will spend a lot of time with the client if the firm is hired. This person should ask good questions about client resources and logistics, especially of his counterpart on the client team.

- **Specialist:** Specialists are there to ask and answer questions in their area of knowledge. If called upon, they must demonstrate deep knowledge of the subject they specialize in.
- **Monitor:** Monitors observe the clients while the clients are talking with or listening to other team members to pick up signals that those speaking to the client may miss. Monitors have the right to interrupt the flow of the meeting, based on such an observation: "Mike, you seemed uncomfortable with that, correct?" or "Mary, it looked as if you had something you wanted to say on this matter." They must exercise this right judiciously and infrequently. Everyone who is not speaking, regardless of what other roles he has, has the responsibility of monitoring. One particularly astute team member who is not expected to do a lot of talking should be assigned this role.

Do all particpants know where they are supposed to sit?

The general rule is for like to sit next to (or across from) like. The client partner should sit across from her counterpart in the client organization, as should the day-to-day lead and the specialists sit across from their counterparts. Before the meeting, during any breaks, and after the formal discussion is over, they should try to establish a personal link with their counterparts.

Other considerations might override this general rule. If your team is comprised of representatives from several firms, as is common with architectural and engineering firms, for example, don't let the representatives of the different firms sit at opposite ends of the table. Look like a team! Make sure that the lead members of the most important organizations sit near each other.

Is responsibility for follow-up clear?

After a sales meeting, each person who attended should be assigned responsibility for follow-up. At the very least, each should send an e-mail to his or her counterpart in the client organization. Of course, these team members should report back any information they get from the clients to the person who owns the pursuit.

Is progress reported back to all team members?

If you want your colleagues to act like a team, you must treat them as one. As the pursuit develops, the pursuit owner needs to brief team members from time to time on what is happening. Yes, I know, this takes precious time. How much more convenient it would be if people could act like team members when you need them to and then lose interest until you need them again on another pursuit. But they won't. You want others to advise you on anything of substance they learn about the clients or the specific pursuit. You owe them the courtesy of providing updates. The extra work will pay off as teams get stronger and stronger with experience.

20 Shortening the Sales Cycle

Selling takes time, and you have only so much time to give, even to selling. It stands to reason that one way to sell more work is to shorten your sales cycle, thereby freeing up hours to sell additional engagements. If, on average, you can covert a lead into a paid assignment in a month, but it takes me six weeks to do the same, at the end of the year you will have sold half again more engagements than I have. Rainmakers know how to shorten the sales cycle.

The rainmakers we interviewed focused on urgent issues where the client wanted to move quickly. As one rainmaker put it to me, every company has three to five critical issues that its people focus on. These issues are driven by the board and the CEO, and everyone owns a piece of them. If you are dealing with one of these issues, you are helping; if you are dealing with anything else, you're selling. Sales cycles tend to be shorter when dealing with one of these core issues. If a rainmaker is unable to link a client's problem to a core issue, she moves on to another issue or to another client.

Chapter 16 demonstrates the importance of linking to a high-level need. This is another reason why you should start your presentation of your services by linking them to a high-level need: It keeps the client focused on the urgency of finding a solution.

Rainmakers are good at keeping the client focused on that urgency and using it to drive the sale to a rapid close. They seek to conclude each conversation with an agreement with the client on a next step that moves the sale closer to closure. They use language like the following:

- There's a lot at stake here, right? And you agree that the next step is to bring your team together with the head of our M&A practice? Good. What can we do to clear people's calendars to make this happen quickly?
- Given what you've said about the importance of this matter, can we afford to wait more than two weeks before we meet again?

- If I might suggest, is it all right if I stop by your secretary's desk on the way out and see if we can work it into your schedule?

Rainmakers are deliberate about how they keep a sale moving. But remember, just because an issue seems important to you doesn't mean that it seems so to the client. A management consultant was once frustrated by his inability to close on a project that would save his client $40 million. He finally asked the client why he wouldn't want to save that much money. The response was simple: "I would, but I have three other initiatives, each of which could save in excess of $200 million, that I am trying to keep our people focused on. We haven't got time for this issue right now."

Rainmakers also resist getting passed down by a senior buyer to someone more junior. Enthusiasm for a project often wanes as you move down an organization from the senior buyer who wants something done. If a senior buyer tries to pass you down to a direct report, resist it by saying something like this.

Could I make a suggestion? This is obviously an issue of importance to you and your company, and it is in both our interests to make sure that nothing gets in the way of getting it resolved. When a senior person asks a direct report to see us, it can sometimes be perceived as undesirable. If the referral is seen as dissatisfaction with what the direct report is doing, our participation will be seen as threatening and that will get in the way of making something happen. I suggest that you host the meeting with Bill and say specifically why you are doing so. That shows your commitment to taking action, which it would be inappropriate for us to express. After that, we can continue the meeting on our own with Bill, if that is what you want. In our experience this approach is most likely to make sure that no one gets distracted from the main issue.

Still, there are times when a client's interest in hiring you for a project seems to stagnate. Here are some things you can do to deal with such a situation:

1. *Determine why interest has flagged.* It is easier to deal with most problems if you know their causes. Ask a friend within the client organization what is happening. Is the client simply distracted by other important issues? Is someone resisting buying your services? If so, who? Is there another issue that must be resolved first? Has a competitor unexpectedly entered the picture? Have the buyers changed at the client company?
2. *Get in front of the buyer.* Unless you talk to the buyer, preferably face-to-face, you will be able to neither get better information nor advance the

sale. If the buyer is distracted by other pressing issues, sometimes just getting face-to-face is enough to help him or her focus on the problem you are interested in. A decision sometimes follows. Good things happen when you spend time with clients. But remember, the reason you use to get face-to-face may have nothing to do with the project you want to discuss. That may have to come up as an aside. You need a reason for a meeting that is urgent enough to make it happen, or you must somehow place yourself in the client's path so that you meet accidentally.

A Hartford-based professional was frustrated by his inability to get a New Jersey-based client to authorize Phase 2 of his work. Though the issue was important, it wasn't as urgent as other things the client was dealing with. Phone calls from the professional went unreturned. Finally, he left a message for the client saying that he would be in New Jersey the following week on other business and asking the client to join him for lunch. Over lunch the client focused long enough on the professional's project to authorize the next phase. Sometimes it just takes getting in front of the client.

3. *Help the client understand the consequences of not acting now.* Ask questions that draw out the consequences of not acting fast. Will problems increase or opportunities be missed? Both the client and you need the answer to this question. If the consequences are great enough, the client's urgency to buy will increase. If they are small, you will understand why you have to be patient.

4. *Determine if you are meeting with the right buyer.* Sometimes buying decisions are delayed because you haven't spent time with the real buyers. If not, you had better get to them. Ask a friend in the client organization who the real decision makers are.

5. *Determine if you have missed a buyer.* If you miss talking to a buyer, that can cause delays in approvals. Read The New Strategic Selling, by Stephen Heiman and Diane Sanchez,[1] for guidance on identifying and categorizing buyers.

6. *Test the client's level of commitment to you.* Test the client's level of commitment by asking for something, such as a meeting with the boss or access to information or something related to the project that will require the client to extend himself. The buyer's level of interest in you can be measured by his willingness to extend himself for you.

7. *See if you can identify a small service to sell now.* Sometimes a client is unready to undertake a large assignment now but will authorize a small one that takes a step toward a solution and provides immediate value. See if you can cut out a piece of your proposed work that meets these criteria and sell it now. Once it is completed, it may be easier to sell the total solution.

A professional firm was talking with the head of human resources at a large automotive company. The client kept talking around the issue but was unwilling to authorize the firm to go ahead with the work. He finally revealed that the president of the company had told him that he was to sell the idea of doing the work to the board at a meeting two weeks away. The HR manager was afraid of embarrassing himself in front of this audience. One of the firm members offered to help prepare the presentation for the board for a small fee, and the client gratefully accepted. The presentation was a success, and the full assignment was authorized shortly thereafter.

Rainmakers know that the longer it takes a client to authorize an assignment, the more time there is for something to go wrong. They move the sale along as quickly as they can.

But sometimes there is nothing you can do to increase urgency. In that case, be patient and stay on top of the opportunity: The client may just need more time to make a decision.

And pursue additional opportunities. You will be more patient with each opportunity if you are pursuing enough so that there is a reasonable probability that one will come in soon, even if others don't. One common reason that a professional can become frustrated with a client's delay in closing is having too many eggs in one basket. This is particularly common among young professionals or professionals just starting their own practices. Almost inevitably, they go through a phase where success or failure seems to hinge on whether one assignment closes. If you are in this situation, remember that this is a normal part of your development and you must push through it by developing a portfolio of opportunities.

Writing a Proposal

When discussions get serious, your prospect will usually want you to submit a written proposal. He may want one for any of several reasons:

- **Clarity:** A written proposal helps clarify his thinking about his needs and how to meet them. A proposal that does this adds real value.
- **Validation:** A proposal provides him with a way to validate your understanding of his issues, your credentials for dealing with them, your approach to dealing with them, and your terms.
- **Formality:** A written proposal formalizes the commitment. The proposal helps sort out marketing hyperbole from fact and commitment. The prospect realizes that most people are more cautious about what they put in writing than about what they say. He can refer to it later if there are any disagreements about staffing, scope, deliverables, timing, or fees.
- **Confirmation:** A proposal shows he has been diligent in his selection. It gives him something to show to others interested in the selection of a professional to confirm what you will do and that you are the right one to do it.
- **Responsiveness:** Your ability to prepare a written proposal tests your responsiveness. This is especially true if you have little time in which to prepare it.
- **Comparison:** A written proposal makes it easier for the buyer to compare professionals competing for his business.

The weight a buyer places on a proposal when he makes a choice can vary from heavy to almost none. You must always assume the former. Make it work for you by doing the following.

Offer to prepare a proposal when you think it will advance the sale.

An agreement to accept a proposal signals a prospect's increased seriousness about retaining you. It implies either that he has gone beyond general discussion to a point where he may be able to make a decision or that he is now willing to submit the proposal to someone else for a decision. If you sense you are getting to such a point, offer to prepare a proposal. If the prospect accepts, it shows that you have read the situation correctly.

If he declines, you have misread him and must figure out how close to hiring you he really is. Try a broad probe, such as, "Your description of the need seems quite compelling, but something is holding you back. Can you share your thinking with us?"

A proposal may also be a way to help the prospect clarify his thinking. I recently used a proposal this way with the head of a consulting firm. We had talked three times about the sales training needs of the firm's partners. He could not clearly state what he wanted, and every suggestion I made ran into obstacles. He seemed to like me and to want to hire me, but he couldn't figure out exactly what he wanted me to do. To advance the discussion, I sent an unsolicited proposal, suggesting that it might give him something to react to that would clarify the problem. It did. Based on the discussion that followed, I sent a substantially revised proposal and was hired.

There is a risk; the prospect may use your proposal as a basis for a formal request for proposals (RFP) sent to several firms. I usually take that risk, believing that if I really help the prospect do his job by helping him clarify his thinking, he will remember me later. Usually I am right. When wrong, I forget about it and move on to the next prospect.

A proposal is primarily a marketing document.

Yes, a proposal can have legal implications, especially if it doubles as a contract. You should be careful to avoid words that imply an unachievable standard of performance, such as saying that you will find the best solution or that you will ensure that something happens. Also avoid words and phrases with a different legal meaning from their common usage, such as "Time is of the essence." Consult a lawyer for details. You should be careful not to promise services that you can't or won't deliver. But you must not let legal considerations blind you to a proposal's fundamental objective: selling your services.

A proposal also has operational and financial implications. Often, preparing a proposal helps the professional think through exactly what he is going to do when he gets hired and how he will make money at it. Do not confuse this benefit to you with what you want a client to get from your proposal. When you actually write the proposal, much of the information you prepare to get you to that point should probably not appear in it.

Lack of clarity about goals is the single biggest reason for weak proposals. Remember that what you want it to do is sell your services.

Treat a proposal as part of a larger marketing effort.

You have worked to gather information on the client's need. Review what you have learned prior to preparing the proposal in order to refresh your memory on details and nuances. If your knowledge has important gaps, try to fill them before you start on the proposal. The need to put your thoughts in writing often helps you recognize information gaps and provides a legitimate reason for calling your prospect to ask additional questions.

You have also worked hard to deliver specific messages to a prospect, messages you will want to reinforce in the proposal.

Decide what image you want the proposal to project.

Should the proposal give the impression that it is simply formalizing an agreement arrived at with a handshake? Should it suggest that you want this project more than a dozen other competitors do? That you are creative? That you are reliable? Its form and appearance will convey these messages. Based on the circumstances of each sale, you need to decide what image you wish to project and build it into your proposal.

If the proposal is really just a formality, make it look like one. Keep it short. Consider a letter format. A major competition, on the other hand, demands something more elaborate. The choice of covers can make you look creative or reliable, expensive or economical. Choose carefully to match the image you want to project.

Desktop publishing technology makes it easy to customize proposals. If you have a scanner, consider using the client's logo on the title page. Design-oriented professions, in particular, have the freedom and resources to prepare covers and dividers with images that relate to the prospect.

Focus on benefits.

Many professionals view the description of the work they will do as the core of a proposal, the real reason for its existence. But prospects don't hire you because of the task you are going to perform; they hire you for the benefits they expect to receive. Your description of the work you will do is only there as a proof—one of several proofs—that you will deliver benefits. Think of why people buy a specific car. They want reliable transportation, comfort, image, and many others things. Engines, interiors, color, and a vast array of other features are but means to acquire these benefits. It is the same with professional services.

Decide what services you should offer.

In many cases, you have some discretion in deciding how large a project and how full a range of services to offer. At one extreme, you can offer only those that meet the prospect's most immediate need while mentioning that you can also help with later needs. The other is to offer a full-service package immediately. The choice you make between these two extremes or some compromise between them depends, in part, on the signals you have received from the prospect about his propensity to spend. (See Chapter 22 for more information on fees.) It also depends on the probability that the prospect well require the full range of services. If initial work might help the buyer decide that no further action is needed, the impression that you will provide this work objectively will be enhanced by a proposal that asks the prospect to commit only to the first portion. A small project can help the prospect get to know you without making a large commitment.

Amplify on your theme and the benefits you will provide.

The standard parts of a proposal are only vehicles for you to show the benefits you are going to deliver and to differentiate yourself from your competitors. Each must fulfill these functions.

Cover letter

The cover letter should introduce your central theme and delineate the major benefits you will provide. It should not run more than a page and a half; a single page is better. This is the place to thank members of the prospect's team who have helped you gather information needed to put the proposal together. If you are submitting a letter proposal, cover these points in the first paragraph.

Executive summary

If the proposal is twenty pages or more, you may wish to add an executive summary, focusing on the prospect's core objectives, the benefits you will provide, your primary credentials for providing them, and the major features of your services. Executives focus on core objectives and high-level benefits more than anyone else.

Project understanding

Variously called the "The Issue," "The Statement of the Problem," and "Background on the Problem," among other names, this section shows that you understand what benefits the prospect needs and why. Whenever possible, start with a statement that defines a high-level corporate objective. ("Allington China seeks to become the low-cost producer in its industry.") Then tie the need you will be addressing to the higher, corporate one. ("As a part of this effort, the distribution department seeks to lower its total operating costs by 15 percent.") This can be followed by a description of specific opportunities to meet that need. (In the example given, this might include references to reduced inventories, more efficient material handling, or improved shipping logistics.) At the end of the section, state that you propose to help solve the problems that you described. ("Crosbie Consulting proposes to conduct the analyses required to help the distribution department reduce its costs by 15 percent.")

Background on your firm and engagement team

This section should prove that you have the credentials to do what you promise. If you have already delivered these credentials in a presentation or some other way, you may choose to keep it brief, but don't eliminate it completely. Provide proof of the following:

- **Your reliability:** You are not a fly-by-night organization. The firm or its staff knows the business because they have been at it for a long time.
- **Your relevant experience:** This is a good place to summarize relevant past experience with short client lists and one or two descriptions (one to three sentences each) of past projects. Refer the reader to an appendix for greater detail. If this section gets too long, the reader will lose the thread of your argument.
- **Your expert's credentials:** A concise summary of honors received, publications, or other relevant expert's credentials may also be appropriate here. Place detailed resumes, if they are needed, in an appendix.

Project outline

This section proves you have an approach that will deliver the promised benefits. In it, you commit to certain work and ask the client to commit time and other resources. It should only be detailed enough to make the prospect feel confident that you will do the job. The level of detail required varies among buyers. The more technically oriented the buyer, the more detail he is likely to want to see. This is analogous to a contractor who wants more detail on the construction of a house he may buy than others might.

Make an effort to tie each major task described in this section to the benefits the client is seeking. When you begin to describe any information gathering you must do, tell the prospect how this will produce a benefit. If developing a consensus is important to him, mention that information gathering is the first step in developing consensus because it involves everyone in the process early. If the nature of the problems the client faces is not fully understood at the time the proposal is written, say that this stage will help ensure that you solve the right problem.

Each task will cost the prospect money; tell him how each one will provide him value. Doing this will differentiate you from the majority of your competitors. The less experienced he is with buying your services, the more clearly he needs to be told. Exhibit 20.1 lists some common elements of a professional project outline. With a specific prospect in mind, see whether you can describe the benefit he will receive from each.

EXHIBIT 20.1 Relating Proposal Elements to Benefits

The column on the left lists elements common to proposals of many professionals, though the precise name of elements varies among the professions. In the column on the right, list primary benefit(s) that a specific prospect will receive from each element. Note that on some engagements there are multiples of some elements (e.g. Analysis, Interim meeting, etc.).

Element	Benefit to Prospect
1. Information gathering A. Internal to client B. External to client	
2. Analysis	
3. Generation of alternative solutions	
4. Interim meetings	
5. Documentation	
6. Recommendations	
7. Final meeting	

Make sure to note key events, such as major review meetings, in this portion of the proposal.

Deliverables

Somewhere within the proposal you need to summarize specifically what the client is going to receive from you by the end of the engagement, or, if this will be an ongoing service, at designated times. This can be incorporated within the project outline, or you can compose a separate section. Examples of deliverables include presentations, reports, analyses, findings, recommendations, plans, and documentation of many sorts. This is a good place to summarize the overall value you are providing.

Assurances

Make clear that you will comply with any legal or other concerns noted by the prospect, which might include demonstrating that you have an affirmative action plan or that you will hold information provided to you in confidence.

Timing

The prospect needs to know how long the work will take and when key events will occur. If he is in a hurry, be sure to show that you are especially qualified to do the work quickly.

Fees

The prospect will want to know what the work will cost. You should quote fees clearly and concisely, avoiding any appearance of evasion. Prospects are extremely sensitive about professionals who promise one fee up front and ask for a larger one later. An unclear fee quote will create the impression that you may do this. See Chapter 22 for suggestions on how to construct a fee quote.

Authorization

At the end, the proposal should state clearly what the prospect needs to do to authorize your work. This can be done by signing a copy of the proposal so that it becomes a contract and returning it to you, requesting a formal contract, issuing a purchase order, paying a retainer, or sending a separate letter of authorization.

Appendices

Use appendices for any information that is so lengthy it might distract from the major thrust of your proposal's argument. An appendix is also a good place to put any information the prospect wants but is unlikely to read in detail. Full resumes of team members, detailed project descriptions, and proofs of the firm's financial stability are all good candidates for appendices.

Use simple language.

The proposal should be easy to read. This means you must use simple language and comply with the rules of usage, grammar, and style. If you have concerns about your English composition skills, ask someone else to edit your draft. Review Strunk and White's Elements of Style (see appendix for reference) once a year. If you do what this small book recommends, the quality of your proposals will improve.

Make it visually appealing.

A proposal cannot sell for you if no one reads it. The easier it is to look at, the more of it people will read. Make it visually appealing. This means your proposal should have the following:

- **An attractive cover:** First impressions count. An attractive cover will induce a prospect to look inside.
- **A logical layout that is easy to follow:** Clearly mark transitions in subject with headers. If the proposal is over five pages, include a table of contents.
- **An easy-to-read format:** Avoid large blocks of text. Keep paragraphs short, generally five sentences or less. Use bullets periodically; they provide relief from standard paragraphs and engage the eye. Leave ample margins.
- **Brevity:** Keep it short. A short proposal is less intimidating than a long one. You can relegate back-up material, the kind of material a prospect is likely to leaf through anyway, to an appendix. Short is relative. Some clients or projects require large proposals. Yours should be shorter than the average submittal, whatever its length.

You may choose to disregard this suggestion if technically oriented buyers will have a primary role in reviewing your proposal. Such people often decide who to recommend on the basis of detailed specifications that require longer submittals.

- **Graphics:** Architects, interior designers, consulting engineers, and others in the built-environment industry use pictures of their work to interest readers. Most professionals can use diagrams, charts, tables, and other graphics to illustrate aspects of their proposals. Readers like it when you do. If you do not currently use graphics in your proposals and your proposals are more than three pages long, spend half an hour brainstorming about what you could include. Consider Gantt charts, flow diagrams, organizational diagrams, maps, and sample deliverables.

Folow the requested format.

Some prospects send RFPs that ask for information in a specific sequence or format. In such cases, comply with the request. If you don't, you will appear unresponsive. You will also offend the author of the RFP, who is likely to pre-screen proposals before others see them, and you will make it difficult for a review committee to compare your proposal to others, which will annoy them. Most proposals that ignore requested formats lose projects.

Occasionally an RFP format will be so ill-constructed that you will find it difficult to follow the requested format without huge redundancies or confusion. If you must violate the format, stick as closely to it as you can and make it clear that you are doing so. For example, after a heading you might note, "This section answers questions 4, 5, and 11b of your RFP."

Customize boilerplate material.

Most proposals incorporate boilerplate. There is seldom sufficient time to write everything from scratch, and content requested by different prospects tends to be repetitive. Use existing materials, but be sure to take the trouble to customize them each time. You must edit resumes to ensure that the most relevant experience is listed first and that material irrelevant to your prospect is deleted. Project descriptions often need recasting to emphasize their relevancy to a particular prospect. Often this can be done efficiently by including the heading "Project Relevance," after which you list key similarities with the prospect's situation or key benefits you provided.

You must discipline yourself to make substantial changes, too. When rushed, you will be tempted to use an old work outline that almost but doesn't quite fit this prospect's situation. This often results in a weakly developed case for why you should be hired. Use the old material to help you plan your project outline, then rewrite it completely for the prospect you are pursuing now.

Hand-deliver your proposal.

Delivering your proposal by hand accomplishes several things. First, it shows the project is important to you. Second, it provides you with another chance to talk with the prospect about his needs. Third, it may give you a chance to present the proposal. A few professionals refuse to deliver proposals any other way. If you can't deliver your proposal in person, follow up by phone to make sure it was received.

Quoting a Fee

You must get paid for your work or you will soon have to find some other way to make a living. Not only must you get paid, you must get paid enough. The economics of a professional practice are so simple they can be reduced to the following formula:

$P = (H$ times B times $R)$ minus C

Where:
H = total hours available
B = percent of those hours that are billable
R = hourly rate
C = costs

If you want more money, you can lower your costs, increase the percentage of your time spent on paid work, or increase your rate. You can also work more hours in a day, provided that you can get paid for some of the additional time. Most of this book focuses on keeping the percentage of your time that is billable high. First, it shows how to get billable work; second, it shows how to get that work efficiently, so that you spend as little time as possible on non-billable marketing. This chapter focuses on your pricing, which determines your hourly rate.

We all want to increase our prices. With higher prices, for the same hours worked, you earn more money. Surely, it's the most desirable way to increase your firm's income. But you are likely to find pricing the most persistently difficult part of selling. Professionals with years of successful selling behind them continue to struggle with pricing. From one direction they are pushed by prospects to get prices down, and from the other they are pushed by their cost structure to get prices up. If you have spent most of your career managing projects to a budget and have suffered through a few that have been under-priced, you are likely to focus on a cost-plus-profit approach. Many professionals do this; many lose sales because they do.

Another group of professionals become so enamored of winning a job that they lose sight of their costs. There is an old joke about an architect who inherited a million dollars. When a friend asked him what he was going to do with it, he responded, "Keep practicing until it's used up." Few of us have a million dollars to spend this way.

The following principles about pricing will help you determine the best approach for your practice.

Your flexibility in setting a price is determined long before you quote a fee.

Pricing starts when you select a profession and a specialty, when you select a market, and when you select a strategy for pursuing that market. Some but not all of this is now beyond your control. You may still have the freedom to define a specialty, shift your market, and choose a new strategy. If you wait to receive an RFP before you think about pricing, your fees will be lower than if you address the issue early.

First, you can create a niche where competition is lower, permitting you to capture higher prices for a while. Apple Computer's creation of the desktop publishing market and later the iPod are two good examples of this. It also happens in the professions. I remember attending a breakout session of 300 people at a conference for strategic planners. George Stalk from Boston Consulting Group, a young man at the time, spoke on time-based competitive strategies. When he finished, at least three quarters of the audience rose and tried to get a private word with him at the podium. Time-based competition was a new concept, and BCG had a temporary corner on the market.

On a less dramatic scale, this kind of differentiation is possible in almost any profession. One New Jersey accountant, for example, developed a specialty in the valuations required for divorce settlements. You must think about your experiences and the needs of your market and look for opportunities to establish a niche.

Second, you can select a market that permits higher margins. Analyze your past projects to see which have been profitable and which have not, and focus your attentions on the profitable part of the market. This can be hard to do, especially if you are in a business in which you receive many unsolicited RFPs, as is true, say, for information systems consulting in the government market. An RFP looks attractive. The prospect has a need and almost certainly has a budget. But if you must compete with thirty to fifty other firms for the work, you had better have a strong reason to believe that you can win before you waste time and money responding. In such an environment, prices are sure to be low. Some of the most important choices you make in marketing concern what projects *not* to pursue. Chapter 23 provides more information on that topic.

Third, you can decide how you will take your services to the market. As I noted earlier in this book, one consulting firm grew over three years from $20 million in revenues to $100 million because it developed a new strategy for taking its business to the market. Defying accepted beliefs about what works and what doesn't, the company developed a cold-calling strategy that allowed it to bid without competition on large projects. Complementing or replacing your current strategy for going to the market can sometimes reap big dividends. Part IV of this book will help you determine what strategies might work for you.

Early discussion of needs often means a better fee.

Early knowledge of a need gives you the chance to learn more about the client, develop a relationship, and help him define a need. You may be able to presell him before the formal selling process begins. When this happens, you can sometimes get yourself sole-sourced for the project or at least be the favored contender in a competition. This usually translates into a higher fee.

I was reminded of this recently when I spoke with a consulting engineer who had been pursuing a university client for many months. Because it is a public institution, the university has to advertise formally for bids. When a project came along that my friend wanted, he wasn't worried about the competition that open bidding would create. "We'll get it," he assured me, "because we understand their problem better than anyone else. I know just what to put in our submittal to make us the right firm to do the work." His early relationship with the client allowed him to compete more on service than on fee.

An infrastructure engineering firm tracked its performance on winning what it called bottom-line-impacting projects (BLIPs). In one year, it won an impressive 60 percent of the BLIPs it went after. Analyzing the data further, management determined that the firm had won a staggering 80 percent of the BLIPs it had pursued for over a year. This is a powerful argument for getting in early.

Selling higher up often means a better fee.

The CEO will pay more for your services than a manager will. Both will pay more than a purchasing agent. Many professionals will ask to speak to a senior executive as a part of the investigation required to define a project's scope and set a fee. The senior executive's contribution is usually valuable, and the professional has a chance to win an ally who will not be price sensitive.

Don't quote a fee any sooner than necessary.

Many clients ask for a quote during preliminary discussions, either because they want to avoid wasting your time and their own if you cost more than they can afford or because they are just curious. Avoid giving a number. You can usually forestall further discussion by saying that your fees vary greatly depending upon the exact services provided and that you will have to learn more before you can give an estimate. If the prospect persists, ask him why he wants to know now. The answer may give you the information you need to deal with his concern appropriately.

When forced to talk about fees early in the process, give wide ranges. Saying that your fee will run between $100,000 and $200,000 tells the client that he won't get away for $5,000 and that he won't have to pay a million, but it also gives you plenty of room to determine the right price later. Be aware, however, that a prospect tends to remember the low end of the range. When you finally quote a figure, remind him of the full range before stating the fee.

Occasionally you may want to quote a range early in the conversation in order to qualify a prospect. You should do this when you seriously question the prospect's willingness to pay or when the cost of pursuit will be high relative to the final fee. While working in Chicago, I used to do this when a small prospect called me from California. I went to see those who weren't put off by the range I quoted, and I avoided several expensive trips to the West Coast for projects I probably could not have won and that would not have been worth much if I had.

You must determine the prospect's fee expectations.

Often buyers expect fees to fall within a preconceived range. This is true whether or not the buyer has ever purchased the kind of service you offer. Once established, these expectations are difficult to change and are a major determinant of what the buyer will pay.

Such expectations come from many sources. The buyer may have talked to your competitors, heard comments made by a peer, made an analogy between your services and some other kind of service he is familiar with, or simply based his expectation on his budget or approval limits. If possible, try to determine what that expectation is before you quote a fee.

Sometimes the nature of a client provides a clue; an investment banking firm will expect to pay more than a discount retailer will expect to. Usually you have to infer a range from answers to indirect questions. You can ask questions like these:

- *How did you hear about my firm?* This is always a safe question, and the answer can help. A referral from a past client suggests a price expectation comparable to the fees paid by that firm.

- *Have you ever worked on a project like this before?* You may not have to ask this question. The answer may be volunteered in discussion about how long the buyer has been on his job or about the need for the service. The more experience he has, the better informed he will be. Information on specific firms he has worked with also tells you about his fee expectations.
- *Is there competition on this project and, if so, who is it?* You may not want to ask this question, and if you do, the buyer may decline to answer. On the other hand, he may volunteer the information, or you may pick up gossip on competition through your network. The more competition there is, the better informed the prospect will be about pricing. A selection of high-end or low-end competitors also gives you a sense of the level of other quotes he is likely to hear.
- *What is your budget?* It is often inappropriate to ask this question, but sometimes your rapport with the buyer will allow you to do so. I recently asked a buyer for his budget, and he told me, "Up to $X without approval, and up to $Y with approval." In the built-environment professions, of course, the expected construction costs and building type provide indicators of the expected budget for professional services.
- *What benefits will your company get from this project, and why do you need it now?* These questions will give you a sense of the value the client expects to get from your work and his level of urgency. All other things being equal, the more value expected and the greater the urgency, the more the prospect will be willing to pay.

Change in expectations means change in scope of services or perception of value.

When the prospect doesn't want to pay what you want to charge, you can either walk away or try to find a solution satisfactory to you both. Sometimes you can educate him on the value of your work, an onerous task, especially if you are up against low-priced competitors. In that case you must not only demonstrate the return he will get from your work but also prove that the return is much higher than he will get from the competitor. For many services this is difficult to do.

Your best bet is to redefine the scope of the service. You can then redesign the project and price it again. When I sold location consulting services, I sometimes had to compete against large construction companies that would practically give away the work in hopes of getting large construction contracts later. Once this happened with a price-conscious prospect planning to move a manufacturing plant. I knew the job would go to my low-ball competitor in a direct comparison, even though I believed my firm's services were superior.

The CEO wanted to move in order to lower labor costs because his company was losing market share to low-cost competitors. "What if moving the plant doesn't reduce your costs enough to make you competitive?" I asked and told him a story about a company that had spent millions to relocate only to have the competition drop its prices still further and maintain a price advantage. The company went bankrupt. This captured my prospect's attention. I was the location consultant, and I was suggesting that a location change might not work! I recommended a low-cost feasibility study to determine whether the company should move, upgrade its manufacturing technology, reengineer its product, or do some combination of these three to meet the competition. I won the job, performed a service that dealt more accurately with the client's need, and, after three phases of work, earned a higher fee than if I had just sold a location study.

Redefining the scope often requires determining the underlying goal that the prospect is trying to achieve. If you understand that goal, you can sometimes see another way to achieve it that will allow you to win the project at a price you can afford. Another way to redefine scope is to ask yourself, "What does the prospect need to meet his immediate objectives?" If you define the scope this way, you can often reduce the work required and demonstrate to the prospect that you will be a good steward of his money, spending it only as it is needed.

Consider alternative ways to construct a price before you make a quote.

The principal approaches for constructing a price are the following:

- Cost-plus
- What the market will bear
- Competitive
- Value-based

Note that here I am referring to pricing approach and *not* the way billing is structured, a related but different issue.

Cost-plus pricing is based on overhead.

This approach is most easily explained in the context of a sole practitioner.

To estimate costs accurately, the sole practitioner must estimate his overhead for a year. This includes rent, utilities, insurance, labor, postage, office supplies, and all other nonreimbursable expenses. He must also estimate the percentage of his available hours that he can bill to clients, the remainder being overhead. With this information he can use the formula shown at the beginning of this chapter to calculate the fees he will have to charge to a targeted annual income.

Exhibit 22.1 provides an example. The consultant must charge $300 per hour ($2,400 per day) if he wants to make $240,000 per year. To price a project, he must estimate the number of hours it will require and multiply it by $300. This is typically done by listing each task to be performed and then estimating the hours required for that task.

EXHIBIT 22.1 Determining an Hourly Rate

Total available hours	2,080		
Non-billable hours	-1,040		
Billable hours	1,040		
Rate per hour	(a) x $ 300	(b) x $ 500	(c) x $ 700
Gross income	$ 312,000	$ 520,000	$ 728,000
Annual expenses	– 70,000	– 70,000	– 70,000
Net annual income	$ 242,000	$ 450,000	$ 658,000

Many larger firms build this kind of calculation into their hourly rates. Thus, in calculating a cost for a project, they only have to add in a figure for nonreimbursable expenses.

A cost-plus price can be structured either as a daily rate or a project fee.

What the market will bear pricing allows pricing flexibility.
Few professionals acknowledge that they charge on this basis, but many successful ones do. This approach will help you increase or decrease your fees, depending upon which you need to do.

If your calculation of a cost-plus fee results in a number that is more than the client will pay, you must either get your fee down or forgo the engagement. First, ask yourself whether you have defined the scope of the project correctly. What specific questions does the client want answered? What outcome is he seeking? What specific deliverables does he require?

You may find that your cost is too high because you are answering the wrong question. This is an easy trap to fall into. My own hit rate increased markedly when I became more effective at defining client need. It resulted in selling more, smaller projects to the same client with higher total fees than I had been able to win in the past.

Next, you must review the list of tasks developed when you originally priced the project to see what can be taken out. For each task, ask these questions: Does the client really want this done? Is it necessary for the completion of the project? Is there a cheaper way to do it? Cheaper ways include using low-cost talent within your firm, outsourcing a task, or asking the client to perform it. You may also be doing things by hand that should be automated, delivering reports instead of presentation summaries, or providing your services in other ways that are more expensive than need be.

Finally, ask yourself, "If I had no other choice but to do this project at this price, how would I do it to make it profitable?" Often this reverse thinking can lead to creative ways to get your price down.

What-the-market-will-bear pricing can also ensure that you do not underprice your work. Some clients and industries are simply willing to pay more than others. Believing that price is one measure of quality, they may pick a competitor if your price is too low. It takes chutzpah to ask for twice your normal rate, but if that is what the prospect wants to pay, you would be foolish not to ask for it.

Competitive pricing is based on expectations.

Competitive pricing is much like the what-the-market-will-bear model except that instead of using your beliefs about what the client is willing to pay to determine your quote, you use your expectation about what the competition will ask for. This can be risky because few of us really know what a competitor is likely to charge. But if the client has chosen high-priced firms to ask for bids, you can quote a higher fee than you might otherwise.

Value-based pricing is based on demonstrated value.

When you charge a client a percentage of the expected or actual value received from your work, you are value pricing. This is how most professionals would like to price, but most don't, for two reasons. First, they may not be able to demonstrate the value of their services. What is the value of an accounting audit? What is the value of a good interior design? It is hard to prove. Second, the market may not let them. A prospect who requests bids from several professionals is, in essence, saying that she can get the same value from any of several firms and so will hire the one with the lowest price. True value-based pricers are typically those firms whose marketing strategy allows them to bid noncompetitively.

Even if you do not see an immediate opportunity to price in this way, it is worth seeing whether you can demonstrate the economic value received from your work. Firms that do this can often find ways to apply the information to win clients at higher fees. Here are some of those ways:

- **Performance pricing:** Some cost-reduction consulting firms get paid a percentage of what they save; some litigators and attorneys who deal in collections matters earn a percentage of the money they get for their clients. Contingency-fee recruiters only get paid if a candidate is hired by the client company. Some professionals feel that they cannot maintain their objectivity with such fee arrangements and look down on those who price this way. Others, including such high-profile firms as Bain & Company, have no difficulty about tying compensation to value. Clients are increasingly looking for this type of pricing.

Clients who think that performance pricing is a good idea must be reminded that it has to be good for both parties.

Because you are putting your fees at risk, you should require a significantly higher premium when you price this way than when you charge a flat fee per project. Contingency fees can best help you increase your pricing when two conditions apply. First, you are more certain of the favorable outcome your work will produce for the client than the client is. This is after all a bet, and the best bets are made when you are more certain you have a winning hand than the client is. Second, there must be a clear, simple, and measurable way of determining your level of performance. Otherwise, you will end up bickering with the client over your fee. Such disputes are distasteful and, in the long run, unrewarding.

To avoid being pushed into a performance fee by a client, you can insist on a higher upside payoff if you do well. If you can't take that approach for competitive reasons, I recommend sounding extremely enthusiastic about the performance-pricing approach and surprised that it's being requested. Say, "You want a performance price? Yes, absolutely. We greatly prefer that approach. It's good of you to suggest it." Your enthusiasm will usually dampen the client's interest, and he will revert to a project fee.

- **Providing testimony from past clients:** One consulting firm I know provides estimates of cost savings before beginning an assignment, supported by data on actual savings produced at other clients. References validate these data. The firm then asks for a fixed fee based on the value it forecasts it will provide.
- **Documenting value for a client:** Whenever possible, a professional should show a client the savings or revenues that have resulted from his work. McKinsey & Company is reported to go to great lengths to do this. This practice undoubtedly accounts for some of the loyalty its clients show; it makes the person who hired the firm look good.

Build price increases into your quotes.

Clients will accept a price increase more readily if they see it coming well in advance. So, if your projects run for a long time, build price increases into your proposals. During its high-growth years, one management consulting firm increased its prices three different ways. All of its contracts committed its clients to a 1.25 percent price increase each quarter, compounding to an annual increase of over 5 percent. Additionally, because demand for its services was so high, the company was able to obtain periodic unscheduled price increases from its new clients and, to a lesser extent, from its old ones.

The third method for increasing its prices was more subtle. As the firm grew rapidly, adding employees at the bottom, its best professionals won frequent promotions. With those promotions came higher billing rates, which the clients had to pay unless they were willing to accept a new face on their projects.

Never sound defensive when quoting or raising your fee.

Many professionals don't quote fees that are high enough or raise prices as often as they should. One firm I know realized that and, in the depths of a recession, put in a 20 percent price increase for new clients. Few balked, and the firm kept growing. They had been charging much less than they should have for years! In professions where there is significant price elasticity, such as management consulting, firms may be able to increase their prices rapidly during boom years. Many are slow to realize this; the fastest-growing firms do. Even in professions like architecture, where elasticity is lower, some firms manage to charge a premium.

The challenge, of course, is to get a premium in the face of client resistance. Identifying the cause of the resistance will help you overcome it. Clients resist high prices because of factors such as the following:

- **Preconceived ideas about what a professional should cost:** The client may think he knows what a particular service should cost based on past experience acquiring what he sees as a comparable service. When this happens, you must educate the client on price structures in your profession.
- **Budgets:** The client company may have already established a budget for a project that is below your asking price. This could be because the client's company is small and the amount is more than it can afford—you shouldn't be pursuing such a client—or because the client doesn't really know what a service is worth. In that case, once again, you must educate the client on your profession.
- **Approval limits:** Your quote may be beyond the buyer's approval limit, requiring him to go to his boss or even to his boss's boss to get your fee accepted. If this occurs, you must help the buyer develop his argument for a larger sum and, if at all possible, get a meeting with the boss. You may need to coach the buyer on language he can use to do this.
- **Doubt about the value of the service:** The client may be concerned that he will not receive value for the money he pays. If he can negotiate a

lower price, he can reduce his exposure. If this is the client's concern, you must educate him on the value you will provide.

- **A tendency to negotiate:** For some clients negotiating is a habit, and in some organizations everyone is expected to push suppliers to lower their prices. If this is the case, inflate your bid so you can reduce it during negotiation, thereby allowing your client to prove his value to his organization. At the same time, negotiate vigorously.
- **Competition:** Competitors will often quote a fee lower than yours to win work away from you, dragging down your price, especially when there is an oversupply of professional talent.
- **Experience with your firm:** A client who has become accustomed to the level of price that you asked for when work was scarce will have a hard time accepting rapid increases when demand for your services goes up. When this happens, you must explain your situation and put in regular increases. Also, resign yourself to earning less from this client than you do from more recently signed ones.

Focus discussion on the value you will provide.

Your best tactic is to defend your price on the basis of the value the client will receive from your work. If the client believes that you will provide sufficient value, he will be more likely to disregard any preconceived ideas he had about what your service should cost. He will be more likely to scrounge up money from elsewhere in his budget to pay for the work or to introduce you to his boss, who has authority to authorize spending such a large amount. His negotiating position will be weakened. He will be less interested in working with competitors. All these good things happen if you can convince him that the value of your service is great enough.

But doing so is hard. The value of some professional services seems especially difficult to prove. For example, how do you calculate the economic value of a well-designed building? One frequently used measure is a building's efficiency as determined by the ratio of usable space to total square footage. But the value of a design is seldom solely a matter of efficiency.

In May 1967, a small, West Coast hotel chain opened a new luxury hotel in Atlanta, a city which at the time was known for the drabness of its accommodations. The exterior, though attractive, wasn't exceptional. The entrance was understated. But guests gasped in fascination and delight when they entered the lobby. Architect John Portman had borrowed a few ideas from Frank Lloyd Wright, extended and adapted them, and come up with the first hotel built around a large atrium. Guest were given a second breathtaking view of the space when they rode up glass-walled elevators. All this was a stunning new concept at the time.

The design was not especially efficient. Other hotel operators purportedly scoffed at the waste of space, and the original investors had gotten cold feet and backed out of the project. But it was a huge economic success because it attracted guests. The hotel became a place that trend-conscious business travelers—and there are many of them—had to see and stay at. As a concept prototype, it revolutionized the design of many luxury hotels built in later years and eventually of more modest ones. It transformed its owner from a little-known firm to a household word. Today, everyone has heard of Hyatt Hotels, and many have stayed at the Atlanta Hyatt Regency or at one of its many atrium-centered progeny, thanks to John Portman.

The design of the hotel was a huge accomplishment—and so was convincing the client that it was what they wanted. I would have liked to have been in the room when Portman explained the value of his mad vision to his clients.

Managers at high-growth firms where we have conducted interviews were good at explaining the value of their work. This was true even in areas where value was hard to measure. One rapidly growing architecture firm I studied for this book conducted extensive research into the value of good design for a specific type of building. Its findings helped it win work at premium prices.

Many firms haven't determined the value of what they do. They have a hard time articulating it, beyond broad generalities. As a result, they cannot justify premium fees.

Here are some suggestions for determining the value of your services:

- **Use the client's currency for calculating value.** "Value," itself, is a slippery term, as a wise man, David Maister, once pointed out to me. It means different things to different people. Of course, the meaning that counts is your client's. If you want to talk value to a client, you must deal in his coin. This is why you ask questions about the client's need, and then listen carefully to the response. By answering your questions, the client tells you his view of the value of getting his problem solved and the value he expects to get from a professional in solving it. In short, he is describing the benefits he hopes to get. The high-level opener (described in Chapter 16) links your services to the core value the client hopes to obtain. The entire sales process, then, should help you understand the value the client is looking for and let you articulate your offering in that same coin. Among the common alternatives are these:
    - *Increased revenues:* Many clients want to grow their revenues. New strategies, business deals, facilities, and other things that clients create or arrange with the help of professionals are designed to bring in money or to create an infrastructure needed to make money.

- *Cost reduction:* Performance improvements, layoffs, redesigns of benefits packages, and facilities consolidations are designed to save money and are also achieved with the help of professionals.
- *Risk reduction:* Many clients will pay a premium if they believe that doing so will reduce the chances of failure. This is especially true of high-risk and complex endeavors. Most clients are willing to pay attorneys higher rates to defend them against a hostile takeover than they are to assist with a standard real estate transaction. They will pay higher rates to architects and engineers to a design a research laboratory than to design a standard office building. In both cases, a part of the premium they pay is to reduce the risk of failure in situations where the cost of failure is high.
- *Speed:* Time has value to many clients. For example, a casino operator knows just how many dollars per hour per square foot of space his business can make from its slot machines, and the number is large. Once the operator has decided to build a new casino, every day its completion is delayed is a day without that revenue. Fast-track design and construction makes sense in this environment, and the operators are willing to pay a premium for it.

- **Provide proof.** The benefits you offer to a client must be determined by what you learn in the sales meeting. But certain categories come up again and again. Among them are the following:
  - *Experiential proof:* The most powerful proof is success of similar work for a similar, former client that a prospective client experiences. Hyatt's competitors only had to see the crowds attracted to the Atlanta Hyatt Regency or the slightly later San Francisco Hyatt Regency in the Embarcadero Center to perceive the value of captivating design. Because they were losing convention business to the hotels, the competitors felt Hyatt's success where it hurt the most, in their pocketbooks. Similarly, an attorney who has represented his clients successfully is likely to get a call from those who sat on the other side of the table when he helped negotiate a good deal. But not all professional work lends itself to such visible proof.
  - *Testimonial proof:* Also effective are strong references from past clients who stress the value received from your work. The more the former client volunteers about the value received, the more compelling the reference. See page 214 for more information about getting effective client references. During the briefing, you can remind clients of the outcome of past projects. I recently briefed a former client on the effectiveness of a coaching program we had provided. I

reminded him of the additional business several of these people had brought in, providing specific dollar values. When called by the firm looking for the reference, he repeated these numbers. We got the new account.

■ *Business cases:* Sometimes a professional can develop a business case for a project. This is often done by management consultants. At their simplest level, these business cases show how the costs of a project compare with expected financial benefits. While the costs projected in most business cases are hard numbers if the client chooses to proceed, the benefits in either savings or additional revenues are usually softer projections. For this reason, they should represent conservative estimates. The more a client is involved in developing a business case, the more ownership he will feel for it.

When you believe your price is fair and right, hold your ground.

If you believe in the value of the service you are offering and the fairness of your price, avoid discounting. Discounting sends the message that you either don't believe in the value you are promising or are a weak negotiator. An accountant tells this story.

A large privately held homebuilder had a reputation for hiring a new auditor every three years to keep fees low. Eventually, our turn came and we won the business. Four years later, the founder-president took me to lunch and told me, "We slipped up! We usually go out to bid for audit services every three years, and your firm has had the business for four. So, I just wanted to advise you that we are going to request bids this year. Of course, your firm will get a chance to bid."

I thanked him for telling me and said that he needn't send us the request for proposal, because we wouldn't be bidding. "Of course you will," the client responded. I said no. Just as it was his business decision to go out to bid, it was ours not to respond. I said that if after four years we hadn't proven the value of our services sufficiently to earn a client's loyalty to us, either we were doing something wrong or it was a bad match. Either way, we shouldn't continue the relationship. I added that I would be happy to meet with him to review the value we had provided over the past four years, and he accepted. At the meeting we obtained a new contract with a price increase.

You will neither enjoy your work nor become successful by working with clients who nickel and dime you. Taking work from such clients absorbs resources that could be better spent elsewhere. Deciding when to turn down work is the subject of Chapter 23.

A prospect is less likely to balk at a fee delivered in person.
When you deliver a proposal in person, you can reinforce the value of your service. You can also observe that prospect's reaction to your fee and explain and modify it as needed. The prospect lacks this support if you send the proposal by mail.

Bill your client as soon as you can.
A client is willing to pay for a service he needs. He will also pay for one just completed, while the memory of value received is fresh. Once a project is completed, the longer he must wait to make a payment, the greater will be his reluctance to do so.

Get clients in the habit of paying from the beginning of an engagement. Asking for a sign-on fee equal to between 20 and 30 percent of the total expected fee is one way of doing this. It will also help your cash flow. Thereafter, submit bills at established intervals.

Conclusion

Too often, professionals consider pricing only after a prospect asks them for a fee. By then much of their flexibility is lost. Pricing deserves to be one of the fundamental issues you consider when you develop a marketing strategy. Good negotiating after you submit a quote can seldom make up for being able to make a profitable quote in the first place.

23 Turning Down Small Work

The more small assignments you take on, the harder it will be to increase your revenues per client. Because it takes almost as much effort to sell to a small client needing small amounts of work as it does to a big client, selling costs as a percent of fees are much higher with a small client. Also, some clients require high maintenance while providing low profitability, sucking up hours that could be better deployed elsewhere. Many rainmakers who have experienced rapid revenue growth made tough decisions about the size and kind of the clients that they would deal with, thereby subjecting themselves to temporary criticism and second guessing. But they stayed the course, realizing that some of the most important decisions concern what work not to take.

Those who take on work that is too small or unprofitable do so for reasons, some of them good and some of them less so. These include the following:

- **Loyalty to old clients:** It can feel mean and ungrateful to turn down an old client whose assignments you valued in the past—even more so, if the client helped you get started or helped you through hard times. It is a hardhearted person who has never caved in and taken a small assignment for this reason. But must you always? There are things you can do to reduce the chances of having to take a job that's too small.
- **Service to a valued client:** If a big client asks you to do a small assignment, you may feel obligated to do so as a part of your broader service, and this obligation increases if you think a competitor might use the opportunity to gain a foothold in the account. This is sometimes a good reason and sometimes not.
- **Portal to a new client:** Sometimes you are the one seeking a foothold. Accepting a small assignment may be the way to get one.
- **Fear that you may later regret turning down the opportunity:** You may not feel secure about other work coming in. The economy could turn

bad, or a big account might end its assignments with you. These things do happen. I know of one firm that turned down work at Nordstrom because the assignment was small, only to find a few months later that its bigger opportunities had dried up. But it isn't nearly so common a problem as the prevalence of the fear suggests.

Many professionals aren't insecure about winning more work; they're just insecure. This is particularly true of professionals who have started their own firms. In the early, lean years, they take whatever work comes their way and are glad to get it. Later, when times are better, they have a hard time breaking the habit. I know. I suffer from this problem myself, and call it the entrepreneur's disease.

- **Discomfort with saying no:** Some people have difficulty saying no to anyone kind enough to express an interest in working with them. They can't find the words—or the courage. They don't want to seem rude or arrogant.
- **Avoidance of the hard work of developing bigger opportunities:** It is easier to respond to an inquiry from a prospective client, no matter how small, than to go out and find a big one. This is the least acceptable reason, though a common one.

Sometimes it makes sense to take on small assignments and small clients, and sometimes it doesn't. To complicate matters, an assignment you should take today may be one you should turn down two years later. Our decision criteria must change with the fortunes of our practice. If we don't change those criteria, we will curtail growth.

When tempted to take on small assignments, especially from small clients, picture a scale weighing the benefits against the costs. On the benefits side are a few small wins, the equivalent of pocket change to your firm. These are real dollars. Weighing in against them are largely risk dollars, less tangible at the moment but able to become real suddenly. The small work reduces time you have for the big pursuits. This is a serious consequence for time-starved professionals. In the worst case, the small assignments can make it impossible to pursue a big opportunity. This happened to an architect I know who was committed to present his design to a small client on the day a big one asked him to pitch his services. The small client declined to reschedule. Feeling honor-bound to keep his commitment, the architect had to pass up the large opportunity.

More commonly, small jobs cut into hours you would have to pursue the big fish. They sap your focus. The selling and startup time required for a small project is often the same as for a big one. Divvying up your time among five small opportunities that together will provide revenue far below that of a big one is of questionable wisdom.

Worse, you may take on a matter for a small client and then let a big one push it aside. This leaves the small client in the lurch and is unethical. A lawyer once took on a matter for our firm and then stopped working on it while he focused on bigger clients. I still steam when I think of the frustration this caused. You don't want a reputation for treating people this way.

There is a subtler cost to taking on small assignments that can do long-term harm to your firm. Psychologically it's hard to negotiate a $5,000 fee with a small client one day and then ask for $1 million from a big one the next. People who consistently try to do that tend to underprice their larger assignments. But if you are always asking for large sums, it gets easier. You get better at it.

To avoid these problems, you must develop a clear description of work you will take and work you won't. This understanding then can become the basis of a policy. Whether it is a private, personal policy or one for your firm depends on your goal or rank. In its heyday, the consulting firm Index set a policy of turning away work that would not have the potential for generating at least $1 million in fees. Some in the firm disagreed with the decision, but after it was made, average revenues per client ballooned. When our little firm, Harding & Company, set a policy of not accepting work below a specific dollar amount, we stopped accepting dozens of small assignments that were a clear distraction.

Next, look for others in your field to whom you can refer the work you turn down. You help two people that way: the client and the professional you refer. Then practice the words you will use to decline an opportunity. Here are two samples:

> I don't think we are a good match for you. We work for much bigger firms and find that it doesn't make economic sense to do otherwise. Could I refer you to someone who might be a better match? Her name is Mary Smith, and she does excellent work.

> We aren't set up to take on a project of this size, and I wouldn't want to because I would be afraid it wouldn't work out for you. We usually refer people to Phil Smith when we can't take on the work. Can I give you his number?

If the person pushes back, help him see the situation from your perspective. The head of a small technology consultancy sounded offended when I told him that we didn't work for companies as small as his. I asked him if his firm took on work from clients with revenues equal to his firm's. He acknowledged that it only worked for much larger organizations and went away satisfied.

Once you recognize that turning away work is best for the client, too, using such language gets easier. Professionals at fast-growth firms even recommend that well-established clients use competitors when the work isn't a good match for them. Mike Palmer, at the time a partner at Diamond Technology Partners, tells this story: "The first thing you always ask is what is best for the client. [A larger investment bank] asked us to do several things that we could have done, but we suggested they use [another firm], who could do the job better and cheaper." Having turned down work and saved the client money, Palmer found that he had earned credibility with the client that helped when he later pursued projects that he wanted.

When You Lose a Sale

I do not love thee, Doctor Fell.
The reason why I cannot tell;
But this I know and know full well,
I do not love thee, Doctor Fell.

—Tom Brown

This may be the best-known rejection of a professional in song or story. Unfortunately, like many notifications, this one is uninformative. I have never heard words so blunt as these myself, but like most professionals, I have been told that the chemistry with my competitor was better, a tactful version of the same thing. And just as in the rhyme, the person who delivers this message always says he doesn't know why. This chapter will help you get beyond such vague statements.

The market is a great teacher, and for reasons I don't fully understand, it teaches better when we lose than when we win. A debriefing on why you didn't get a job is the market telling you what you are doing wrong. Only a fool would ignore this source, the only one that really matters. Smart people want to get every drop of help they can.

When you lose a sale, try to do the following.

Understand the prospect's mind-set.

When a prospect calls to give you the bad news, his words are influenced by recognizable inhibitors:

- **Time:** The call to you is a necessary distraction. The prospect wants to get it over with as quickly as possible so he can get back to the business at hand. His objective, then, is to keep the conversation brief, and he will choose the reasons he gives you for his decision accordingly.

254

- **Good manners:** Just as you would be reluctant to tell a casual acquaintance that he smells, prospects will avoid telling you anything that might offend.
- **Self-interest:** Prospects don't want an argument. The decision is made and irreversible. It is simplest to give you a reason that is unarguable.
- **Self-esteem:** Sometimes giving the reason would embarrass the prospect. If the project was wired from the beginning, or if the senior executive chose someone else for a selfish or petty reason, the notifier is unlikely to tell you. If he wasn't really party to the decision and doesn't know why his boss decided as she did, he may not want to admit it.
- **Confusion:** Often the notifier doesn't fully understand why the decision went the way it did. He only senses it.
- **Unconscious behavior:** Some people are extremely averse to confrontation. They seldom speak directly to anyone. This is a deep-seated psychological condition that you cannot change.

Given these inhibitors, the chances of getting good information on why you lost a sale are slight unless you handle the situation carefully. Remember that the prospect feels about as comfortable telling you why you lost as you would explaining to a neighbor why he wasn't invited to your party.

Try to convince the prospect to talk to you like a Dutch uncle.

A Dutch uncle is the person who has the relationship and feels the duty to give a vainglorious teenager stern and candid advice about his behavior. That is what you want the prospect to do. To do it, the prospect must feel that he has the relationship and the duty. He must feel that doing so won't be too painful. Only such feelings will overcome the inhibitions that keep him from giving you good information. Getting him in this frame of mind underlies many of the following guidelines.

For starters, you must really want this kind of talking-to. You won't always like what you hear, and you will have to sit there and take it. When this happens, remember it is what you don't hear that hurts you the most.

At its worst, a marketing problem is like a cheating spouse; friends know but don't tell you about it. One successful architectural firm almost went bankrupt after the president and primary marketer retired. His successor, who wanted to fill his shoes, took the lead in all the firm's marketing efforts, but his abrasive manner drove away prospects. He could have solved the problem with training or by transferring the marketing lead to someone else, but he didn't want to hear he had a problem. The accountant who told me this story had tried to fill the Dutch uncle's role and found that his help was unwelcome. Don't react this way. We all need Dutch uncles from time to time.

Try to set up a special interview for the debriefing.

Before calling to give you the bad news, the prospect has decided what he will say to get the job done quickly and painlessly. At best, he plans to give you partial information; at worst, he intends to lie. To push him beyond this initial explanation risks exposing him. He will withhold cooperation rather than let that happen. Also, if he must notify several others who lost the bid, he will be anxious to get on to them.

For these reasons you should not try directly to overcome resistance to getting good information during this first conversation. Rather, listen to his brief explanation and then try to set up a separate time for a face-to-face or phone interview, using words like the following:

> Obviously we're disappointed at the news; we really wanted to work with you. But we understand that you had to make a decision and wish you every success. If we can be of any further help, let me know. I do have a favor to ask. Once a project is lost, it's lost. The only thing we can get from the time and effort invested is information on how we can do better the next time. We have a set of debriefing questions that we like to ask when we lose. Could I arrange a half-hour conversation with you to go over them? It would be a great help.

These words inform him that you accept the decision and are not going to argue and that you bear him no ill will. They also let him know that the debriefing is a standard procedure, so that he doesn't feel singled out.

If he agrees to the meeting, schedule it immediately. He may say that he doesn't see what more information he can provide. If so, respond that you have found such meetings extremely helpful even when the prospect feels as he does, and repeat your request. Once he gives you a commitment, thank him and get off the phone.

I have had prospects totally revise their explanation of why I lost a sale during a follow-up meeting. This would not have been possible had I asked all my questions during the initial phone call because reversing themselves so quickly would have embarrassed them. Of course, if the prospect insists on doing it then and there, you must comply.

Occasionally a prospect will agree to a meeting, ask you to call back in a week to schedule a time, and then not take your calls. Move on. He wouldn't have given you good information if he had met with you.

Claim any relationships that will get you better information.

You may have a relationship with the prospect that creates an obligation on his part to give you better information. If so, use it. You can sometimes make claims on a relationship that would have been inappropriate during the sale.

If the prospect has been a client in the past, for example, ask for a follow-up meeting on the basis of the good work you have done previously. I once lost a sale at an insurance company that was the carrier for my firm. During the sale, we never mentioned this relationship. We suspected the prospect knew of it and that he would take offense if we claimed it.

Once we lost, I felt differently. I politely pointed out the relationship—we had been right; he was aware of it—and said we had not felt that it was appropriate to make an issue of it during the sale, but that now I was making a request as a customer, not a vendor. I wanted good information on why we had lost the sale. He understood me and respected my earlier discretion. He gave me one of the best debriefings I have ever had, one that was instrumental in fixing several problems in my firm.

You may be able to make a claim on friendship. If the prospect used to be in private practice, you may be able to make the claim on the basis of his understanding of your need for this help. By making such claims tactfully, you are freeing the prospect to talk to you more candidly than he might otherwise, that is, to talk to you like a Dutch uncle.

The debriefing will not lose anyone a job.

A prospect naturally fears that if he speaks candidly, his words will hurt someone. This is an unfair burden to put on him. No one should lose a job for making mistakes on a few sales. (Unemployment rates would rise steeply if this were a general practice.) Instead, you seek the prospect's help in identifying ways in which you and your teammates can improve. If I sense any hesitation, I usually say something like this.

> This is not a witch hunt. That's not the way this firm operates. We all want to get better. That is deeply built into our culture. We can sit around and guess what went wrong and maybe even be right some of the time, but it means more when we hear it from someone in the market whose opinion we trust.

Plan your questions in advance.

When you get a formal debriefing, use the prospect's time well by knowing what you want to ask. I always work from a questionnaire for two reasons. First, it ensures that I cover what I want to know. Second, if I am meeting face-to-face, it confirms my claim of a formal debriefing process.

A sample list of questions is provided in Exhibit 24.1. Note that Part A starts the interview with several open questions. These give the prospect the chance to say what is on his mind on any subject he chooses. Narrower questions might focus his response too quickly and bias his answers.

EXHIBIT 24.1 Debriefing Questionnaire

Company Name: _____

Interviewee: _____   Title: _____

Address: _____

_____

_____

Interviewer: _____   Date: _____

Part A: Overview. Introduce with the statement: "I would like to ask some general questions first."

1. Why did you select the other firm?

_____

_____

_____

_____

2. What did they do especially well during the sales process?

_____

_____

_____

_____

3. Where could we have been better?

_____

_____

_____

_____

Part B: The Sales Process. Introduce with the statement: "I would now like to ask how we compared with the competition in some specific areas." You may have to prime responses with additional questions, such as, "Who did you talk with at each firm at this stage?" or "How did each firm make you feel?"

4. Initial phone contact discussion of the project:

_____

_____

_____

_____

5. Fact-finding visit to your office:

_____

_____

6. Your visit to professional offices:

7. Brochure and other marketing materials:

8. Presentation
   a. General comments:

   b. Participants:

   c. Format:

   d. Visual aids:

   e. Q & A:

9. Proposal
   a. General comments:

   _____

   _____

   _____

   _____

   b. Appearance:

   _____

   _____

   _____

   _____

   c. Understanding of issue:

   _____

   _____

   _____

   _____

   d. Description of scope:

   _____

   _____

   _____

   _____

10. Fees:

   _____

   _____

   _____

   _____

11. Follow-up:

   _____

   _____

   _____

   _____

12. Additional comments:

   _____

   _____

   _____

   _____

Part C: Specific Concerns. Introduce with the statement: "To finish up, I would like to ask you a couple of questions we had on specific concerns about our performance." Since these concerns are situational, you must develop these questions yourself.

13. Concern A:

_____

_____

_____

_____

14. Concern B:

_____

_____

_____

_____

Once the prospect has answered these questions and elaborated on any issues that they raise, I tell him that I want to review the sale from beginning to end, then ask the questions in Part B. The answers to these questions help in two ways. First, they tell you about the relative importance of different issues. If he can talk at length about presentations but can barely remember proposals, it tells you that the proposals didn't weigh heavily in the decision. Second, they keep him talking, and when he talks, he gives information. Often he is unaware when he tells you something important. He may even provide a clue to something he is unwilling to say. That you presented without visual aids while everyone else used slides is useful competitive information, whether or not it affected this sale. In responding to these questions, the prospect will sometimes give you information that you can combine with information drawn from other sources to identify a problem.

In Part C, saved for the end of the interview, I ask any questions that test theories I have about the loss. What effect did a specific mistake have? Would it have helped if we had brought the president along? Questions like these might bias the interview if asked earlier.

Never disagree with or debate what you are told!

Never disagree in a debriefing, and never debate. The instant you do, the prospect will clam up. He is giving you information as a favor, and disagreement implies that you don't appreciate it. He doesn't want to argue; he has better things to do.

This doesn't mean you have to agree with everything he says. You must only accept it as his understanding of what happened. If you don't see how he can feel as he does, choose nonargumentative language to learn more. "That's interesting. Tell me more." "I'm not sure I understand. Tell me more." "We certainly don't want to give that impression. Can you tell me what we did that gave it?" These words show you won't argue and that you are truly interested in learning more without implying agreement.

Write down what you hear.

Take detailed notes on what you hear during a debriefing. Over the years I have learned that it is much easier to remember good news than bad. Note taking helps ensure that you remember both. Also, the full value of what you learn may only be apparent with time. As noted, a response may only be meaningful when combined with other information you may not yet have. I keep a file of post mortems and review them about once a year to refresh my memory and see whether they can tell me anything new.

Discount certain information unless you can determine what it means.

An explanation of why you lost may be true or may simply show that the prospect feels inhibited about telling you the truth. Treat the following comments with caution:

- *You lost it on price.* Maybe you did. Then again, maybe this is the least controversial explanation available. Try to find out how great the difference was. Ask the prospect if he has any opinions about why your price was higher. Did you misunderstand the scope?
- *Price didn't make any difference.* If the prices were close, this is probably true. If yours was high by a wide margin, it probably means, "I don't want you to think I'm cheap." You probably failed to justify the price differential with added value.
- *You were second choice.* And so was everyone else. Only accept this one if you get details about why you were second and someone else was third. Usually this statement reflects a well-meant desire to make you feel better and nothing more.
- *It was a close decision.* Maybe, but he probably just doesn't want you to feel bad.
- *Their chemistry with our people was better.* Sometimes this, like price, is simply an easy excuse because it is difficult to argue with. Sometimes it is a kind version of the words used with Dr. Fell. There is a reason, but the prospect is uncomfortable telling you. In some cases, however, it is a true statement and the prospect really doesn't know why. He only senses it. That is because chemistry derives from his feelings about how you look,

how you behave, and what you say. He may be summarizing his reaction to many little things he is not fully aware of. Your detailed questions on the sales process may help draw out an answer. Reflect especially on whether your looks, words, and actions made you seem: a) compatible with the prospect's culture, b) as if you cared about him personally, and c) as if you would be enjoyable to work with. If this phrase is repeated often, get professional presentation coaching.

- *I wanted you to get it, but the others voted for your competitor.* Read this as, "I want you to like me." It is probably untrue.
- *I don't really know why. When things could easily go either way, it's hard to say.* This person is probably extremely nonconfrontational. If so, you will never get useful information from him. Try a few additional questions to confirm whether this is true. If it is, thank him and try to get a debriefing with someone else.
- *You presented well, but the others on your team didn't.* The prospect will find it extremely difficult to criticize the debriefer. To do so would require overcoming what he has learned since childhood about good manners. The debriefer always gets higher marks in a debriefing than his teammates. Don't let it go to your head. He is probably just being polite.

Debrief as many people as you can.
If several people participated in the hiring decision, interview as many of them as you can. Each will have a different perspective, and some may feel less inhibited than others. Use your questionnaire with each.

Don't expect all debriefings to be worthwhile.
Not every debriefing will provide you with helpful information, but not every one has to. If only 20 percent give you insights into what you need to improve, you can make tremendous progress. Most will help at least a little. Breakthrough debriefings are rare, and they only happen if you make a practice of debriefing every time you lose a sale.

Send a gracious thank-you note.
After your debriefing, or when you realize that you won't get one, send your prospect an e-mail thanking him for the opportunity to compete for his project. Tell him that you appreciate his time and help and wish him success on the project. Make it as personal a note as you can; a form letter will be seen as one.

This is good manners and also good business. Your prospects today are probably pretty much your prospects for the future. You want to be considered the next time he has a need, and the chances of that happening will improve if you accept the loss graciously and retain a friendship. Every so often a competitor will foul up a job. It will be more likely to come to back you if you have accepted the first decision gracefully.

Put each loss behind you and go on to the next sale.

The harder you worked to win a job, and the closer you came to winning, the worse it feels to lose. You must learn what you can from it, put it behind you, and go on to the next one. Good marketers bounce back quickly.

Everyone who sells has slumps. When this happens to you, remember that marketing is a numbers game. Though skilled marketers will win more jobs than poor ones, even they have slumps. The rules of probability ensure that during some periods you will hit a string of unusually difficult situations, while at others sales come more easily. You are not necessarily performing better when you are hot. You may simply be luckier.

That is not to say that you should wait for the slump to pass and take no other action. You should increase your inquiries into why you are losing. There may be a good reason; a competitor may have found a new and exciting approach, or client needs may be shifting. But good marketers adjust to such changes and bounce back and win again.

I once had a losing streak in which every prospect I touched seemed to choose a competitor or postpone his project indefinitely. It drove me crazy. I rethought everything I did, completely revamping my approach to the market. In a few months the slump ended, and I began to win again. To my surprise, a number of the projects that I thought I had lost came back to me. This forced me to make a decision. I could either abandon the improvements I had made on the grounds that my reason for making them now seemed invalid, or I could retain them, believing that the basic reasoning behind them was good even if they had been initiated for wrong reasons. I chose the latter and have never regretted it.

Professional markets are extremely competitive. You have to work constantly to stay ahead. This means you must always be looking for ways to improve. You must always be questioning what you are doing. Just don't question yourself.

PART IV

From Tactics to Strategy:
What Works and What Doesn't

The first three parts of this book are devoted to specific marketing and sales techniques. The professional who wants to develop new business must become proficient in at least some of them. Marketers market. By doing the things described in the preceding chapters, you can become a marketer, and you can sell. You will see results. Marketing is a numbers game, and anyone who speaks or publishes often, keeps in touch with past clients, makes cold calls, or performs other marketing tasks will get some business. The more skillful you become, the higher your batting average will be, just as a batter improves if he practices his swing.

But that is not enough. Individual marketing events must be built into a larger strategy if they are to have a lasting and large impact on your career and on your firm's development. The better your strategy, the more often you will score, just as a batter will hit more often if he makes informed decisions about when to swing, when to pull, and when to bunt.

Strategies are implemented by the allocation of resources. When you decide to write three articles, give one speech, and hold a seminar, and at the same time you decide not to send out any mailings, you are making a strategic decision, whether or not you recognize it as one. In a world of infinite resources, strategy would not be a concern because you could do everything you want to do, but for most of us time and money are scarce. Spending them on one task means we forego some other.

This portion of the book describes marketing strategies to help you select the right mix of tactics. We will look at strategies for both individuals and firms, recognizing that for the sole practitioner, the two are indistinguishable.

In researching these chapters, I have made studies of several groups. First I have identified marketing stars in several professions, people who showed a knack for marketing early in their careers and developed into lead marketers and rainmakers for their firms. Some of these individuals have been described in the case examples that begin chapters in the preceding parts of this book. Looking at the entire group, I have been able to draw conclusions about the development of successful personal strategies.

Second, I have interviewed rainmakers and people who have observed them. At this point, I have information on more than 300 rainmakers, spread broadly across the professions.

Third, I have looked at a large number of firms in a single profession, consulting, interviewing roughly fifty people in more than thirty organizations. These interviews have been complemented with experience and selective interviews with other professions and anecdotal information gathered over a thirty-year career.

When developing a strategy, you must understand the underlying logic to sales strategy that explains how firms and individual professionals attain rapid revenue growth. This logic is covered in Chapter 25.

Once you understand that logic, you can look for opportunities to gain relatively easy successes, successes that help you deal with the professional's perennial shortage of time and money. Chapter 26 explores ways to do so, describing the simplest of marketing strategies. Such strategies have been the foundations of many professionals' marketing careers.

You will also want to look closely at yourself, assessing both your personal inclinations and abilities and any specific gaps in your skills or credentials that need filling. Chapter 27 provides tools for making such an assessment.

Next, you must look at your services and market. As is shown in Chapter 28, different kinds of services and markets lend themselves to very different marketing strategies. Pick the right strategy, and you will see an ample return on your marketing; pick the wrong one, and you will waste your time, as many have before you.

These different levels of consideration—the simple mathematics of a sales strategy, your personal abilities and needs, the nature of your service, and the strategy selected by your firm—create a complex environment within which you must develop your own strategy. Any reasonable strategy is better than none. Strategies needn't always be new and exciting. I have interviewed many successful rainmakers who used deceptively simple strategies.

In creating a strategy, there are no extra points for originality and no penalty for doing something simple or fun. What matters is that you have a clear understanding of what you want to accomplish and how you will accomplish it and then that you execute to the plan. My goal is to give you the understanding and tools to become a rainmaker.

25

The Logic of a Sales Strategy

For the past fourteen years, the other members of my firm and I have studied rainmakers, professionals successful at generating new business.[1] Along the way we learned of a few rainmakers who achieved sales with compounded growth rates of over 20 percent per year, year after year. A few achieved compounded growth rates of more than 50 percent per year. With that kind of growth, it didn't take long for many of them to build large practices, and, in some cases, large firms. These were the super rainmakers, and they caught our attention.

We wanted to understand how they could achieve such explosive revenue growth. It wasn't about any specific ways they went to market. Beyond some broad generalizations about doing good work, it wasn't readily apparent what these firms had in common that would set them so apart from other firms in their professions. When we finally figured it out, the answer was surprisingly simple. A little reflection will show that there are three things you can do to increase your sales:

- *Increase the size of your network.* All other things being equal, the person who talks about his services with 200 people will sell more than the person who talks with only 100. We will call this variable N, or network size.
- *Increase the percentage of people you know who actually buy from you.* The person who gets business from 5 percent of the people he talks with (which include some old clients he hangs on to and new ones he brings in) will sell more than the one who gets business from but 2 percent, once again, all other things being equal. We call this variable B, or percentage of buyers.
- *Increase the fees you earn from each client.* The person who earns $150 from each client will make more money than the one earning only $100. Call it F, or average $ per client.

A professional's revenue, then, can be written as the product of these three variables. That is:

Revenue = N x B x F

where N = network size, B = percentage of buyers, and F = average $ per client

The trick is to increase N, B, and F at the same time. If you do, the impact is profound, because you get geometric growth.

Exhibit 25.1 uses a simple model to show the impact. Professionals A, B, C, and D all set out to make their fortunes, all starting from the same place (Exhibit 25.1A). In year one, all have networks of 100 people they talk to about their services; all actually sell business to 2 percent of this network; all sell each client $100 worth of services. After year one, all try to increase their sales, but each uses a different strategy.

EXHIBIT 25.1A Geometric Sales Growth Model

Four professionals must increase their sales. All four start from the same point in Year One:

- Network Size: 100 people
- Percent Buyers: 2%
- Revenues Per Client: $100

EXHIBIT 25.1B Geometric Sales Growth Model

Assumptions Table: Growth Rate Per Year

	A	B	C	D
Size	20	0	0	20
Percent Buyers	0	1 percentage point	0	1 percentage point
Average $ Per Client	0	0	5%	5%

EXHIBIT 25.1C Geometric Sales Growth Model

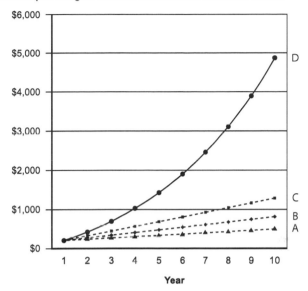

Results Graph: Doing All Three at Once Creates Geometric Growth

As the assumptions table (Exhibit 25.1B) states, Professional A grows his network by 20 people each year for ten years while the variables of percentage of buyers and average sales per client remain fixed at year-one levels. Professional B becomes increasingly effective at selling, selling to 1 percentage point more of her network each year without growing her network or increasing her sale per client. Professional C increases his average billings per client by 5 percent a year without growing his network or increasing his closure rate. As can be seen in the graph (Exhibit 25.1C), all three strategies result in similar slow growth lines.

Compare them to line D, which shows what happens to Professional D who works hard and grows all three variables simultaneously. Her sales take off like a rocket. Geometric growth occurs when you multiply variables with increasing values with each other. That, in effect, is what rainmakers do.

This simple little model and the logic that underlies it have many profound implications for a professional firm and for individual professionals. Not all are relevant to the content of this book, but let's look at two that are.

The model begs a question: If the trick is to grow these three variables at the same time, why don't more professionals do it? That's because, if easily said, it's not so easily done. That is primarily for two reasons.

Execution poses problems.

Try to deliver on all three yourself, and you quickly find that succeeding in one area makes it harder to succeed in another. Say, for example, you grow your network rapidly from 20 to 100 people. Now you have to divide your attentions among five times as many people as you did before. That takes time, often meaning that you have less time to devote per contact. If, at the same time, you want to increase the percentage of people in your network who buy from you, you find you have a direct conflict. Increasing the chances that someone will buy from you usually requires spending more time on them. One effort, growing your network, pushes you to spend less time with each contact, while the second effort, increasing the percentage of people in your network who buy from you, pushes you to spend more time with a small number of them.

As you grow your network, the average quality of the contacts tends to decline at first, with quality measured in terms of the ability of a contact to hire you. This also works against your ability to increase the percentage of contacts that hires you. As you succeed in one of the three areas required to achieve geometric sales growth, succeeding in the other two areas gets harder.

Many professionals are best at one thing.

The three different ways to grow revenue also require dissimilar skills. Most of us are strong in one of the three areas. Some people might excel in two, but few are good at all three. Professional firms are notorious for expecting their people to do everything including selling, managing, and doing. They tend to expect their senior people to be able to handle any kind of selling situation imaginable. We all tend to be good at some things and not so good at others.

Fortunately, you don't have to be good at all three. Many people make great contributions to their firms by excelling in one or two areas. They team with someone else to fill out areas where they are weak. A partner at the German office of a management consulting firm aggressively grew his network and sold work to new clients. But he proved unable to convert these clients into the large accounts the firm wanted. Another partner at the firm was brilliant at developing accounts but had never been able to go out and find new clients. When the two partners teamed up, the office experienced a breathtaking rise in revenues. And the careers of both men soared.

Unfortunately, stories like this one are the exception.

It is possible for a professional to be only average at growing revenues in two ways, say network size and dollars per client, and to compensate for this middling performance with huge success in the remaining area, say the percent buyers. A thought leader sometimes succeeds this way.

We can now look back on the skills and methods described in the first three parts of this book from a new perspective: They provide the ways to grow revenues in one of the three ways we have been discussing. It is obvious how the subjects covered in some chapters tie to one of the three variables. The chapters on how to manage a sales meeting (Chapters 14 through 18) will help to increase the percentage of your contacts who buy from you. Chapters 13, 22, and 23, on cross-selling, turning away small clients, and pricing, show ways to increase your revenues per client.

But in other cases it's not so clear. Does writing an article help you build your eminence and so predispose prospective clients to hire you (thereby increasing percentage of buyers), or does it inspire some prospective clients to find you and meet you (thereby increasing network size)? Obviously, it can help do both. Also, for one article you might conduct some background research by interviewing prospective clients, while for a second you don't. In the former case the article clearly helps you grow your network. In the latter, it is less clear.

Still, the subjects covered in preceding chapters are the building blocks for growing the three variables. The remaining chapters of this book describe how you can assemble these tactics into a strategy.

Simple Strategies That Can Help You Now

Professionals cite lack of time as the single biggest obstacle to marketing. You have to bill a high percentage of your time to earn a profit, leaving few hours for marketing. This means that you must use what marketing time you have efficiently and effectively. Experienced marketers squeeze as much impact as they can from each hour they spend on marketing. Two principal means for doing so are leveraging and running campaigns.

Leverage your limited time.

Leveraging is simply using the same hours to complete several marketing tasks. It offers you the advantages of a two-for-one sale. Sometime these two-for-one efforts even help work on two of the growth variables that were the subject of the preceding chapter. Examples of leveraging include the following:

1. *Use a speech as a basis for an article.* The time you spent preparing the speech will greatly reduce the time required to write the article. Often a professional association that has asked you to speak will be glad to publish the speech in its journal. If not, someone else may.
2. *Give the same speech to different groups or through different modes of delivery.* This economy has been used by politicians and speaking professionals since time out of mind. A little reflection or research will often provide you with at least two or three additional groups that would be interested in the speech you have just prepared for one audience. You may also be able to use it in a Webinar. If you can prove that the speech went well with the first group (with a thank-you e-mail or summary of speaker evaluations), you have ammunition to convince someone else to give you a podium.
3. *Use the same article for several publishers.* You have to be careful of copyright limitations, as well as editors' fears of being scooped by competing publications, but if you are careful, you can often use the same article for

different publications. Never offer an article to a journal without noting that it has been published elsewhere. Never do so without informing the publication in which it first appeared of your interest in using it elsewhere. Often the editors of the journal in which it is first published will be happy to authorize reuse, especially if their journal is referenced as the original place of publication. As one example, I once published a speech on analyzing labor markets in a personnel journal and in one directed at corporate real estate managers. The latter was interested because labor markets were crucial to selecting new corporate locations. The journal directed at corporate real estate executives was willing to reference the publication in which the article had first appeared.

4. *Using a similar article for several publications.* You can often adapt a single article for quite different audiences. An article on outsourcing call centers for the insurance industry might be very similar to one for the banking industry. Each will have examples from companies in the appropriate industry, and each may require a few changes in emphasis to customize it to a specific audience, but the underlying content will be much the same. In such cases, you don't have to seek permission from the journal that published the first article before you offer it to a second, nor must you advise the metal-stamping journal about the previous publication of a similar piece in the plastic injection-molding journal.

5. *Use a blog entry as the basis for a longer article.* Blog entries tend to be short. You can cover the topic in more length in an article.

6. *Allow a blog entry to be republished in an electronic magazine.* Electronic magazines are frequently looking for short, insightful pieces and are happy to reuse your blog entries. Within six months of starting my own blog, I was able to recycle several entries that way.

7. *Give a speech at a professional association meeting you will be attending.* If you are going to devote the time to attend a professional association meeting, you might as well apply to speak. You will receive greater recognition if you go as a speaker. Moreover, speakers generally have an easier time meeting and talking with others at a conference. It is understood that they are making a contribution to the organization, they have at least minor celebrity status (often evidenced by ribbons attached to their name tags), and they are participating as experts in a particular area.

8. *Conduct a survey at a professional association meeting and use it as the basis for a press release, article, or white paper.* This works particularly well if you have a booth at an exposition or are speaking to a large group. You will be there anyway, so you might as well use the opportunity to gain information that can be used for future marketing. By promising a copy of the survey results to those who provide their names and addresses at the bottom, you can also generate a list of qualified leads.

9. *Use conversations you have at an association meeting as the subject for a blog entry.* Listen well for issues of interest to the other participants at the association meeting, follow up with good questions, and you have the raw material for a blog entry. You may even be able to quote some of the people you met. Getting approval for the quotes gives you an excuse for recontacting them, and many people like to see their names in print.

10. *Use a press release as a basis for an article or speech.* Once a press release has been used or rejected by the media, get as much additional value from it as you can.

11. *Use an article that results from a press release and mentions your firm as a mailer.* This is a good way to remind your market that you are seen as an expert by the media.

12. *Use a reprint of an article you wrote as a direct-mail piece.* This saves the time of creating a mailer.

13. *Turn a speech into a white paper and use it as a direct-mail piece.* This is the same as the first suggestion in this list except that you do your own publishing. This can be done when you do not have time to wait for publication or when a speech is unpublishable for an acceptable reason— such as that it is focused on too narrow an audience for a publication to find attractive.

14. *Ask a network contact to speak at a seminar.* You help that individual, whom you are trying to cultivate, by providing market exposure. At the same time you gain a speaker for your seminar.

15. *Ask a client with whom you want to build a strong relationship to speak at a seminar.* He may enjoy the recognition, and you gain a speaker.

16. *Ask a client with whom you want to build a strong relationship to share a podium with you.* He may welcome the exposure, and you will get to work with him while preparing the presentation. Working together builds relationships.

17. *Ask a client with whom you want to build a strong relationship to author an article with you.* He may appreciate the exposure, and the joint authorship will enhance your credibility.

Whenever you undertake a marketing task, it is worth reflecting on how the time you are expending can be leveraged. But leveraging does not apply to marketing tasks alone. You can also leverage activities not related to marketing. Here are some examples:

• *Turn a business contact into a network contact.* Most professionals have contact with vendors, subconsultants, clients, and other professionals who serve their clients, and some of these people can be useful network contacts. When you identify people with this potential, see whether you can help them, and follow the other networking rules that will allow you to make them a part of your network. For example, a New Jersey accounting firm that handled the personal accounts of several attorneys at a New York law firm held a party for the law firm's partners to inform them of the accountants' corporate experience. When one of the lawyers later needed to refer a corporate client based in New Jersey to an accountant, he referred it to the firm that had held the party.

- *Use research conducted for a client as the basis for a speech, Webinar, press release, or article.* This is the most common leveraging technique. Some forms of research, like surveys, lend themselves to this kind of use. Whenever a survey is contemplated for a client, its marketing value should be considered *before* you design the survey questionnaire in case a few questions need to be added to increase its marketing value.
- *Use research as a basis for cold calls.* If you have surveyed companies who might make good clients, offer to discuss the results with them as a reward for participating.
- *Turn a training session into a speech or an article.* If you train other professionals, you may be able to leverage the work required for a half-day training session into a speech or article.
- *Turn an internal training session into a seminar or Webinar.* Of course, you will not want to give away company secrets. If you can avoid doing so, the internal training program you have created can sometimes have marketing value.

Experienced marketers make the most of the nonmarketing work they do for marketing advantage.

Finally, there may be things you do for social reasons that can be leveraged into a marketing activity. The combination of business with golf provides a hackneyed but real example. I once helped a social acquaintance sell a training assignment through an introduction and endorsement. She has since become a useful business contact and a part of my network.

Design a campaign.

A campaign increases the impact of your marketing by delivering your message several times to the same people. It helps your market retain your message and associate it with you. Many of the leveraging techniques described in this chapter can be used to create a campaign. For a successful campaign, you must have a target market, a message, and a series of events to deliver the message to the market.

A campaign I directed at the insurance industry included four articles, a speech, a direct-mail program, and cold calls. Over two years, work from this industry went from almost 0 to 20 percent of my office's revenues.

Professionals commonly use several kinds of campaigns:

- **Direct mail/e-mail:** Perhaps the most obvious example is a direct-mail campaign. A single mailer is seldom adequate to imprint a message about your firm on the minds of recipients. As noted in Chapter 3, you will generally need to deliver your message three or four times over a short period to have an impact.
- **Speaking:** In businesses characterized by a large number of regional associations, a campaign to speak at a large number of them can be an effective method of building your reputation and developing leads. You can leverage the time required to prepare for such a campaign by using the same speech over and over.
- **Cold calling:** This is particularly important when you have a market that consists of a relatively small number of large organizations to whom you want to deliver a specific message. In such cases, direct contact is probably the most cost-effective method. An architecture firm developed a strategic alliance with a mechanical, electrical, and plumbing engineering firm to deliver a specialized service to the pharmaceutical industry. Cold calls at each company in the industry were an important factor to the alliance's success.

Many campaigns are based on more than one marketing technique. A firm that has developed a specific skill, service, or knowledge base will wish to get the word to the market repeatedly through a variety of methods.

As the founder of a large European consulting firm put it, "You have to be present in people's minds. It's like a mosaic, with the pieces including seeing you mentioned in an article, receiving a letter from you, or hearing you give a speech." A campaign will help you capture client mind-share and use your scarce marketing hours efficiently.

Self-Marketing: Experts Make Themselves

Larry and Alice were both in trouble—for different reasons. With one year on the job, Larry was 50 percent billable, when the target for entry-level professionals was 75 percent. Project managers didn't find him productive and weren't anxious to have him on their projects.

Alice, a senior project manager, billed over 80 percent of her time, putting in long hours every day and on weekends. Given her experience and compensation, she should have been bringing in new clients, but she never found the time. She was always too busy producing work—some of it was work that Larry should have done.

The head of the practice met with each separately and began by asking them how they thought they were doing. Larry's response was enlightening. An ambitious young man, he perceived that long-term success in the firm would be based on marketing. He was anxious to prove himself in this area. The practice leader educated him on the economic logic of the firm and showed him why, at this stage in his career, his most crucial need was to market himself internally to project managers by demonstrating high productivity, remaining highly billable, and developing the experience that would, in a few years, permit him to market effectively on the outside.

The practice manager next sat down with Alice. She perceived that she was doing well, though she was concerned about the long hours. The manager reviewed the economic logic of the firm with her, showing that at her level a certain amount of selling of new business was required. She protested that she didn't have time, and he committed to lighten her work load.

Within six months, Larry had transformed himself into one of the firm's most productive associates. His labor was eagerly sought by several project managers, he billed over 80 percent of his time, and he still made time for a little marketing. During this same period, Alice made little progress. Though the practice leader steered new work to other managers, he found that Alice volunteered to relieve others of some their burdens, informally taking on the work he had tried to protect her from. When he mentioned this to her, she protested that the work had to get done and that she had been obliged to help the other project managers.

When the firm had to lay off employees because of a downturn in business, Larry kept his job and eventually developed into a fine marketer. Alice lost hers because at her compensation level, the firm could not afford her unless she brought in enough business to support herself. There were other capable managers who could run projects.

Events like these are common in large professional-service organizations. Careers are made and broken by the compelling logic of a market that demands high production of professionals at the same time that it demands sales. It is a logic that relentlessly weeds out many fine professionals like Alice, allowing only a few the chance to reap the rewards of becoming a partner with a major firm. The logic works equally well for the sole practitioner, who must both sell and produce work to stay in business.

Interested in developing talent for professional firms, I once wrote down a list of all the successful marketers of professional services I knew well and reviewed their careers to see whether I could identify any commonalty in their histories. My objective was to learn from the experiences of these stars and find a way to transfer it to others.

I learned the following.

The stars were universally high producers early in their careers.

These people threw themselves into client work early in their careers. Sought after by managers because of their productivity, they rapidly developed a strong experience base. They sought independent experience in which they could work directly with clients and were eager to demonstrate an ability to manage client relationships. As a young lawyer, Mike Schell, later a partner with Skadden, Arps, Slate, Meagher & Flom, preferred to work on the firm's less-prominent merger and acquisition projects instead of the larger and more prestigious ones, which were followed carefully in the business press. "On the big projects I would have been the fifth face on a six-headed totem pole and likely would have had little contact with the client. I felt I got a lot more out of the smaller projects where I could be a principal player, work directly with the client, and have a central role in all the work."

In most firms, professionals who can demonstrate an ability to earn client confidence are given increasing responsibility. As a partner at another large firm put it, "Finding young people who are acceptable to clients is a key issue for the partners because if you don't, your time is fully taken up by existing clients and you can't do any marketing." The stars filled this need.

The experience they gained by working many projects allowed them to talk more knowledgeably to prospects when they had the opportunity and to develop their own anecdotes, so essential to marketing services. Because of this knowledge base, they were included on sales teams early, thus increasing their market exposure.

The stars showed an intense interest in marketing early in their careers.

These people were more than reliable producers of work and managers of client relationships. They also had a strong desire to bring in new business. Each developed an approach to marketing and stuck with it. Each found special ways to assist in the marketing effort. Some became superb relationship marketers, deliberately converting one-time projects with clients into long-term firm relationships. Several became skilled networkers, bringing in leads from their contacts outside the firm. Others used still different techniques, but each had a concept of how he or she could bring in business and worked at it steadily. Colleagues in their firms soon viewed them as specialists in specific marketing activities. When opportunities requiring these activities arose, they were asked to participate.

The stars took great care to credential themselves.

All of the stars updated their bios regularly, ensuring that this most fundamental of marketing documents reflected their full experience. This was particularly important early in their careers, when each additional assignment significantly expanded their experience base.

Their craving for credentials showed itself in different ways. One professional had earned degrees in architecture, engineering, and business and was working on his CPA accreditation when workload resulting from career success forced him to reassess his priorities. Another was a joiner of associations and became known as an expert among the members with whom she worked on committees. Several published or spoke frequently.

All the stars found ways to improve their firms' services.

Sensitive to client needs, the stars were more interested in making their clients happy than in rigid rules about how to do an assignment. They responded to client concerns and, in doing so, found ways to improve their firms' services. One consultant developed an add-on service that eventually became a substantial revenue source. Another overhauled the way cost comparisons of alternative solutions were made. An architect enhanced his firm's programming effort by developing specialized knowledge of a specific building type. An attorney solved a legal problem in a way that the partner in charge of his project had doubted would work.

These improvements didn't just help clients. They lowered production costs, increased revenues, or increased service value without increasing costs.

The stars became specialists.

The stars were seen as specialists early in their careers, often, though by no means always, in areas in which others in the firm showed little interest. This had crucial benefits. First, they were increasingly selected to work on projects requiring their specialty; because they were easy to market to clients, their knowledge in the area was thereby also increased. Second, as experts, they gained selling and marketing opportunities because they were the logical individuals to speak for the firm on the subject of their expertise. Many of the stars developed two or more areas of expertise during their careers, adding one after another. In all the professions it is increasingly important to develop such specialization both as firms and as individuals. A specialization is often a prerequisite for an emerging marketer to get opportunities to sell. Take these examples:

- *An attorney was brought into a firm specializing in bankruptcy law to broaden its commercial practice.* At first he billed himself as the individual who did all of the firm's nonbankruptcy commercial work. This did not work well. It proved so hard to claim expertise in such a wide area that even his partners couldn't figure out how to pitch him to their clients. When he began to develop an expertise in labor law, the situation changed. He became a credible expert. The other partners began to refer him business.
- *An architecture firm established a program to develop specific second-tier personnel as marketers, but the firm found that it only succeeded with specialists, including one who had not been identified for development.* The need to succeed at sales was so great that senior personnel almost always bumped the generalists from sales calls and presentations because the seniors were perceived to have a higher probability of winning. Specialists seldom got bumped because they had knowledge and credentials that the seniors didn't.
- *A partner at a Wall Street law firm found that he could get opportunities to speak and to meet with clients because of his specialty in a specific area of securities law.* Sometimes the work that resulted had little to do with this specialty, but the specialty got him in the door ahead of competitors.

The stars saw the benefits of becoming specialists and didn't resist the label, as some of their peers did. They didn't resist concentrating their work in one or two areas at the expense of broader experience.

Beyond these points there was little the stars had in common. Certainly all were ambitious but seemingly for different reasons. Some wanted money, others recognition, and still others worked largely for the fun of building a practice. Some were extroverts, some introverts, some highly polished, and at least one somewhat folksy. A few were good managers, others were not, but they all brought in business.

The characteristics of the stars can be used by other professionals seeking to develop a personal marketing strategy. As Robert Louis Stevenson said, everybody lives by selling something. At different points in a professional's career, he sells different things to different people. Early in his career, a professional in a large firm *sells his production skills to partners* and other senior personnel in the firm. People seen as unproductive seldom last long enough to prove themselves as external marketers. Somewhat later in a career, the professional is asked to participate in client meetings and selective sales presentations. This happens first when the client wants "to see the one who actually does the work." In these circumstances, the professional's primary task is to *sell himself to existing or prospective clients.* Still later in his career, the professional markets projects that will largely be done by others. At this point in his career he must *sell the firm to prospective clients.*

Defining the track this way explains why star marketers bill so many hours early in their careers. They know that this is the best way to sell themselves to senior firm members and earn opportunities on the assignments that most interest them. Skills and experience gained from working these assignments form the basis for credentials, and credentials form the basis for marketing.

I have refined this career track into the following four-step hierarchy of development needs for the aspiring marketer:

1. *Skills:* These are gained through training, often on the job from more senior professionals, though they are sometimes self-taught. They are demonstrated by an ability to complete specific tasks efficiently and effectively. They can be technical skills, such as a particular analytical ability; process skills, such as the ability to gain consensus; aesthetic skills in some professions; and marketing skills.

2. *Experience:* This is gained by doing many assignments with limited guidance from more senior professionals and is demonstrated by an ability to apply a skill to new situations. Having it means you can be sold to others in the firm and to prospective clients as a key player in a project team.

3. *Knowledge:* Gained by thinking about experience and through research, it is developed largely on one's own or through discourse with other experienced professionals. Knowledge is demonstrated by an ability to draw inferences from experience that go beyond technical proficiency. Knowledgeable professionals are the ones who expand their companies' practices by modifying old services and developing new ones and by devising marketing programs.

4. *Expertise:* One message stands out from the experiences of the stars: Experts make themselves! Gained largely by the professional's promotion of his or her knowledge, experience, and skills, expertise is demonstrated by a recognition of your status as an authority by others. Note that an expert doesn't have to have the most experience in a field; he or she simply has to promote his or her experience more effectively than others do.

To develop a personal marketing strategy, you must first determine where you are on this hierarchy. Exhibit 27.1 is a simple form that you can use as a tool. Make copies and fill out the form for each area in which you want to present yourself as an expert. This can include expertise by industry (such as banking, automotive, or not-for-profit), functional area (securities, human resources, tax accounting, power plant design, or sales force compensation), process skill (negotiating, managing, facilitating), and marketing (public speaking, article writing, networking). Define specializations as narrowly or as broadly as makes sense given your firm and market. So, for example, an insurance industry specialization might benefit by being narrowed to property and casualty or life and health companies, to mutual or publicly held companies, to large or small companies, or some other segmentation.

EXHIBIT 27.1 Personal Evaluation Form

Area of Expertise: _____

_____ .

Target Market: Who would be interested in this area? Note types of clients, others in the firm, outside business contacts, and so on.

_____

_____

Expertise: What proof do you have that you are an expert? Include degrees, certifications, number of past clients in the area, publications, memberships, speaking platforms, testimonial letters, and so on.

_____

_____

Knowledge: What specialized knowledge do you have as a result of your experience? Is there anything that differentiates your knowledge from that of others with similar experience?

_____

_____

Experience: What experience do you have on which knowledge can be based? Include client work, previous employment, and any other appropriate experience.

_____

_____

Skills: What specialized skills do you have of value to the market? Include both technical and process skills.

_____

_____

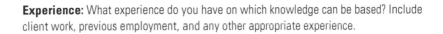

If you find yourself thinking, "I can do it all," beware. Maybe you can. But that is not the point of this exercise. Now you are trying to evaluate your level of expertise in specific areas, and expertise is defined by your markets' view of you, not your own view of yourself. You can start anywhere on the form you wish; I often find it best to begin with knowledge, since this category best describes what I would like to sell.

Don't be concerned if you have little to put down in some categories. The main purpose of the exercise is to identify gaps you must fill. If your credentials are weak, you now know that they must be improved, and a first step in your marketing strategy should be to do so. Credentialing activities include writing and speaking. I would also recommend writing and speaking if your knowledge is weak, because doing these things will force you to articulate what your experience has taught you.

If your experience is weak, you must find a way to increase it. Perhaps you should ask senior people in your firm for the opportunity to work on projects that will develop it. In the architectural industry, firms can gain experience through teaming arrangements in which one team member offers geographical proximity, client access, or superior design, while the other brings experience and expertise. A series of successful team arrangements can give a firm the experience needed to become an expert and dispense with further teaming. If you lack skills, you must seek further education.

Exhibit 27.2 shows a personal evaluation form filled out by an architect who specialized in research laboratory design. Note that his expertise is based, among other things, on working on twenty laboratory projects. Other individuals may have more experience than he does, but that is not a major concern as long as he promotes his experience better than they do or can differentiate what he has to offer in ways of importance to his clients. Others may also have written more extensively on laboratory design. The way he uses his publications for marketing is more important than the quantity he has produced. Nevertheless, this individual might conclude that he needs more publications or speaking opportunities to further enhance his stature at this point in his career. He might also place a priority on building nonpharmaceutical experience or decide to specialize further in the pharmaceutical industry.

EXHIBIT 27.2 Sample Personal Evaluation Form

Area of expertise: Research laboratory architecture

Expertise:
- List of 20 laboratory projects
- Reprint of article on laboratory design in *Industrial Research & Development*
- Member of ISPE
- List of five speaking engagements
- Juror on panel to select "Laboratory of the Year"

Knowledge:
- How to program a research laboratory
- Implications of changing technologies on laboratory design
- Language used by researchers when discussing facilities issues
- Typical facilities concerns of researchers and alternative design solutions
- Names of leading specialists needed to support work

Experience:
- Work on 20 laboratory projects (15 pharmaceutical)
- Work with most noted research lab design consultants

Skills:
- Architectural programming
- Laboratory layout
- Consensus building
- Explaining laboratory requirements to nonspecialist architects

---

Next, use the material from your personal evaluation form to create a bio for yourself describing your expertise in a particular area. This bio can be used when you are selling yourself to prospective clients, seeking speaking engagements, and being introduced at speaking engagements, as well as for other marketing purposes. If your firm has a standard format, use it. If not, invent your own. Review your bio. Does it sound convincing? Do you have enough credentials, and have you used them effectively to prove your expertise? What does it tell you about the self-marketing that you should be doing?

Create a personal marketing plan.

The personal evaluation is an important first step to creating a personal marketing plan. Such a plan must do four things:

1. Build your credentials
2. Disseminate those credentials to prospects
3. Get you information on prospect need
4. Get you face-to-face with prospective clients

The first two parts of this book are devoted to marketing techniques that can help you achieve these objectives. A strategy selects a mix of activities to achieve all of them. For example, publishing articles is an excellent way to accomplish the first requirement and will help with the second, but it does a poor job of getting you information on prospect need or getting face-to-face with prospective clients. That is why a marketing strategy can seldom be built on one technique. In selecting a mix of techniques appropriate for you, you must consider several things.

First, you must consider where you are in your career and what your existing credentials are. Younger people must concentrate more on building experience and credentials. Their experience, as reflected by their bios, often looks thin. Often they are not expected to bring in much business and so can devote more time to building their experience, credentials, and reputations. Seasoned practitioners have experience and are often under more pressure to bring in work. Building experience is usually less of an issue than effectively using their experience to win new clients. They need to spend more time on generating leads and getting face-to-face with prospects.

Second, you must reflect on your personal abilities. Do you write well and enjoy it? If so, article writing offers a possible avenue. If not, you must either find writing help or abandon this approach. Do you like the idea of public speaking, or does it make you acutely uncomfortable? Are you a sociable person, a natural networker? If so, networking becomes a particularly attractive alternative. It sometimes pays to ask others, people whose judgment you respect, where they think your talents lie. Friends can provide a reality check.

If you review the case studies that begin the chapters in the first part of this book, you will see that most of these star marketers began by doing something that came easy to them, relative to the alternative approaches. Most built upon one key ability, adding others as their skills and reputations developed. Doing something for which you have a natural ability will help you market efficiently early in your career, when the demands to remain highly billable are greatest.

Third, you must be sure that the marketing tasks you set yourself are achievable. Because you must produce work at the same time that you seek to develop new business, a large portion of your marketing effort must be interruptible. Few professionals can afford the luxury of dedicating themselves solely to marketing for a three-month period. They work on a marketing project in fits and starts because they are always being interrupted by the demands of paying clients. If your marketing plan does not take this into account, it will fail.

The first part of this book focuses on showing how specific marketing tasks can be structured so that they are interruptible. Many of the formulas described in Chapter 1 provide a structure that makes it possible to write an article in pieces, in short chunks of time such as when a canceled meeting gives you an unexpected half hour, while in a plane, or between 7:00 and 8:00 A.M. before the phone begins to ring. Similarly, Chapter 8 describes techniques used by others to maintain a networking effort in spite of production demands. Your personal strategy should include activities of this type that allow you to make incremental progress.

That does not mean you should always steer clear of large projects. Writing a book is a major marketing achievement for many professionals and a worthwhile goal. However, it is also a huge undertaking requiring many hours of work over an extended period. Even after you finish writing it, a year can pass before you see it in print. Writing a book can easily be a two- to three-year process. If authoring a book represents the main focus of your marketing effort, you will have to wait a long time before you see any results from your work. Thus, if you depend upon your marketing to bring in business, you must employ some additional methods to carry you while you wait for the book to appear.

Depending on the level of support you can call on, other marketing activities can also require long periods before you see results. Preparing a two-day seminar, which requires arranging for speakers and facilities, preparing content, acquiring a mailing list, preparing a mailer, sending the mailing, and many other tasks, is also a major undertaking for an individual. Yet you see no benefits from all that effort until the seminar is completed. No new business can be expected from any of your work until then.

Compare these activities to making a cold call on a prospect once a week.

Each visit has stand-alone value—you learn about a particular prospect and deliver a message. Even if your program is interrupted by production needs, the value of visits you have made remains and may result in new business. Incremental benefits can come from direct mail, speaking, article writing, public relations, and networking campaigns. With so many approaches to choose from, every personal marketing plan should include techniques that permit incremental benefits.

Finally, your personal marketing plan must take into account the special characteristics of your market and services. This is so important a subject that the next chapter is devoted to it.

With these considerations in mind, review Parts I, II, and III of this book and set out three or four key goals for yourself for the next year. They should be so stated that your performance can be measured. Examples of such goals might include:

- Publish one article.
- Meet with twenty other partners in the firm (roughly one every two weeks) to discuss cross-marketing opportunities.
- Devote one hour every Tuesday morning to making networking telephone calls.

Create a separate page for each goal in a log and establish tasks and completion dates required to complete them. For example, since most articles take an average of six months to appear in print, you must submit one or two finished pieces over the next five months to have reasonable assurance of meeting the goal of publishing one within a year. Set a deadline for submittal and work a schedule back from there. If you are going to meet with twenty other partners to discuss cross-marketing, you must schedule time for setting the appointments. You need as much discipline in structuring your marketing work as you do in working for your clients. Monitor your progress toward your goals twice a week.

28 Market-Based Strategies

Charlie found the secret—a new way to sell his firm's services that would bring in millions of dollars in additional fees. He learned of it from an ebullient, some-what eccentric consultant who had devised the method. A cautious man, Charlie checked references on the system at other firms which had used it. Their responses convinced him. They had seen a dramatic increase in sales from the approach, which relied on sophisticated telemarketing techniques to get senior marketers in front of prospects.

Charlie pushed hard to have the system adopted at his firm. He arranged a meeting between his boss and the marketing consultant. He pitched the system to his partners. The consultant was hired and the system put in place. One year and many thousands of dollars later, the firm abandoned it. It had not produced a single new project in all that time. What had gone wrong?

While researching this book, I asked many professionals what they would like to see in it. One said, "I'd like to know what works and what doesn't. I've spent money trying a lot of things. For many of them, I don't know if they paid off or not. For others that clearly didn't work, I don't know if it was because of my execution or because they just wouldn't work for [a firm in my practice]."

My friend's concern is valid and, I suspect, common. One hears a lot of conflicting statements about marketing techniques in the professions. A few I have heard include:

- You really can't market this business. Cold calling doesn't work for law firms.
- Cold calling doesn't work for consulting firms.
- We built our (new law) office by cold calling.
- Our cold calling program is the source for almost all of our new (consulting) clients.

288

- We network with a lot of people, but I really couldn't say how valuable it is.
- Networking doesn't work for someone new in the profession because all of the best relationships have been taken.
- Clearly the quantity and quality of leads we get from networking are better than from any other source.
- We had a publicity program, but it didn't produce any results.
- Getting your name mentioned in the press is one of the most important things you can do.
- I spend a lot of time and money putting together a newsletter twice a year, but I don't know if it does any good.
- (Our newsletter) is the spearhead of our whole effort to keep our name constantly in front of our clients.

Many of the conflicting views result from treating a whole profession as the basic unit for analysis of what works and what doesn't. Because each profession is so diverse, approaches that work for one firm or practice often don't for another.

Take, for example, the two characteristics of client need shown in Exhibit 28.1.

EXHIBIT 28.1 Characteristics of Prospect Need

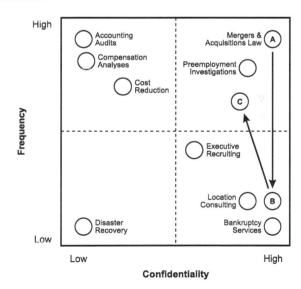

The vertical axis shows the frequency of need. Companies need accounting audits annually. Compensation analyses are also required frequently. Some companies have an ongoing need to investigate all prospective employees. In contrast, most companies select sites for major new facilities at most once every three or four years. If lucky, they will never need assistance from a bankruptcy attorney or from a turnaround expert who will help them recover from a disaster.

The horizontal axis shows the confidentiality of the need (not to be confused with confidentiality of the actual work performed by the professional). Everyone knows that companies have an annual need for audits, that they must conduct compensation analyses frequently, and that they would like to reduce their costs. No call for secrecy there. Likewise, when a disaster occurs, it becomes public rapidly. Other needs for services, however, must be confidential. Companies will often confidentially identify a replacement before firing an executive. Companies planning a move know that if word leaks out, their employees will be upset. They will be subjected to political pressure to stay, and real estate prices may rise in the areas where they want to buy a site. Many firms do not want it known that they hire an investigator to check out the people they plan to hire. If they are suffering from financial troubles and fear bankruptcy, they will want to minimize publicity and the associated risk of scaring customers and creditors.

Over time, and sometimes cyclically, the characteristics of prospect needs may change. As shown in Exhibit 28.1, during boom years in mergers and acquisitions activity, some companies are under constant threat of takeover, while others are almost constantly seeking acquisitions (Circle A). During downturns, there are fewer buyers and sellers (Circle B). Eventually, as interest in mergers and acquisitions recovers, so does activity (Circle C).

Companies falling in different quadrants of Exhibit 28.1 face different marketing challenges, even if they are in the same profession. (See Exhibit 28.2.) The more frequent a company's need, the more loyal it tends to be to the firm it works with. Working together regularly, client and professional establish deep relationships. The less frequent the need, the lower the loyalty. The more confidential a need, the fewer firms a company is likely to talk with before making a selection. By comparison, pursuit of publicly known needs can be a free-for-all. These variances result in very different marketing concerns that require different marketing approaches for companies in the different quadrants.

EXHIBIT 28.2 Key Marketing Challenge Based on Client Need

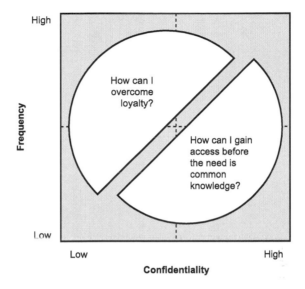

They also explain why, as described in the anecdote from the beginning of this chapter, the cold-calling program didn't work at Charlie's firm when it had at others. The firms where it succeeded sold solutions to a need that all prospects readily acknowledged and that occurred with moderate frequency. These combined characteristics resulted in prospects that were not unduly loyal to any one vendor, that had a relatively high probability of identifying a need on each call, and that shared a willingness to talk about that need. Charlie's firm solved infrequent, confidential problems. The probability of calling a prospect at the time it had a need was slim. The chances of reaching someone within the company who knew about the need were slimmer still, and the likelihood that anyone would talk about such needs with a total stranger was almost nonexistent.

The degree to which technique selection varies by firm is further illustrated in Exhibits 28.3 and 28.4. The former, developed for a location consulting firm (a firm that helps its clients find locations for plants, offices, and warehouses), arrays a variety of marketing techniques against two factors: the cost per contact and the adaptability of the technique to the infrequent and confidential needs of its clients.

EXHIBIT 28.3 Technique Selection Criteria for Location Consulting

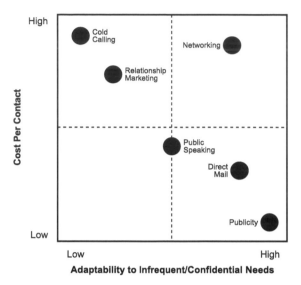

EXHIBIT 28.4 Technique Selection Criteria for Utility Consulting

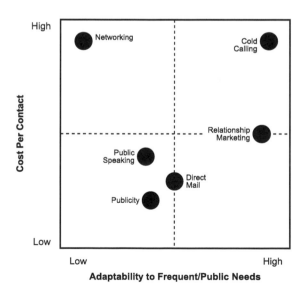

Exhibit 28.4 shows how a utility consulting firm (one consulting in many functional areas to electric power, natural gas, and telephone companies) faces a very different situation because the needs of its market are frequent and public. In this case, relationship marketing with existing clients is highly adaptable and quite cost effective because the consultants have frequent business reasons to meet with their clients. Cold calling also works well, though it is expensive, because the firm can count on a relatively high percentage of the prospective clients it contacts having a need for the firm's services and on their willingness to talk about these needs. Publicity is less adaptable to the utility consultant's situation than it was for the location consultant because the subject matter the utility consultant deals with is of less interest to a broad public. This means that the firm has to work harder and incur greater expense to attract publicity. The cost per contact from publicity is therefore higher in this case.

Analyses like these will not select techniques for you, but they do provide insights into why some techniques work well and why others don't. More importantly, they help you identify obstacles that have to be overcome to make a technique work.

Confidentiality, frequency of need, and cost per contact are not, of course, the only variables that influence what marketing techniques will work and what won't. Others include the average revenues per sale, the degree of geographic dispersion of your market, whether the decision maker's identity is easily identified, whether your firm's name is known, the number of competitors in your area of expertise, the size of your firm relative to others in the profession, and the characteristics of the industry you sell to.

The dynamism of professional markets ensures that almost every rule about what works and what doesn't will have exceptions. General statements, as long as they are seen as general, do hold. Here is how market and service variables generally affect the desirability of alternative marketing approaches.

Cold calling is costly.

Cold calling costs more per contact than any other approach. This means that it works best if the value of adding a client is high, either because your engagements cost a lot or because you can expect a long-term relationship once you have been hired. It works best with needs that are frequent and public. It also works best when your market is sufficiently geographically centralized for the time and expense of making a single visit to remain low.

When these conditions do not prevail, cold calling is less likely to work. Also, when there is extreme loyalty to another firm, cold calling alone is unlikely to overcome it.

Publicity depends on media appeal.

Some practices have more media appeal than others. When I worked at a location consulting firm helping companies like Toyota, United Technologies, and Citicorp select sites for new plants and offices, we received media attention because our work resulted in new jobs and taxes. Yet a firm that supported us, one that consulted on the movement of furniture and equipment, received little, because its work had little apparent impact outside the company that was moving. Services that are difficult to understand also have low media appeal, as do those of interest to very small segments of the population. The larger your firm relative to competitors in your profession, the easier it will be to attract attention because the media tend to seek comments from large organizations.

While all this is true, public relations is a far more flexible and resilient marketing approach than many others. You may not be able to gain access to major national media unless your service meets some of the preceding criteria, but you can still get attention from regional or trade press. Creativity, persistence, skill at helping reporters, and careful selection of media targets can ensure almost any firm media attention.

Relationship marketing works best when the client frequently needs your services.

Relationship marketing works best when the need for your services is frequent and, at times, intense, resulting in a business reason for maintaining contact around which you can build a relationship. Lawyers who represent unions, for example, find that intense, close work during an election followed by the frequent contact needed to deal with ongoing legal needs provides a strong basis for developing relationships.

Relationship marketing works best for geographically centralized markets because it is easier to keep in regular, face-to-face contact when distances are short. It is particularly valuable if perceptions of service quality happen to be low in your profession because then it serves as a differentiator. I know of a mechanical, electric, and plumbing engineering firm that has built a strong niche for itself on this basis.

Networking works best when there are many potential clients in an area.

Among the most resilient and flexible of marketing techniques, networking works for a large number of firms. It will work best if your market is geographically centralized or if those who service client needs related to your own are centralized. New York, for example, as the Mecca of the securities industry, has a well-functioning network of professionals that service publicly held corporations throughout the United States. For firms located elsewhere, this network can be more difficult to access.

Networking also works best if you can capture a strategic relationship that provides leads exclusively to you. Networks can function so efficiently that leads and introductions flow rapidly through a profession. Every local law firm is likely to refer two or three accountants rather than one. By giving out the lead to several firms, it hopes to receive leads from each of them in return. The same practice applies when accountants refer lawyers or when banks refer either lawyers or accountants. All would like to receive exclusive leads from banks but seldom get them.

The more specialized the service a firm offers, the fewer competitors a network contact is likely to be able to refer when he uncovers a need. The improved ability to capture a strategic network is one of several reasons for specializing. The greatest beneficiary of the formal networking group I once belonged to was an independent consultant with a specialized niche in an area of purchasing. Because almost all companies could use his services, and because the other members of the network knew no one else who offers them, he received a larger number of leads than anyone else in the group.

Exclusivity can also be formally arranged between two firms, and many have made major marketing leaps because they have captured such a relationship. When exclusivity is agreed to, there are often market pressures to violate it. This means that some ability to enforce the arrangement may be key to its success. This is the case whenever two firms in related areas merge. Alternatively, it may result from a special and powerful tie unobtainable by others, such as the relationship between McKinsey & Company and its alumni it has helped place at client companies.

When the need for a service is infrequent or confidential, networks can also be an effective way to reach a market. This is especially true if you can identify someone who has an ongoing relationship with a prospect and thus is likely to learn about a need when it occurs. For example, a disaster recovery consultant will usually develop networking relationships with property and casualty insurance companies.

Professional associations provide access to far-flung clients.

Trade associations help you overcome the difficulty of networking in a geographically dispersed market. At least once a year, the members come together at the same place, and committee work provides reason for more frequent conversations. Because all associations feel pressure to bring in new members, it can be hard to establish exclusivity at such a group.

Seminars, Webinars, and conferences require a big number of potential attendees.

Because seminars, Webinars, and conferences are marketed through direct mail, and direct mailings usually have low response percentages, success requires a large list of prospective attendees relative to the size of the audience you require. Such a list requires a market with at least one of the following:

- **Frequent and expected need:** If you know you are going to have a need and that you will have it soon, you have an incentive to find out how to deal with it. You can probably identify a list of people who will have to address such a need.
- **An infrequent need being faced by many firms all at once:** This can result from a change in laws. For example, one law firm drew 200 Mexican companies to a conference on the North American Free Trade Agreement. It can also result from a fad. Numerous seminars and conferences have been run on management fads for zero-based budgeting, benchmarking, reengineering, e-commerce, and governance. In such cases you can probably identify a list of people who might have an interest in a timely seminar or conference.

In contrast, it is much harder to attract an audience of prospective clients for a seminar on preparing for bankruptcy or tornadoes—examples of infrequent, difficult-to-predict needs.

Seminars, Webinars, and conferences also work best when mid- and lower-level personnel can have an influence on the purchase of your services, given that these groups make up the bulk of most seminar audiences. Because most seminars are marketed through direct e-mail, you must also be able to identify logical categories of buyers for whom you can acquire lists.

Public speaking and article writing attract varied audiences.

The more audiences you can identify that might have an interest in your message, the more likely public speaking will work for you. Some fields offer many more audiences than others. Economic development consultants, for example, can speak to several national trade associations, five or six associations serving multi-state areas, state-level groups, groups serving portions of large states, individual economic development organizations, and chambers of commerce. Many of these groups will pay expenses and an honorarium to someone with a message. An accomplished speaker can obtain as many opportunities as he can handle. By comparison, a professional who specializes in work for electric power utilities will have many fewer opportunities. Public speaking will thus make up a smaller portion of his marketing mix.

The same logic holds for article writing. For some practices there are many possible outlets; for others, there are few. The more geographically dispersed your market, the more attractive both of these approaches will be because they allow you to reach a wide audience at modest cost. Similarly, the less frequently a prospect is likely to need your services, the more you will wish to stress public speaking and article writing because attendees and readers will self-select on the basis of interest.

Direct e-mail is a flexible tool to be used in many ways.

Because direct e-mail can be used to achieve several different objectives, it can produce value for most firms. As a lead-generating vehicle, it works best in geographically dispersed markets for services of moderate or low value. Because of its low cost per contact, it offers an affordable way to reach a large, dispersed market. As a way to remind past clients and prospects of your services and continued interest, it can work with any market.

Know your market to determine what you must do.

Services and markets vary greatly from firm to firm, and these differences must be taken into account when developing a strategy. A law firm specializing in family law faces a very different market from one specializing in securities law. An architect who designs nothing but public schools must market in very different ways from one that has built an international reputation for design excellence. An information systems consultant sells in different ways from a turnaround consultant.

You cannot select the right strategy for your market unless you know your market and service. A surprising number of professionals doesn't. A traffic engineer once told me how surprised he and his partners were when they first did an analysis of their client base. The results, calculated on actual contract dollars, differed substantially from the partners' perceptions. They were far more dependent on a small number of clients than they realized. The analysis demonstrated that the firm needed to diversify while devoting extra attention to the limited number of key clients that supported it.

Long ago I did a study of the geographic spread of consulting clients of the firm I was working for. Viewing ourselves as a national organization on the brink of becoming international, we were chagrined to learn that 80 percent of our business came from within a three-hour drive of our offices. The story that begins this chapter provides yet another example of a firm that did not fully understand the implications of its market on the effectiveness of alternative marketing approaches.

We all have a tendency to fool ourselves into believing our firms are bigger and more broadly based than they actually are. These self-deceptions can hurt us badly if we act as if they were true. Similarly, a growing firm may not realize immediately that its new size changes the market it sells in and the marketing opportunities available to it. If you have not done an analysis of where your business comes from, do so now. Here are some questions to answer:

Answer these questions to determine your business mix.

- What percentage of my business do I get from different kinds of clients (by industry, by geography, by service, by size of company, by title of the buyer, etc.)? What kinds of clients are most profitable? What has the trend been?
- What percentage of my business do I get from my three, five, and ten largest clients? What has the trend been?
- What is the average size of my contracts? What percentage of my business do I get from contracts within specific size ranges, such as $50,000–$100,000 or $100,000–$250,000? (Note: You must set ranges that are meaningful for your firm.) What has the trend been?
- What is the average size of my total billings to specific clients for a year? What has the trend been?
- How would I like to change any of the above? Rank these changes in order of importance.

Determine your service and market characteristics.

Every professional needs to be able to answer one key question: What are the characteristics of my service and market?

To some extent, this answer will depend on the information you collected on your business mix. Fill out the form shown in Exhibit 28.5 for each major service you offer. This exercise will help you select a mix of techniques that you can work at consistently over time. Remember, it is through consistent work over time using techniques suited to your practice that you get results.

EXHIBIT 28.5 Practice Assessment Based on Market Characteristics

Rate the suitability of each marketing approach for your practice.

Low-Flexibility Techniques: Ratings should average 2 or lower to warrant using as a central part of strategy.

Cold Calling
   a. *Frequency of need*

1	2	3	4	5
At least annual				Less than once every three years

b. *Confidentiality of need*

1	2	3	4	5
Always highly public				Always highly confidential

c. *Value of sale over next three years (You must create your own scale, depending upon the size of your firm.)*

1	2	3	4	5
Always highly public				Always highly confidential

d. *Geographic dispersion of market (relative to location of salespeople)*

1	2	3	4	5
Always highly public				Always highly confidential

Relationship Marketing

a. *Frequency of need*

1	2	3	4	5
Always highly public				Always highly confidential

b. *Intensity of contact*

1	2	3	4	5
Requires frequent, intense contact				Requires infrequent contact

c. *Value of sale over next three years (You must create your own scale, depending upon the size of your firm.)*

1	2	3	4	5
Always highly public				Always highly confidential

d. Geographic dispersion of market (relative to location of salespeople)

1	2	3	4	5
Always highly public				Always highly confidential

Medium Flexibility Techniques: Ratings should average 3 or lower to warrant using as a central part of strategy.

Seminars and Conferences—either (a) or (b) must apply, but not both
  a. Frequency of need

1	2	3	4	5
At least annual				Less than once every three years

---

b. Time sensitivity of need

1	2	3	4	5
Many people need to know now				Few people need to know now

---

c. Confidentiality of need

1	2	3	4	5
Many people need to know now				Few people need to know now

---

d. *Geographic dispersion of market* (applies to short seminars only)

1	2	3	4	5
Highly concentrated				Highly dispersed

Trade and Professional Associations
a. Geographic dispersion of market

1	2	3	4	5
Many people need to know now				Few people need to know now

High-Flexibility Techniques: Warrant using if other approaches are inappropriate and rating on single factor is not 4 or 5.

Networking
a. Geographic dispersion of market

1	2	3	4	5
Many people need to know now				Few people need to know now

Publicity
a. Media appeal of practice

1	2	3	4	5
Many people need to know now				Few people need to know now

Public speaking and articles
a. Number of identifiable forums

1	2	3	4	5
Many				Few

The exercise is designed to stimulate your thinking, not to be a recipe for a strategy, because strategies do not lend themselves to recipes. Neither should it be used to preclude ever using a technique. Perhaps the exercise suggests that cold calling or seminars do not show high promise for your practice. This should not prevent you from using them once in a while, if circumstances seem to recommend it; we all need to preserve a healthy opportunism when marketing. They should simply not be a part of your strategy.

Answer these questions to characterize your current marketing effort.

- Where have your leads come from (publicity, client referrals, direct mail, network contacts, etc.)?
- What has the trend been?
- Are their other people selling to your market who have successfully used lead generating approaches that you haven't?

Several firms I have worked with have protested that they don't know where most of their business comes from and that the information is unobtainable. In each case, a focused effort has produced the information. If you don't know the answer to this question, you probably haven't tried hard enough to find it. Of course, a lead can come from several sources at once (say, your reputation and a speech). If this is the case, and the client cannot tell you which was most important, use your best judgment to assign a weight to the importance of each. What is the trend for each source?

Answer these questions on the competition.

- Who are your major competitors?
- How many projects have you lost to each of them? Why?
- Has the number and mix of competitors been changing?
- Where do your major competitors get their leads from? How is their business distributed among client types?

This information is harder to learn, but you don't need precise answers. Ask the competitors' former employees. Ask others who know them, such as past clients and vendors.

What does all this tell you about the strategy you should be adopting?

Conclusion: Becoming a Rainmaker

In many ways, selling is more fundamental to being a professional than doing or managing the work that follows. Professionals who sell must see the client's big picture. To win, they must understand how the work they are being asked to do fits into a client's larger world. The understanding you gain during a sale places you in an unequaled position to structure and oversee all work that follows. The more unusual the assignment, the more likely this is.

Those who are out in the market selling are also those most likely to see opportunities for new services and practices because most ideas for such advances come from the market. They are the ones who most quickly pick up warnings of market changes to which a firm must adjust. They are often the visionaries of their organizations.

Professionals who sell are also primary implementers of firm plans. Decisions to expand into new markets, to offer new services and to establish strategic alliances mean nothing by themselves. Sales give them substance. A firm's carefully developed procedures for advancing professionals up the hierarchy to partner also mean nothing if firm revenues cannot support promotions.

A professional who does a superior job of bringing in new business is seen as more than a salesperson. Her special powers make possible the way of life of the firm, the small society of which she is a part. *Rainmaker* is a fitting title for one who makes such a contribution.

The objective of this book is to give you the understanding and the tools you need to sell. If you develop the skills; if you can understand that marketing is a numbers game that requires working through many small losses to win later; if you can establish the discipline needed to keep yourself in the market; if you can cheer yourself on until you succeed, then you, too, can become a rainmaker.

303

Appendix

Further Reading and Information

Article writing and writing in general

Strunk, William, Jr., and E. B. White. *The Elements of Style*. New York: Macmillan Publishing Co., Inc., 1979.

If you follow the guidance given in this short book, your English composition will improve noticeably. It has become the standard source on this subject, recommended by teachers and writers because its advice is so sound and reasonable.

Bacon's Business Media Directory: Print and Broadcast Business Media. Chicago: Bacon's Information Inc. Published Annually. Also available online at http://us.cision.com

This directory provides the most complete listings of magazines available. It gives basic information on what publications are available in a particular field and tell you what they cover and how to reach them. Too expensive for most people to buy and not carried by all libraries, to find this book you may have to go to your public relations department or firm.

Public speaking and presenting

Jacobi, Jeffrey. *How to Say It: Persuasive Presentations*. New York: Prentice Hall, 2006.

This is a concise, easy-to-carry reference book on speaking and presenting.

www.simswyeth.com/Blog

This blog offers regular, well-written entries on a wide range of public speaking and presenting issues. (The capital "B" in Web address is case-sensitive.)

Networking

Sneider, Susan R. *A Lawyer's Guide to Networking*. American Bar Association, 2006.
    Not just for lawyers, this is a short how-to book on the subject.

Albert-László Barabási. *Linked: The New Science of Networks*. Cambridge, MA: Perseus Publishing, 2002.
    This is an accessible review on the theory of networks.

Gladwell, Malcolm. *The Tipping Point: How Little Things Can Make a Big Difference*. Boston: Little Brown & Company, 2000.
    This well-written layperson's description of how fads are created has a lot in it that is relevant to networking, if you view networking as making a fad of yourself or your firm.

Selling

Rackham, Neil. *SPIN Selling*. New York: McGraw-Hill, 1988.
    This is a classic on face-to-face selling, used by many professional firms.

DiMisa, Joe. *The Fisherman's Guide to Selling: Reel in the Sale—Hook, Line and Sinker*. Avon, MA: Adams Media, 2007.
    This book achieves the rare combination of being a helpful how-to book while also being entertaining.

Heiman, Stephen E. and Diane Sanchez. *The New Strategic Selling*. New York: Warner Books, 1998.
    Another classic, this book is the best ever written on how to figure out what you need to do next to win a complex sale, for example, one with several buyers, several meetings and competition.

Notes

Introduction

1. Wittreich, Warren J. "How to Buy/Sell Professional Services." *Harvard Business Review*, March–April 1966. p. 129.
2. Dennett, Tyler (Ed.), *Lincoln and the Civil War in the Diaries and Letters of John Hay*, New York: DaCapo, 1988. p. 179.

Chapter 1

1. *Bacon's Business Media Directory: Directory of Print and Broadcast Business Media.* Chicago: Bacon's Information Inc. Published annually. Also available online.
2. Westlake, Donald E. "Champing at the Bar." *New York Times Book Review*, 12 December, 1990.
3. Rose, Mark. *Shakespearian Design.* Cambridge, MA: The Belknap Press of Harvard University Press, 1972.
4. Branch, Taylor. *Parting the Waters: America in the King Years, 1954–63.* New York: Simon & Schuster, 1988. pp. 76–77.

Chapter 2

1. Branch, Taylor. *Parting the Waters: America in the King Years, 1954–63.* New York: Simon & Schuster, 1988. pp. 76–77.
2. Toastmasters International is an organization with many local chapters. To find one near you, go online to *www.toastmasters.org.*
3. *National Trade and Professional Associations* is published by Columbia Books, Inc., Washington, D.C.

Chapter 5

1. Blumberg, Donald C., "Getting Customers to Ask for Your Services." *IMCommunicator,* January 1994, p. 3.

2. *Bacon's Business Media Directory: Directory of Print and Broadcast Business Media.* Chicago: Bacon's Information Inc. Published annually. Also available online.
3. Hiaasen, Carl. *Tourist Season*, New York: Warner Books, 1986, p. 371.

Chapter 10

1. Wolf, William B., *Management and Consulting: An Introduction to James O. McKinsey.* Ithaca, NY: Cornell University, 1978, p. 42. This thin book captures some of what his colleagues knew of McKinsey after his death. It is a valuable resource for those interested in the consulting profession.
2. This term originates in graph theory, but it has been popularized by Malcolm Gladwell in his book, *The Tipping Point: How Little Things Can Make a Big Difference.* Boston: Back Bay Books, 2002.

Chapter 11

1. For a layperson's description of power curves and networks, see Albert-László Barabási's *Linked: The New Science of Networks.* Cambridge, MA: Perseus Publishing, 2002.
2. Barabási, *Linked*, p. 87.
3. Barabási, *Linked*, p. 95.
4. Wolf, William B., *Management and Consulting: An Introduction to James O. McKinsey.* Ithaca, NY: Cornell University, 1978, pp. 42–43.
5. Kanigel, Robert. *The One Best Way: Frederick Winslow Taylor and the Enigma of Efficiency.* New York: Penguin Books, 1997.

Chapter 12

1. Harding, Ford. *Creating Rainmakers: The Manager's Guide to Training Professionals to Attract New Clients.* New York: Wiley, 2006, pp. 19–27.

Chapter 13

1. Harding, Ford. *Cross-Selling Success.* Avon, MA: Adams Media, 2002.

Chapter 14

1. I have taken these components from Peg C. Neuhausser's *Corporate Legends and Lore: The Power of Storytelling as a Management Tool*, New York: McGraw-Hill, Inc., 1993, pp. 33–25.

Chapter 15

1. A good book on selling is written entirely around the fishing metaphor. See DiMisa, Joe. *The Fisherman's Guide to Selling: Reel in the Sale—Hook, Line and Sinker.* Avon, MA: Adams Media, 2007.

2. I have adapted the terminology from Raymond L. Gordon and his book, *Interviewing Strategy, Technique and Tactics,* Homewood, IL: The Dorsey Press, 1975.

Chapter 20

1. Heiman, Stephen E., and Diane Sanchez. *The New Strategic Selling.* New York: Warner Books, 1998.

Chapter 25

1. More details on the findings of this research can be found in my other books:

Harding, Ford. *Creating Rainmakers: The Manager's Guide to Training Professionals to Attract New Clients.* New York: Wiley, 2006.

Harding, Ford. *Cross-Selling Success.* Avon, MA: Adams Media, 2002.

Index

309

Made in the USA
Lexington, KY
05 March 2012